FOOD LOVERS'
GUIDE TO
PITTSBURGH

FOOD LOVERS' SERIES

FOOD LOVERS'
GUIDE TO
PITTSBURGH

The Best Restaurants, Markets & Local Culinary Offerings

1st Edition

**Sarah Sudar, Julia Gongaware,
Amanda McFadden & Laura Zorch**

Guilford, Connecticut

Editor: Kevin Sirois
Project Editor: Heather Santiago
Layout Artist: Mary Ballachino
Text Design: Sheryl Kober
Illustrations by Jill Butler with additional art by Carleen Moira Powell and MaryAnn Dubé
Maps: Alena Joy Pearce © Morris Book Publishing, LLC

ISBN 978-0-7627-8117-1

Printed in the United States of America
10 9 8 7 6 5 4 3 2 1

All the information in this guidebook is subject to change. We recommend that you call ahead to obtain current information before traveling.

Contents

Recipes, 247

Appendices, 268

About the Authors

Sarah Sudar is passionate about two food groups, cupcakes and french fries, and is obsessed with savoring a cup of coffee after dinner. She recently received her master's degree in journalism and mass communication (along with Julia) and is happy to report that she is actually using her degree wisely (by writing this book). When she isn't writing about food, she is a freelance writer and blogger, focusing on fashion and style.

Julia Gongaware is an accomplished eater and holds a master's degree in journalism and mass communication. When she's not searching for her next great food adventure, which in her case usually involves a cheeseburger, she's researching social media trends for the health care industry. She resides in the heart of Pittsburgh's Little Italy.

Amanda McFadden has a lifelong goal to eat her way across the continental United States and she's making good progress. That being said, Pittsburgh is still one of her favorite spots to do just about anything, especially eat. When Mandy isn't stuffing her face with the city's best pizza, she is scouting out her next travel destination and working as a digital marketer for one of Pittsburgh's leading manufacturing corporations. Mandy resides in Mt. Lebanon and can usually be found with an ice cream cone in hand.

Laura Zorch has never met a sugary treat she didn't like. Fact: Her body is composed of 80 percent water and 20 percent cake. Laura holds a master's degree in arts management from Carnegie Mellon University, which helps in her day job as an arts administrator.

Acknowledgments

We'd like to set our forks down for a moment and declare our appreciation for everyone who has accompanied us on this journey of caloric magnificence. To all the chefs—your commitment to producing exciting kitchen feats is awesome and your efforts are not unnoticed. To our publishing team and editor, Kevin—you officially owe us roomier pants after this undertaking, but we'll let that slide since you've made our dreams come true. To Mark, our favorite Drunk Yinzer—your editing prowess sobers us. To the people of Pittsburgh and the city itself—you really are the best; and that, friends, is the whole delicious truth.

Sarah Sudar: So, thinking about who all to thank is kinda hard and I promise to make this short before the music starts to cut me off. I'd like to thank my parents and my entire family for teaching me how to cook and bake, especially my father, who often demands a fresh loaf of bread in the oven. Huge thanks and hugs go out to all of my friends who helped me "research" for this book. You know who you are and you are welcome. Special shout-out to Sarah for helping me set (and achieve) goals I never thought possible. To Julia, Laura, and Mandy—thank you for your hard work and tolerating my project management skills (xoxo). My last thanks go out to the city of Pittsburgh and the chefs, restaurants, and people calling it home. Yinz are awesome.

Julia Gongaware: Never would I have imagined I'd have the opportunity to live and share my dreams with so many people I love and admire. To my mom, dad, and brother: Thank you for your encouragement, support, and giving me the confidence to use my voice to express what's always been in my heart. To my eating companions: Without you I would have had to eat all that amazing food all by myself. And even though we all know I could have, it was so much more fun with you. To Sarah, Laura, and Mandy: Thank you for helping me discover my love of food and writing. This adventure has been so very amazing with you three by my side.

Amanda McFadden: Thanks to those with whom I've shared many a great meal, to those who have shown my taste buds no boundaries, and to those who have not passed judgment when I've clearly fed myself well past the point of full. Thanks to those who allow me to choose the restaurant and to those who trust my palate enough to ask my opinion and advice. Thanks to my mom and dad for putting delicious food on the table, and thanks to each of my six siblings for letting me be the one to go back for seconds. Thanks to all my favorites, especially those who join me in my daily ice cream adventures. Thanks to Sarah, Julia, and Laura for sharing my passion for Pittsburgh, food, and writing enough to hop on board the eatPGH train. Thank you everyone, from the bottom of my heart (and my belly), for being there while I feed my appetite for life.

Laura Zorch: It is not often that I find myself in a word vacuum. But, as I try to express my gratitude to all the folks who continuously bless my life, I can't seem to maneuver over my keyboard to plunk the right configuration of consonants and vowels. "Thanks" just doesn't seem to cut it. So, if you have eaten with me, laughed with me, and shared with me through this process, know that you make my heart happy. I owe you all a huge high five. A special note of appreciation goes out to my mom and dad, whose unconditional support and love never cease to amaze. Two kinder people I have yet to encounter, nor do I expect to do so. My last, and heartiest, bit of gratitude is reserved for three fantastic diners: Sarah, Julia, and Mandy. While I am still grasping for an appropriate level of thankfulness in a turn of phrase, I did manage to find one fitting word for you ladies: famous. Thanks all. It has been fun (and filling).

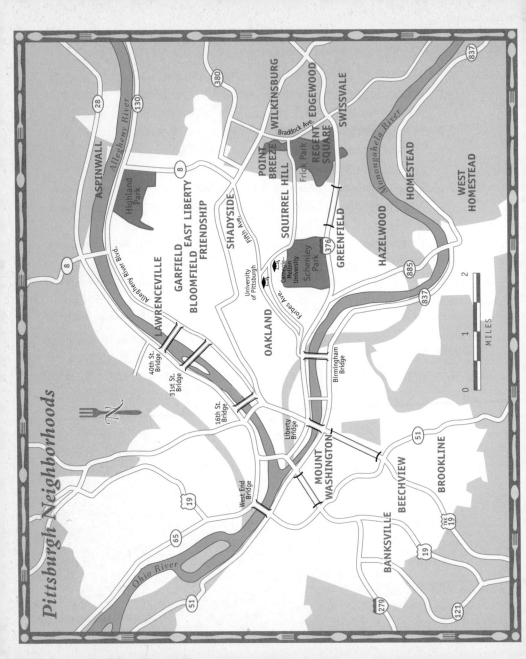

Pittsburgh Neighborhoods

Introduction

This just in: Pittsburgh is all kinds of awesome. This once belea-guered steel town has transformed into a place that people are talking about—in only the best ways possible. The city's technology, health care, education, arts, and music scene are continuously evolving with every passing year. The cuisine is also evolving within our fair city. Pittsburgh restaurant legends have laid a solid culinary foundation, encouraging a continuous stream of newbies to take risks applauded by stomachs everywhere! Creativity and sustain-ability are on the rise, but most importantly, the Pittsburgh food scene has remained unpretentious and relatable, just like the people. The variety available runs the gamut of cuisine, flavor, and price, allowing both novice and expert foodies to experience culinary bliss.

Pittsburgh has become more than a city with a rich blue-collar, sports-loving history. It has matured and become a destination that attracts people from far-off lands while wholeheartedly embracing its own. It's our favorite place and hopefully soon to be yours, n'at.

How to Use This Book

Have you ever traveled to a new city and tried to pack the very best it has to offer into your agenda only to find out it wasn't actually the best? We're here to give you the scoop on all things food in Pittsburgh and offer our local insight so you can focus on the important stuff, like lifting a fork to your mouth.

We divided the city of Pittsburgh into regions based on their proximity to Downtown. Downtown is the central hub of our city since that's where many 'Burghers work, attend sporting events, and go to fancy performances at the theaters. From Downtown, we venture around the city to neighborhoods in the North, South, and East. We then head into the suburbs because there is some pretty tasty food way outside the city limits. In each of these sections, you will find some of the following:

Foodie Faves

These are our favorite restaurants; the places you can often find us dining in and recommending to friends, family, and strangers.

Landmarks

The places that make up the fabric of our city. If you want an authentic Pittsburgh culinary experience, hit up any Landmark we have listed.

Specialty Stores, Markets & Producers

The go-to places for produce, baked goods, and specialty products. They are located beyond the Strip District, Pittsburgh's most well-known neighborhood for specialty food markets, and we'll help you find them.

In addition, we have included the following to help satisfy your hunger:

Stadium Food

CONSOL Energy Center (home of the Pittsburgh Penguins), Heinz Field (home of the Pittsburgh Steelers), and PNC Park (home of the Pittsburgh Pirates). We love our sports teams and we break down the eateries in each of the three main stadiums.

Local Drink Scene

Pittsburgh has a myriad of local distilleries producing beer, wine, cider, whiskey, vodka, and even seltzer water. Nothing goes better with local fare than a locally made refreshment.

Recipes

In case you want to cook like the pros, we have a selection of recipes from our favorite restaurants, created by the geniuses inside the kitchens.

Price Code

Our price guide is according to the average price per entree at each restaurant.

$	less than $10
$$	$10 to $20
$$$	$20 to $30
$$$$	more than $30

The city of Pittsburgh is made up of 90 neighborhoods, each filled with so many nooks and crannies that it could take a lifetime to see them all. Our solution: If you're only visiting for a short time, get lost with the help of our book. After stuffing your face, take time to explore the neighborhood. If you do, you'll get to experience the true fabric of Pittsburgh through our charming architectural wonders, our eclectic specialty shops, and our locals! Stop by one of the restaurants, bars, or specialty shops we mention and chances are you'll run into someone who lives right around the corner. And we bet he or she will give you the history of the neighborhood, Pittsburgh, and show you a Steelers tattoo whether you ask to see it or not.

To get to the many neighborhoods mentioned in this book, there are a variety of modes of transportation. The Golden Triangle, also known as Downtown, is the core of the city. It's booming with life during the week and is one of the easiest locations to find several modes of transportation to get you around the city. Downtown itself can easily be tackled by foot, bike, or pedicab. Plus, the Strip District, Station Square, and the North Shore are all within walking distance. To see what's on the other side of the Monongahela River, catch the T or walk over the Smithfield Street Bridge (it's the blue one) to the South Side and take one of the two inclines, the Duquesne Incline or the Monongahela Incline, up to Mount

Washington even if it's only for the view. The T can also take you to the North Shore as an alternative to walking over the Allegheny River on one of The Three Sisters bridges. Catch this North Shore Connector at Gateway Station Downtown and ride to your choice of two stations near PNC Park, Heinz Field, and Rivers Casino.

Pittsburgh isn't laid out on a grid system like most cities. We do things our own way here with an abundance of one-way streets, tunnels, and bridges. If you're looking for a mode of transportation that quickly climbs all of our hills and eases navigation frustration, we suggest taking the Port Authority of Allegheny County buses to the neighborhood destinations we've recommended. Buses are available for neighborhoods including, but not limited to, Bloomfield, Downtown, Highland Park, Lawrenceville, Mount Washington, Oakland, Point Breeze, Regent Square, Shadyside, South Side, and Squirrel Hill. Information on accessing public transportation can be found at the Port Authority website: www.portauthority.org.

If you have a hankering for some fresh air or just want to experience the city from a different perspective, we suggest renting a bike. Countless trails run through the city, but the Three Rivers Heritage Trail (www.friendsofthe riverfront.org/files/heritage_trail .html) runs for 22 miles alongside all three Pittsburgh rivers (the Allegheny, Monongahela, and Ohio Rivers) and can take you to many of the neighborhoods mentioned in this book. Plus, a few

hours of pedaling will surely work up an appetite! For more information on all things two-wheeled, visit www.bike-pgh.org.

Keeping Up with Food News

Looking for more local flavor? Pittsburgh media loves to eat and
there is plenty of information to be had. Here are some of our
favorite reads:

Print Media

Edible Allegheny, www.ediblecommunities.com/
allegheny. *Edible Allegheny* is a magazine dedicated to seasonal, local food, and local agriculture. The magazine has featured stories, a dining
guide, recipes, and a calendar of events. The calendar of events is important to view if you are
looking for a food-related activity to try out while in
town. This magazine shouts out local food bloggers and social
media users in the "Online Dish" feature in each issue (eatPGH was
featured in the magazine last year). There are a ton of local food
bloggers reviewing restaurants and testing recipes, and we love that
this magazine is letting the locals know about them.

Pittsburgh City Paper, www.pittsburghcitypaper.com. Free
paper here! This alternative weekly newspaper hits street boxes

all over the city and online every Wednesday. It delivers a hearty dose of music, culture, and regional news with a zesty tongue. The newspaper is the go-to resource for foodies because of its large listing of local restaurants complete with restaurant reviews. Be sure to check out the "On the Side" feature that offers a quick glimpse into a variety of food-related subjects. If you're looking for a cocktail, this is also a great place to start. It has an extensive online happy hour listing and even its own iPhone application called Cocktail Compass (download it on iTunes for *free* by searching for "Pittsburgh Cocktail Compass"). The app uses GPS-based tracking to find the happy hour nearest to your current location. And if you have a little too much fun at happy hour, the app can even call a cab.

Pittsburgh Magazine, www.pittsburghmagazine.com. This monthly magazine is the go-to publication for everything happening in Pittsburgh. *Pittsburgh Magazine* hosts the Best Restaurants Party, which is the must-attend food event every year. Besides letting you know what shows are coming to the Cultural District in Downtown, the magazine offers up restaurant reviews with beautiful photos of the food and restaurants, recipes by Pittsburgh's celebrity television chef, Chris Fennimore, and other bits of foodie information in each issue. There's also a comprehensive listing of area restaurants in the back of each magazine issue. Online at *Pittsburgh Magazine*'s website, you can use the restaurant finder to locate a specific restaurant depending on neighborhood location and cuisine type.

Pittsburgh Is Cool, N'at

Pittsburgh is cool, and our city has been recognized for being so from some famous sources. Yes, the city has won its fair share of sports championships, including six Super Bowl victories, three Stanley Cups, and let's not forget about the Pirates' five World Series wins.

Besides being known for outstanding sports, Pittsburgh has been receiving recognition as one of the most livable cities in the United States (a few times) and as one of the must-visit cities in the world in 2012. With the help of VisitPittsburgh.com, below is a list of some of the city's recent accomplishments.

- #1 cheapest last-minute getaway (Hotwire, 2012).
- One of the top 20 best trips to take in the world in 2012 (*National Geographic Traveler*).
- #1 family fun destination (*ABC City Guides for Kids*, 2012).
- Portland "Out," Pittsburgh "In" for 2012 (*The Washington Post*).
- One of the top 5 places to retire in 2012 (*US News & World Report*).

***Pittsburgh Post-Gazette* Food and Restaurants sections,** www.post-gazette.com. Every Thursday, the Food and Restaurants sections of the newspaper and website receive a major update. And every Thursday morning, our eyes are reading both. The "Little Bites" section will fill you in on the upcoming happenings and specials at local restaurants. Be sure to read Munch, the PG's undercover food critic, who goes a new restaurant each week and writes

- Most secure city among large metro areas of 500,000+ residents (Farmers Insurance, 2011).
- One of the top 10 best cities for sports (*Sporting News,* 2011).
- 2nd bicycle-friendly city (League of American Bicyclists, 2011).
- #1 best city to relocate in America (CNBC, 2011).
- #4 best city for working mothers (*Forbes,* 2011).
- #4 best airport in the country—Pittsburgh International Airport (*Travel + Leisure* Magazine, 2011).
- One of the country's most underrated cities (Yahoo Real Estate, 2011).
- One of the top hottest areas for jobs (Monster.com, 2011)
- Most livable city in America (*Forbes,* 2010).
- Most livable city in the US (*The Economist,* 2009).

Need we go on? If these don't make you want to immediately pack your bags and head to the 'Burgh, then the food will. So keep reading. We are sure you will want to pay a visit after you hear all about the pierogies, specialty sandwiches, and local brews our city has cooking up!

a quirky column about his experience. And possibly the matriarch of Pittsburgh restaurant reviewers is China Millman. When she reviews a restaurant, you know the restaurant has "made it," even if the review is less than stellar.

Table Magazine, www.tablemagazine.com. One of Pittsburgh's premier food publications, *Table Magazine* can be found at grocery stores and markets across the city. This quarterly magazine is chock-full of local chef interviews, recipes, and health and wellness tips. It is more than just a food magazine, this lifestyle publication is dedicated to showcasing stories behind local cuisine, restaurants, and agriculture. The magazine's online site features recipes, local events, and an extensive guide to the BYOB restaurants in the city.

Online Media

eatPGH, www.eatpgh.com. Oh, hey, it's us! Just four ladies who are eating their way through Pittsburgh. We review restaurants and are definitely not afraid to let you know what we like (or don't!) about a dining experience. We keep things local, because Pittsburgh is so full of innovative flavors, there's no need to wander. Sometimes, recipes or a food event we've attended will pop up, but we mostly dish about our dine-outs. Why make food when you can make a reservation? For more information on how awesome we are, head to the blog.

IheartPGH.com. If you're in the 'Burgh and looking for a fun food event or just something to do in general, check out the I heart PGH blog. Our pal Lindsay at http://iheartpgh.com has been blogging about everything Pittsburgh since 2005. Besides blogging about local happenings, Lindsay and the other I heart PGH bloggers do a pretty darn good job covering local foodie events and restaurant news. It's sure to have something that interests you and your palate.

Popcitymedia.com. Pop City is a weekly e-newsletter that focuses on the latest business development, technology, arts, and innovation news in the city. Oftentimes, there is mention of local restaurants opening up or articles about really cool Pittsburghers that are worth reading. You will fall in love with the city a bit more every time you read the e-newsletter. We warn you, Pittsburgh passion is contagious.

thedrunkyinzer.com. If there's one thing we Pittsburghers love as much as food, it's beer! So do the three guys that write The Drunk Yinzer blog. Not only do they scour our city for the best brews and spirits, they also take to the road and report back on how other cities compare, refreshment wise. They also spend time making brews of their own. We like to catch up with these guys from time to time to find out what new craft beers exist and what we should be drinking with our meals.

VisitPittsburgh.com. Visit Pittsburgh is the tourism site for Allegheny County and the surrounding areas. It has a wealth of knowledge about what's going on in and around Pittsburgh. You can find where to stay, eat, and what to do while you are here all at this one-stop website. When venturing to a new city, you should always have a good map. Visit Pittsburgh's website has a rad interactive map of Pittsburgh that is worth checking out. The Visit Pittsburgh staff is active on Twitter (@vstpgh is the main account) and always eager to answer your questions and tell you the cool things about the city.

Festivals & Events

Since Pittsburgh is a melting pot of cultures, the city hosts a variety of ethnic food festivals and food events. Whether eating gyros at one of the Greek food festivals, learning how to step dance at the annual Irish festival, drinking craft beer amongst reclaimed building materials at the Steel City Big Pour, or becoming a fine spirits connoisseur at the Pittsburgh Whiskey & Fine Spirits Festival, there is practically a different food-related event or cultural celebration each month. Here is a list of some of our favorite festivals and events to attend:

February

South Side Soup Contest, www.southsidepgh.com. In February, Pittsburghers bundle up in their parkas, boots, mittens, and hats, and head to the South Side for the annual South Side Soup Contest. A ticket to this "soup crawl" gets you samplings of the best soups from participating eateries and the chance to be a judge for the best bowl. Be sure to get your tickets early because even though it's cold out, this soup crawl is a sellout. Walk from bar to restaurant to diner to pub and get your soup on. There are usually 20-something soups to try so keep your feet moving if you plan on making it to all of them. Keeping up with the times, the Soup Contest has gone green with compostable cups and spoons.

March

Farm-to-Table Conference, http://farmtotablepa.com/conference. It's all about healthy food at this conference. Aimed at helping consumers lead healthier lifestyles and learn about fresh food origins, the Farm-to-Table Conference offers cooking demonstrations, presentations, a farmer's market, and vendors. At the conclusion of the conference, a local food tasting takes place bringing together farm exhibitors and like-minded locavores to enjoy local food, wine, and beer samples.

May

Saint Nicholas Greek Food Festival, www.stnickspgh.org. Each spring, Saint Nicholas Greek Orthodox Cathedral in Oakland hosts one of the larger Greek food festivals in the area. The smell of gyros fills the Oakland air, bringing out students and residents to the cathedral. Outside the cathedral, tents are set up to seat diners. Inside the church's large hall, the food line is typically long, filled with people all waiting their turn for moussaka, lamb souvlakia, and spanakopita. An insider's note: Since the lines can be very long, pre-order your Greek meal online or via fax. See website for details.

Pittsburgh Folk Festival, www.pghfolkfest.org. The Pittsburgh Folk Festival celebrates the diversity of cultures that make up the Pittsburgh region. At the Folk Festival, you can see dance performances from a variety of ethnic dance troupes and dine on ethnic food from practically all over the world. Get a little bit of India, a little bit of Croatia, and a little bit of the Philippines all on one plate, among other ethnic fare. Feel free to dance in the crowd of people when you hear a folk song you like. In addition to dancing and food, there are educational exhibits, an international market-place, and cooking demonstrations.

Pittsburgh Wine Festival, www.pittsburghwinefestival.com. If you love a glass of wine, then this is the festival for you. Held every May at Heinz Field, the Pittsburgh Wine Festival has two tastings. The VIP Tasting features wines that are unavailable in the Grand Tasting, and the crowd is smaller, allowing you more one-on-one time to talk wine with the experts. The Grand Tasting follows and typically attracts over 2,000 people. Wines from all over the world are available for sampling, along with food and entertainment.

July

Slovenefest, www.snpj.org/Slovenian-Culture/Slovenefest. Western Pennsylvania has a large contingent of Slovenians. So much so that the Slovenian National Benefit Society (SNPJ) makes its home here in Enon Valley, Lawrence County. Once a year, in mid-July, the SNPJ throws Slovenefest—a food, music, and culture extrava-ganza at its headquarter location. If button box bands, awesome Slovenian doughnuts, and polka dancing are your flavor, get in on the Slovenefest action! Everyone is welcome.

August

McKeesport International Village, www.mckeesport.org. For over 50 years, the City of McKeesport has been celebrating the diversity of Pittsburgh cultures and ethnic groups by turning a neighborhood park into an international village, complete with food, entertainment, and neighborhood camaraderie. Ethnic fare cooked by patrons from cultural organizations and church groups representing Serbian, Lebanese, Slovak, Chinese, African-American, and a variety of other nationalities is at your disposal for eating. Though there is a small fee charged for admission into the International Village, parking is free. Be sure not to leave your appetite in the car.

September

Bloomfield Little Italy Days, www.bloomfieldnow.com/little-italy-days. Traces of Italy are always present throughout the neighborhood of Bloomfield, but each September the area explodes with Italian heritage. A parade winds through the streets, traditional Italian music is played, and food vendors line Liberty Avenue during this family-friendly three-day festival. You can even watch a few games of bocce while you nosh on a sampling of deep fried risotto balls and Italian hot sausage.

Coors Light Kickoff and Rib Festival, www.steelers.com. The Annual Coors Light Kickoff and Rib Festival is our city's celebration of the start of the Steelers football season. Rib vendors from around the nation venture to Pittsburgh with their racks, smokers, and sauces ready to take on hungry Pittsburghers of all ages. Admission is free, and activities, games, and entertainment are available for the entire family.

Oktoberfest at Penn Brewery, www.pennbrew.com. Can't make it to Munich? Try Penn Brewery for your Oktoberfest-ing! The event takes place over two weekends in September. Whichever weekend you choose, you can enjoy house-made seasonal craft brews, live music, and some of the best German food in the city. Nothing says Oktoberfest better than pretzels, 'kraut, and beer! Penn Brewery looks out for the vegetarians as well, offering meatless sloppy joes because to veggie lovers, 'wursts are the worst.

Pittsburgh Irish Festival, www.pghirishfest.org. Since 1991, the Pittsburgh Irish Festival has been dedicated to generating aware-ness of Irish heritage in Pittsburgh. The festival runs for three days (the weekend after Labor Day) and features live entertain-ment (dance and music), shopping, educational activities, curragh racing, Irish bingo, and, of course, delicious food. Who doesn't love dauber bingo and food? We do! Irish specialties are obviously on the menu, including sausages, corned beef, boxty pancakes, cab-bage, potato soup, desserts, and much more. Definitely a taste of Ireland in the 'Burgh.

Pittsburgh Lebanese Food Festival, www.pgh
lebanesefestival.com. The Pittsburgh Lebanese
Food Festival is a three-day weekend at Our
Lady of Victory Maronite Catholic Church in
Carnegie. Dine in or take out tons of Lebanese specialties like kibbee, lamb, grape leaves, spinach pies,
falafel, tabouli, and hummus. Hungry yet? Orders can
be placed in advance online if you are in a hurry and can
be delivered if you are ordering tons of goods (and you just
might after reading that list).

Steel City Big Pour, www.constructionjunction.org/pages/
bigpour. Held each year at Construction Junction, the city's coolest
place to find reclaimed bath tubs, shelving, and mantels, the Steel
City Big Pour is the must-attend craft beer event in the city. Get
tickets early—it sells out fast. Tickets are priced at two categories:
regular admission (gets you all the craft beer samples you can
handle) and designated driver (gets you all the locally made nonal-
coholic drinks you can handle). Proceeds from sales go toward sup-
porting Construction Junction's mission of conservation through the
reusage of reclaimed building materials. Inside this huge party, you
get access to craft beer samples, food from local eateries, live art
and music, raffles, and a good-ole' time with tons of Pittsburghers.
If you are drinking, be sure to try the Steel City Big Pour specialty
brew, which is made every year by East End Brewing Company.

November

GoodTaste! Pittsburgh, www.goodtastepittsburgh.com. If you are looking for the largest food and cooking extravaganza in Western Pennsylvania, you found it at GoodTaste! Pittsburgh. This annual cooking event features live demonstrations, cook-offs, samplings from local restaurants, and appearances by celebrated television chefs. In addition, there are cooking workshops, foodie goods available for purchase, free product samples (be sure to get your reusable tote bags ready for the goodies), a marketplace for holiday gifts, and events for the kids. If you can't wait until November, GoodTaste! Pittsburgh holds an event in June called "Hometown Homegrown," presented by GoodTaste! Pittsburgh and the Heinz History Center, where the neighborhoods of Pittsburgh are celebrated through food. See website for more information.

Pittsburgh Whiskey & Fine Spirits Festival, pittsburghwhiskey festival.com. A festival for the spirits, and we ain't talking about the boogity-boo kind here. The annual Pittsburgh Whiskey & Fine Spirits Festival is for spirits connoisseurs who want to sample  cordials, gin, rum, tequila, scotch, vodka, and of course, whiskey, from around the world. Attendees ranging from novices to experts pack Heinz Field and sample hundreds of fine spirits, as well as cuisine from local restaurants and chefs. If you are a novice and want to learn how to become a scotch drinker or want to add whiskey connoisseur to your resume, attend this event.

December

Lawrenceville Joy of Cookies Cookie Tour, http://lvpgh.com/
lawrencevillejoyofcookiestour. Free things fill our heart with joy.
So do cookies. Enter Lawrenceville Joy of Cookies Cookie Tour.
The Lawrenceville Joy of Cookies Cookie Tour is a free event held
for four days (Thursday through Sunday) during the first weekend
in December that helps boost the neighborhood's economy. The
purpose is to host an "un-mall" experience, urging shoppers to support local, independent businesses. The tour consists of galleries,
shops, restaurants, bakeries, and other businesses in Lawrenceville
and an official map is drawn up each year. You can visit
over 30 businesses on the map at your convenience,
collecting free samples of cookies and cookie
recipes along the way. In addition to the
cookie tour, there is a cookie mall bake
sale, typically on the Saturday of the
weekend tour. Proceeds from the bake
sale are donated to local community
organizations.

The Nationality Rooms Holiday Open House, www.pitt
.edu/~natrooms. Every winter, the Nationality Rooms at the
University of Pittsburgh hold a Holiday Open House. Admission to
the event is free, and you can tour all 29 Nationality Rooms inside
the Cathedral of Learning. During this open house, each Nationality
Room is decorated in the holiday traditions of each room's heritage.

Be sure to stop by the Early American Room on the third floor of the Cathedral because it is said to be haunted. Spooky! Live performances by ethnic dance troupes, ethnic food, and a global marketplace are also set up during this event in the Commons Room of the Cathedral. A definite go-to event if you are looking to learn more about a variety of ethnic cultures (and feast on some tasty delights) all in one place. Dates vary.

Pittsburgh Magazine Best Restaurants Party, www.pittsburgh magazine.com. Each year, *Pittsburgh Magazine* gathers Pittsburgh's best restaurants and throws one large party, appropriately called the Best Restaurants Party. The party is typically sold out so be sure to get your tickets early! This is definitely the best way to sample some of Pittsburgh's most delicious plates. Over 50 restaurants are on display, offering sample after sample after sample of their noteworthy cuisines, including the top 25 restaurants as determined by *Pittsburgh Magazine*, as well as winners of the annual Readers Poll. Be sure to go on an empty stomach because the samples are filling and will leave you wanting seconds, thirds, and fourths.

Pittsburgh Fish Frys. During the Lenten season in Pittsburgh, many of the locals flock to fish frys held at churches and other organizations. At these fish frys, you can find fish sandwiches, fish dinners, fried shrimp, chowder, macaroni and cheese, coleslaw, french fries, and much more, all for relatively low costs. Of course, there are a lot of tasty fish sandwiches at restaurants and bars, but during Lent, you should try to get to a fish fry. Since there are so many fish frys held around town during Lent, we simply cannot pick a favorite, because they are each worth a try at least once. For an extensive list of fish frys, local television news station KDKA puts together a thorough list each year at http://pittsburgh.cbslocal.com/.

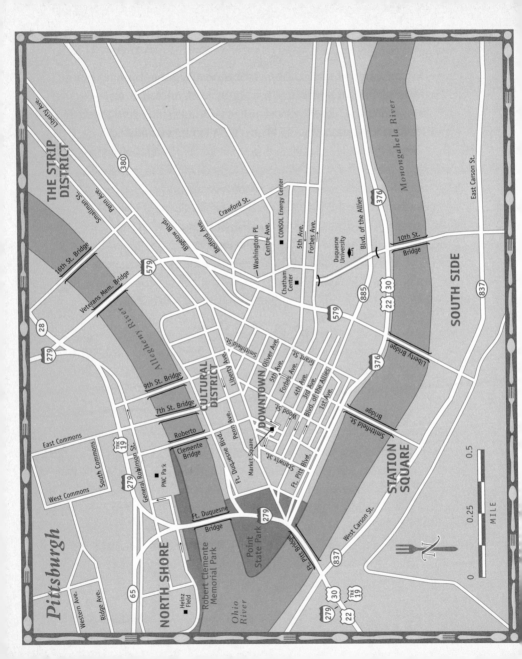

Downtown Pittsburgh & Station Square

Downtown Pittsburgh, like the rest of the city, is in the midst of a renaissance. While it may be running a couple of paces behind some of the area's more vibrant, populous boroughs, "Dahntahn" is second to none in culture and unique eateries.

Much of Downtown's resurgence as a solid place to dine relates directly to the influence of The Pittsburgh Cultural Trust. The Trust began transforming dilapidated buildings in the late 1980s. Now, these spaces like the Benedum Center, O'Reilly Theater, Harris Theater, and Heinz Hall bring crowds Downtown in droves for entertainment. The Trust's galleries, Wood Street Galleries, Space, 707 and 709, and Future Tenant, facilitate cutting-edge art experiences in a neighborhood once filled with adult video stores. With the recent addition of the August Wilson Center for African American

Culture, Downtown has become a cultural oasis. It comes as no surprise that the Downtown Cultural District restaurants would be equally as impressive. The District boasts dining spots that thrill theatergoers, art aficionados, and anyone with a rumble in their bellies.

Renovations to Market Square and Point State Park add to the dining ease of Downtown with locales that offer outdoor seating in warmer months and friendly neighborhood haunts. Downtown's neighbor across the Monongahela River, Station Square, a riverfront entertainment mecca, features mainly big-box dining establishments, but a few gems are worth the short walk over the seriously beautiful (and blue) Smithfield Street Bridge.

While you may hear that traveling to Downtown is like scaling Mt. Everest (it takes both skill and practice), that is more myth than fact. Downtown is drivable and bike friendly, parking is plentiful and cheap after 5 p.m., and you will most likely run into Pennsylvania's state flower (the construction cone) only once or twice. Don't let a little navigation stand between you and a taste of the 'Burgh's Golden Triangle.

Foodie Faves

Backstage Bar at Theater Square, 655 Penn Ave., Pittsburgh, PA 15222; (412) 325-6769; http://trustarts.org/visit/facilities/backstage/; International; $$. The Backstage Bar at Theater Square combines eclectic food, fine wines and spirits, and live music in the heart of Pittsburgh's Cultural District. What could be classier than that? Stop by before or after a show for a glass of red and enjoy the sound of local jazz floating between the tables and chairs. Among the hushed whispers and soft laughter, you can feel the excitement and energy in the air. If you're there for a full meal, order the pizza margarita or barbecue pulled pork on a pretzel bun. If you're looking for lighter fare, we recommend the gourmet cheese platter, hummus and olives, or tiramisu and coffee. Backstage Bar has several great brews on tap, and the bartenders are always happy to chat with you about the current and upcoming shows or the local music acts that have taken the stage in the past. It will be a backstage experience you'll want to brag to your friends about.

Braddock's American Brasserie, 107 6th St., Pittsburgh, PA, 15222; (412) 992-2005; www.braddocksrestaurant.com; American; $$$. Braddock's American Brasserie, located in The Renaissance Hotel Pittsburgh, is a fine place to grab a cocktail or enjoy a great meal before a theater show in Pittsburgh's Cultural District. The restaurant is located next to Byham Theater near the Allegheny River. By far, the best item on the menu are the braised short rib pierogies with creamed leeks in "I think I've died and gone to heaven" pan juices. You will want multiple orders because no one at your table will want to share after they have their first bite. Besides the pierogies, Braddock's serves breakfast, lunch, and dinner entrees that are reminiscent of American comfort food, but with a modern flare. If you make it past the appetizers of pierogies or grilled Strip District kielbasa with sauerkraut and assorted mustards, you can't go wrong with the crab cakes or the house-made potato gnocchi and lobster. See Executive Chef Dean Gress's recipe for **Short Rib Pierogies** on p. 249.

The Carlton Restaurant, 500 Grant St., Pittsburgh PA 15219; (412) 391-4152; www.thecarltonrestaurant.com; Steakhouse; $$$. The Carlton serves lunch to busy businessmen and women and dinner to the crowds that gather for the multitude of events in the city. Located in BNY Mellon Center, the restaurant is in close walking distance to CONSOL Energy Center and several hotels. And, if you want to grab a meal here before your theater showing, The Carlton offers complementary limo service to events happening in the Cultural District. The restaurant is best known for quality steak and seafood dishes, hearty pasta plates, and an extensive wine list. Menu items change daily and are based on seasonal ingredients, providing patrons with the freshest meals possible. A trip to The Carlton is worthy of at least two courses. Entrees include veal with a bleu cheese crumble, swordfish and scallop BLT on ciabatta bread, and buffalo pot roast with chicken and apple sausage. Remember the menu is in constant flux so be sure to call ahead.

Chinatown Inn, 520 3rd Ave., Pittsburgh PA 15219; (412) 261-1292; www.chinatowninn.net; Chinese; $$. We've heard many a tale be told of Pittsburgh's once thriving Chinatown. Today, all that's left is one little restaurant with a big reputation, Chinatown Inn. The restaurant has ample seating, but since the food is straight out of tasty town, there's almost always a lunchtime line. The service is fast and friendly though, so don't let a little wait deter you. At Chinatown Inn you can score yourself a lunch combo with beef, poultry, or seafood. Vegetarian? They've got you covered. One of our favorite combos is General Tso's tofu served with fried rice and a spring roll. The portions are the perfect size, which will leave you with just enough room to polish off a fortune cookie and a cup of tea before you leave. Here's another selling point—free lot parking Mon through Fri after 6 p.m. for dinner.

The Common Plea Restaurant, 310 Ross St., Pittsburgh, PA 15219; (412) 697-3100; http://commonplea-restaurant.com; American; $$$. Picture yourself in a courtroom drama. After a hard day's work, you need a meal that can satisfy the hunger you built up whilst lawyerin'. Nestled amongst Pittsburgh's courthouse and City-County building, The Common Plea is an upscale, old-world joint that would fit the bill in that scenario or, you know, a normal "I'm hungry" scenario. While the decorative wallpaper and low-lit atmosphere may provide a bit of an intimidation factor, the menu is hardly unapproachable. Angel hair onion rings with bleu cheese make for a bright start, and entrees of pasta, chicken, or pork chop could make any law-abiding citizen swoon. Bring your appetite for either lunch of dinner in exchange for a quality meal. Just a little quid pro quo.

Diamond Market Bar & Grill, 430 Market Sq., Pittsburgh, PA 15222; (412) 325-2000; http://diamondmarketgrill.com; American; $$. Thanks to the owners of Primanti Bros., Diamond Market Bar & Grill is serving up delightful dishes in the heart of Market Square. Pittsburgh-made potato and feta pierogies served with cabbage and olive sour cream; macaroni and cheese made with cheddar, gruyère, and pepper jack cheeses; and Iron City mussels served in a sauce made from Iron City beer are just some of the noteworthy appetizers on the menu. We recommend you bring a big appetite when you come to visit because you'll be greeted with barbecue sandwiches of hand-pulled pork, hand-pulled chicken, and beef brisket; Angus burgers; and hot turkey sandwiches. To complement whichever sandwich you choose, you can order fresh-cut fries with a variety of toppings, like cheese curds and gravy, or sweet potato wedges seasoned with brown sugar, cinnamon, and cayenne pepper. House-made soups, handspun milk shakes, and apple and cabbage slaw round out a unique yet down-home menu that gets four thumbs up from us.

Elements Contemporary Cuisine, Four Gateway Center, 444 Liberty Ave., Pittsburgh, PA 15222; (412) 251-0168; www.elements cuisine.com; American; $$$. With a farm-to-table philosophy, Elements Contemporary Cuisine is bringing the suburban and rural farms of Pennsylvania to hungry Downtown eaters. Unique to Elements is the "Elements of Meat, Cheese, and More" menu where diners can create their own charcuterie board from a wide variety of fancy cured meats (such as duck speck, sopressata, and venison salami), cheeses, and "more," including olives, anchovies, prunes, and pickled peppers, to name a few. You can create your own board of 3, 6, or 12 selections. A full platter can be ordered for $90 if you are feeling swanky. Try to make it to Elements during happy hour and enjoy specials on drinks and half-price pizzas in the restaurant's lounge. In the vast dining room, opt for the tasting menu for $30 which includes three courses: featured soup or salad, choice of entrée, and dessert. See Executive Chef Robert Courser's recipe for **Jumbo Lump Crab Rangoon** on p. 248.

Franktuary, 325 Oliver Ave., Pittsburgh, PA 15222; (412) 288-0322; http://franktuary.com; Hot Dogs; $. Imagine, if you will, a gourmet hot doggery that resides in the basement of a church. It's a reality if you live in Pittsburgh! At Franktuary, you can get an all-beef dog, a locavore (organic grass-fed all-beef dog from Volant, Pennsylvania), or a veggie dog. We say go for the Pittsburgh dog, with a smooshed pierogie and coleslaw, and their Buffalo Dog, with Frank's Buffalo Wing Sauce and bleu cheese dressing. Make your dog or dogs into a meal and add homemade pierogies or have a religious experience with a bowl of heavenly vegetarian baked beans. The Franktuary also makes homemade soups and serves up scoops of Oakland's Dave and Andy's Homemade Ice Cream for those of you who

Pittsburgh Must-Eat Cheat Sheet

There are so many of our favorite restaurants in this book, deciding where to eat can be tough! To make life a little easier, here's a cheat sheet for the must-eats in our city. Whether you are here for a weekend or want to experience a quintessential, Pittsburgh culinary tour, we suggest you eat the following:

1. A **Primanti Bros.** (p. 63) sandwich. Choose from a variety of meats and order the sandwich as it comes, no exceptions.
2. Crepe pancakes from **P&G Pamela's Diner** (p. 62). These thin saucers of goodness overfill the plates and are the perfect start to any day in the city.
3. A fish sandwich. During Lent in Pittsburgh, churches and various organizations have fish frys and these are the places to get a great fish sandwich. When you are in town during the other 325 days of the year, head to the Strip for a Wholey Whaler from **Robert Wholey Market** (p. 73).
4. French fries from **Essie's Original Hot Dog Shop** (p. 282). The amount of fries per order will blow your mind. Period. We prefer these after a few cold ones and you should enjoy them like that too.

need a little something sweet after your meal. You can also find the Franktuary rolling around via bicycle, delivering dogs Downtown, and, best of all, it has one of the city's only food trucks. As one of their many taglines exclaims, "Franks be to God!" See Owner Megan Lindsey's recipe for **Sweet Onion Sauce** on p. 252.

5. Pierogies. We like pierogies a little too much in this city, as they are all over the place, even running around during a Pirates game. **Pierogies Plus** (p. 225) are the best in our book, but you can find them at almost any Pittsburgh dining establishment with both traditional and nontraditional fillings.

6. A Pittsburgh Salad, which can be found at tons of our city's eating establishments. Now, what makes a salad Pittsburgh is that it has french fries on top of it, usually with cheese and either chicken or steak (or both) and all the traditional salad fixings. Try one of our favorites at **The Elbow Room** (p. 134).

7. Tacos! If you are in the Strip District, you must stop by **Reyna's** (p. 72) taco stand and get at least two tacos. Because standing in the long line for just one is absurd.

8. Beer. Beer it up all day if you must. Try **Penn Brewery's** (p. 244) flagship Penn Pilsner and **The Church Brew Works'** (p. 177) Pious Monk Dunkel.

9. A specialty hot dog and Duck Fat Fries at **Station Street Hot Dogs** (p. 170).

10. **Prantl's** (p. 181) Burnt Almond Torte. Get the full-size version. And don't be ashamed if you don't want to share.

George Aiken Company, 218 Forbes Ave., Pittsburgh, PA 15222; (412) 391-6358; Southern; $. George Aiken Company has been a household name in Pittsburgh for over 50 years. George opened several restaurants throughout the city, including the famous Georgetown Inn on Mount Washington. George Aiken is the last of its kind: a cafeteria, found in Market Square. Press your nose against the glass and your mouth will start to water over Southern-style fried chicken, mashed potatoes, green beans, macaroni and cheese, hotcakes, and coleslaw. You can order a chicken or fish platter and you'll get two sides and a roll. The toughest decision will be which sides to choose from. Top your meal off with a chocolate, strawberry, or vanilla milk shake made with Turner's milk from the well-known Western Pennsylvania dairy farm.

Habitat Restaurant, 510 Market St., Pittsburgh, PA 15222; (412) 773-8848; www.habitatrestaurant.com; International; $$$$. Habitat Restaurant brings a level of sophistication to Market Square. The locally sourced restaurant is on the second floor of the swanky Fairmont Hotel. Grab a seat by the window and watch passersby on the street below or pull up a chair by the kitchen and watch the sous chef put the finishing touches on meals like the unbelievable roasted butternut squash soup and fresh and fabulous Asian salad with rice noodles, Asian pear, almonds, crispy wontons, bean sprouts, carrots, and miso dressing. Servers carry unique silver amphibian pitchers for water and present exquisitely prepared appetizers, entrees, and desserts. If you visit Habitat for lunch, a must order is the Executive Express, a platter with the soup, salad, entree, and dessert of the day. Get an order of their sweet potato fries on the side—you won't want to miss them. See Pastry Chef James Wroblewski's recipe for **Carrot Cake with Cream Cheese Icing and Caramel Sauce** on p. 261.

Las Velas Mexican Restaurant, 21 Market Sq., Pittsburgh, PA 15222; (412) 251-0031; www.lasvelasmex.com; Mexican; $$. Margarita-o-clock starts at approximately 5 p.m., Mon through Fri at Las Velas Mexican Restaurant in Market Square. It features fresh-made sangria and offers a variety of $5 cantina fare sure to make your hour even happier. *Flautas* stuffed with chicken, peppers, cheese, and more; *sopecitos* topped with ground beef or chicken, salsa, onions, cilantro, and cheese; and veggie nachos are just a few of the options available. If happy hour isn't your style, swing by early for lunch or late for dinner. We suggest the *tacos del paisa*, otherwise known as fish tacos, good at any time of day. Three tacos come loaded with freshly breaded tilapia, shredded cabbage, pico de gallo, and a creamy chipotle sauce. And let's not forget about the side of rice and beans.

Lemon Grass Cafe, 124 6th St., Pittsburgh, PA 15222; (412) 765-2222; Cambodian; $$. Tucked in the bottom floor of a parking garage, Lemon Grass Cafe serves Cambodian cuisine that's packed with flavor in a small location. The service is efficient and the prices are cheap. Lemon Grass Cafe is open for lunch and dinner, and since the service is fast, you can be sure you won't miss an important meeting or adventure in the city. For lunch, you get your choice of an entree with rice, the spicy house lemongrass soup, and a spring roll. We warn you that the soup is quite spicy, so be prepared. There is also the coconut lemongrass soup that is worth a try if you dig coconuts. For vegetarians, we recommend the fresh broccoli in an amazing brown sauce that is so good you will want to lick your plate clean. This is a definite must-eat-at restaurant, especially if you have a soft spot for Cambodian.

Madonna's Authentic Mexican Food, 431 Smithfield St., Pittsburgh, PA 15222; (412) 281-4686; Mexican; $. If you're in search of authentic Mexican cuisine in Pittsburgh, look no further than Madonna's. Madonna's is a cash-only joint, so leave the plastic at home. Order up a grande supremo burrito (that's a large, loaded burrito—meaning it comes with beans, Mexican rice, fresh-cut salsa, sour cream, cheese, and house-made guacamole, which you don't want to miss). You get your choice of chicken, steak, ground beef, veggie, or fish. Save the fish for when you're not in a rush, as it takes a bit longer to cook, but is totally worth it. The menu also features tacos, quesadillas, salads, and nachos, so there's something for absolutely everyone who enjoys Mexican cuisine. Madonna's is one of the best places Downtown to grab a quick, inexpensive, and well-made meal. You'll get it served with a smile too, as the service is top-notch!

Market Street Deli & Grill, 2 PPG Place, Pittsburgh, PA 15222; (412) 471-5851; www.marketstreetdeli.com; Deli; $. If you're in the market for a fresh and hearty Downtown lunch, Market Street Deli & Grill is the ticket. Reminiscent of a deli or grill found in many New York City neighborhoods, Market Street serves up fast and inexpensive lunches so you can get back to your busy schedule. Their daily specials can range from a buffalo chicken wrap to classic deli sandwiches like the reuben or club. What makes this deli different than your average run-of-the-mill sandwich shop? Its homemade Parmesan potato chips and their piping hot, homemade soups. If your palate is craving something fried or grilled, simply peek around the deli counter and order a loaded cheeseburger and fries from the grill. They'll get you in and out in no time.

Meat & Potatoes, 649 Penn Ave., Pittsburgh, PA 15222; (412) 325-7007; www.meatandpotatoespgh.com; Gastropub; $$–$$$. Meat and potatoes? Yes, please! The simplest of American eats gets a hip upgrade at one of the newest locales to join the Cultural District foodscape. Chef Richard DeShantz opened the gastropub in 2011, and the space has been packed ever since. Meat and potatoes are not the only thing on the menu, but carnivores will be delighted with the many meat-heavy options. Standout dinner entrees include the bolognese gnocchi with pancetta, short rib, and pork shoulder and the 34-ounce rib eye for two or for a very hungry one. This joint provides some 1930s atmosphere to go along with your meal; we're just glad it is no longer Prohibition. Brunch is also served on Saturday and Sunday, complete with all-you-can-drink Bloody Marys at the bar! See Meat & Potatoes recipe for **Chicken Potpie** on p. 257.

Nine on Nine, 900 Penn Ave., Pittsburgh, PA 15222; (412) 338-6463; www.nineoninepgh.com; American; $$$$ (Bar Nine: $$). If you are looking for a restaurant with a romantic atmosphere, and impressive food, then Nine on Nine is the place to go when

Downtown. The intimate dining room serves elegant hot and cold starters and entrees, complete with a Theatre Menu and a Chef's Tasting. *Note:* Reservations are strongly recommended for the dining room on weekends and during evening theater performances. In the dining room, the risotto made with wild mushrooms and truffles is the perfect starter. For an entree, try the prime strip with Kobe beef cheek pierogies (we just can't get enough pierogies in this city). If you can't get reservations in the dining room, the adjacent Bar Nine is just as fantastic. The bar has its own small, more casual menu consisting of refined bar food, including Kobe sliders, bar olives, and lobster macaroni and cheese. Though the prices may be a bit expensive, the atmosphere, food, and drinks are definitely worth every penny, and then some!

NOLA on the Square, 24 Market Sq., Pittsburgh, PA 15222; (412) 471-9100; www.nolaonthesquare.com; Creole; $$–$$$. Downtown restaurateur extraordinaire Yves Carreau (the man behind **The Sonoma Grille,** p. 40, and **Seviche,** p. 39) opened this tribute to New Orleans in Market Square. With cuisine dubbed as "Nouveau Creole," Pittsburgh now gets a taste of the bayou. If you're like us and sometimes dream of catchin' a gator with your bare hands, perhaps ordering alligator off the menu will go a ways in satisfying that longing. If your fantasies aren't as rough and tumble (and, quite frankly, weird), try the seafood jambalaya, gumbo, or our favorite dish, Scallops Mac Daddy, made with fresh cornucopia pasta, scallops, and a whole lot of delight. To add to the jazzy NOLA decor, live music is offered at least twice a week, usually on Friday and Saturday nights. No voodoo magic will be needed to make you want to dine here more than once.

Olive or Twist, 140 6th St., Pittsburgh, PA 15222; (412) 255-0525; www.olive-twist.com; Neighborhood Bar; $$. **Martinis!** The name of this bar really says it all, doesn't it? Sure, there is food too, like the buffalo chicken spread served with pita chips in a martini glass, and the Olive or Twist calamari, but really, it's all about the drinks at this spot. Olive or Twist's martini menu has a few martinis that boast Pittsburgh pride, including the Keystone Dirty made with Pittsburgh's own Boyd & Blair Potato Vodka and olive juice. For any non-martini drinkers, there's a healthy list of specialty cocktails, wine, and beer. The downstairs bar and restaurant is small and narrow, so be patient when ordering your drinks in a sea of Pittsburghers. We are all trying to get our martinis, too. Olive or Twist also has a private second-floor lounge that can be rented out for large parties.

Our Daily Bread, 320 6th Ave., Pittsburgh, PA 15222; (412) 471-3436; www.ourdailybreadpgh.org; Cafeteria; $. **Not all church basements are created equal, and Our Daily Bread, located on the ground floor of the First Presbyterian Church of Pittsburgh, is proof. The no-frills cafeteria will leave both your belly and wallet full and has been a warm helping hand in the Downtown community since 1932. It's just like your high school cafeteria only with way less drama and a greater sense of community. Rows of tables filled with a diverse crowd line the old basketball court. Home-style cooked meals like meat loaf with mashed potatoes, burgundy beef over noodles, and fish with macaroni and cheese are sure to warm you up on cold Pittsburgh days. Each day homemade soup like wedding and chicken rice are available as well as a salad bar to accompany your meal. You pay by weight, but most of the hearty lunch options end up under $6, a price we can all be thankful for these days.

Papa J's Centro, 212 Blvd. Of The Allies, Pittsburgh, PA 15222; (412) 391-7272; www.papajs.com; Italian; $$. You'll get a brief glimpse of Victorian-era Pittsburgh when you walk into Papa J's Centro Downtown. The rich mahogany woodwork is only the start of the history lesson. The building dates back to 1860 and once housed a brothel and possibly a stop on the Underground Railroad. "So I hear this place used to be a brothel" is always a great conversation starter. Once you're ready to eat, don't skip out on the fresh bread basket accompanied by an olive oil-balsamic mixture made for you tableside by one of the seasoned waiters. Follow your loaf of bread with the wedding soup made with carrots, celery, spinach, pastina, chicken, and veal meatballs. And for the main course, choose from several American-Italian standards like margherita pizza, pasta with basil pesto cream, or eggplant Parmigiano. If the folklore and food aren't enough, Papa J's Centro hosts a Comedy and Acoustic Open Mic night during the week. You probably should start working on your act now just in case. Additional location: Papa J's Ristorante, 200 E. Main St., Carnegie, PA 15106; (412) 429-7272.

Salonika Gyros, 133 6th St., Pittsburgh, PA 15222; (412) 261-4770; Mediterranean; $. Salonika Gyros is a great place for gyro lovers. The classic lamb gyro is our favorite, but all varieties are sensational and quite sizable. Vegetarians are also welcome at Salonika, and we recommend the falafel sandwich on pita bread. There are several Greek side dishes served, like spanakopita, lemon potatoes, grape leaves, and hummus with pita. We always make sure to order an ooey-gooey triangle of freshly made baklava! Salonika can get quite busy during the lunch time rush, and due to its convenient location to the many Pittsburgh theaters, it's equally abuzz with patrons in the evening hours. But there's plenty of room for all! This is a great place to fill your belly on a budget.

Seviche, 930 Penn Ave., Pittsburgh, PA 15222; (412) 697-3120; www.seviche.com; Latin American; $$. Named after raw seafood marinated in citrus juices, Seviche brings a vibrant, Latin flavor to Downtown while serving small plates and tasty cocktails to a typically sharp-dressed crowd. The dish to try is obviously the spot's namesake, which you can view being created at a specialty bar. The seviche is prepared in several forms, from the traditional to the "Fire and Ice" (for those feeling particularly spicy and ready for some habañero action). For non-seafood fans, the grass-fed beef tacos are a standout on the tapas menu. The tacos may be bite-size but are big on flavor. Be sure to order a drink, such as the Mango

Mojito, one of our favorites. Get your salsa dancing on from 9 p.m. to midnight with live music on Monday and on Thursday for live Latin Jazz from 7 to 10 p.m.

Six Penn Kitchen, 146 6th St., Pittsburgh, PA 15222; (412) 566-7366; www.sixpennkitchen.com; American; $$$. Whether you're looking for brunch, lunch, dinner, snack, or cocktail, Six Penn Kitchen is sure to satisfy your craving. Here, the menu changes frequently but always seems to include a specialty burger (sometimes even served on waffles and corn bread), fish, chicken, lamb, and a vegetarian entree, like falafel. The complimentary bread basket is stocked with several varieties to please the palate. For starters, order a few items off the Snacks and Sides menu, such as the "tots" with sage aioli, the macaroni and cheese, and the house-made pretzels. Six Penn Kitchen is known for serving food made of ingredients from local and sustainable farms and suppliers in the Western Pennsylvania region. The restaurant has two levels of dining, including two bars, a private dining room on the second floor, and a rooftop lounge with stellar views of the city, especially at night during Pirates fireworks.

The Sonoma Grille, 947 Penn Ave., Pittsburgh, PA 15222; (412) 697-1336; www.thesonomagrille.com; American; $$$. The Sonoma Grille is a little slice of the West Coast right along Penn Avenue. Stocked with over 1,000 wines, this place makes it easy to get distracted and perhaps drink your meal. But the food should certainly steal some of your attention. The menu of Cali-inspired dishes is built on the strengths of locally sourced ingredients, so it adapts as the seasons change. Start your meal with the wild mushroom flatbread or seasonal flatbread, prepared depending on the ingredients of the season. Entrees range from duck and pork loin to diver scallops and lamb. Expect to be treated fabulously from start to finish, as the service is as excellent as the roving bread basket. Sunday at Sonoma features a lively Jazz Brunch with Pittsburgh-area musicians. For a reasonable set price of $22, you get a breakfast cocktail, all the makings of a solid meal, and a live concert. The wine, the atmosphere, and the food could trigger some California dreaming, but the sights and sounds of the 'Burgh will make for a pretty sweet reality.

Sree's Foods, 701 Smithfield St., Pittsburgh, PA 15222; (412) 860-9181; www.srees.com; Indian; $. Downtown Pittsburgh is filled with countless upscale restaurants but also has a few unassuming spots that could easily be overlooked. Sree's Foods ranks high on the overlooked list. Tucked into an oddly shaped building on a busy corner, Sree's Foods serves authentic Indian cuisine for lunch. For around $5 you can sample various Indian staples like spinach black-eyed peas, eggplant curry, and tomato dal. Mrs. Sree prepares all the food, mostly vegan and vegetarian options, daily based on a philosophy she and her late husband, Mr. Sree, incorporate into each dish: that food is life. Their attention to spice and flavor elevates the dishes to the next level and creates that slow satisfying burn that will keep you craving more. Additional locations: See website.

Taste of Dahntahn, 535 Liberty Ave., Pittsburgh, PA 15222; (412) 224-2240; http://tasteofdahntahn.com; Diner; $$. Think soda shop, circa *Back to the Future Part II*, kind of futuristic but nostalgic at the same time. That's Taste of Dahntahn. You won't be able to miss it with the huge neon-colored sign with an arrow pointing you into the front door. Inside, you get a diner that is bright, sunny, and a menu filled with menu items like the Iron City Wedge, iceberg lettuce, gorgonzola cheese, tomatoes, peppered bacon, and creamy red wine vinaigrette, and The Swanky Sirloin Sammich, shaved sirloin, cheddar and provolone cheeses, roasted red peppers, caramelized onions, and Dahntahn's homemade 58 mayo. The oval bar has soda shop-style stools and features some great local beers on tap, perfect for when you need a drink after work or a day of "Dahntahn" shopping. Breakfast, lunch, and dinner are served up 7 days a week. Plan to stick around for a while. You can sit, eat, and chat for hours and then ride your DeLorean into the sunset.

Tick Toc Restaurant, 400 Fifth Ave., Pittsburgh, PA 15219; (412) 232-2307; Diner; $. Tucked into the corner among men's clothing on the first floor of Macy's department store is the Tick

Toc Restaurant. It's a hidden Downtown gem and classic Pittsburgh. The menu looks like it hasn't changed since it was first penned and the same goes for the patrons. If you're mid-shop and have a hankering for a tuna melt or want to reminisce about the good ole' days, Tick Toc will help you in both departments. There's a lunch counter as well as a dining area that's usually full during the lunch rush. The menu features diner standards like meat loaf, open-faced turkey sandwiches, and liver and onions. We suggest the chicken potpie. Large chunks of chicken, peas, and carrots are in a rich creamy sauce and topped with a flaky round of puff pastry. It's accompanied by a spinach salad topped with mandarin oranges and dressed with its signature sesame dressing. Pair that with a classic milk shake or malt, and you have a perfect midday lunch break.

Verde Good Beans, 412 1st Ave., Pittsburgh, PA 15219; (412) 523-8885; Breakfast and Lunch; $. The instant you walk into Verde Good Beans on 1st Avenue, you enter a sort of euphoric state. The decor is happy and homey and you feel as if you know the staff on a personal level, like you're childhood friends. Open for breakfast and lunch, their menu changes daily so look them up on Facebook and Twitter to see what the specials are before you pop in. They serve sustainable, organic foods and local coffees and teas. Order up one of their hearty soups or stews and pair it with a create-your-own panini. One of our favorite dishes is their black bean pumpkin soup,

PITTSBURGH FOOD TOURS

If you are like us, you may sometimes find yourself stuffing your stomach so full of good food, you don't want to move. So much so, you may tell yourself, "I need to go walk this off immediately." Well, grab your walking shoes and your fanny pack and go on a Pittsburgh food tour where you can eat, walk, and tour the city's neighborhoods and countryside. There are two main food tour groups in the area: **'Burgh Bits & Bites,** focused on touring the city's neighborhoods and eateries by foot, and **The Fork and The Road, LLC,** focused on touring Western Pennsylvania's countryside with day bus trips out to the 'Burbs and beyond.

'Burgh Bits & Bites Food Tour (www.burghfoodtour.com) offers tours of Pittsburgh's neighborhoods, including Bloomfield/ Little Italy, Brookline, Lower Lawrenceville, Mount Washington, the Strip District (typically on Friday and Saturday) and a wine tasting tour in the Strip District on Friday evenings. Private tours are also available for large groups. Each tour takes you on a stroll, where you learn about local history while tasting local cuisine from eateries along the route. Tickets must be purchased in advance, and tours happen rain or shine. See website for all the details.

which you can enjoy from a tiny bistro table or curled up in an over-stuffed chair. Its quirky decor makes us smile almost as much as the fact that they have Mulberry Creamery gelato and about a million specialty smoothie and coffee drinks on the menu.

The **Fork and The Road, LLC** (http://theforkandtheroad
.com) offers bus tours to the Laurel Highlands, Greensburg and
Latrobe, and Bedford County. On these day or half-day tours, you
board charter buses to these suburban locations and visit a variety of
eateries, including restaurants, bakeries, farms, markets, and other
local food producers. New to the tour lineup are adventures closer
to the city, McKees Rocks and Homestead, which offer tourgoers
history of Pittsburgh steel mills along with culinary explorations in
these neighborhoods. In the Homestead tour, you can experience
a Western Pennsylvania Cookie Table. Traditionally showcased at
wedding receptions, a cookie table is just what the name suggests, a
table (and usually multiple tables) of homemade cookies. Experiencing
one outside of matrimony is indeed a special treat. See website for
tour dates and details.

If exploring the local craft beer scene is more your
thing, then get onboard the **'Burgh Brews Tour by
Molly's Trolleys** (www.mollystrolleyspittsburgh.com).
Boarding the 1920s-era trolley will take you to three
stops, including two local breweries and one distillery or
cider house. See website for more information and tour
availability.

Winghart's Whiskey and Burger Bar, 5 Market Sq., Pittsburgh,
PA 15222; (412) 434-5600; www.winghartburgers.com; Burgers; $$.
Walking into Winghart's in Market Square is kind of like walking into
Cheers, where everybody knows your name. Okay, so the Winghart's
crew doesn't know our names (yet), but they're great at making you

feel welcome. Winghart's doesn't offer up much seating, aside from a few tables in the back and a lunch counter up front. However, it offers specialty burgers you'll want to eat for breakfast, lunch, and dinner. Two of our favorite burgers are named after the owner's friends and family, like the Denny Double Blue with bleu cheese dressing and crumbles, and The Shipwreck with brie, caramelized onions, arugula, bacon, and white truffle aioli. The burgers come wrapped in paper and not on a plate, so a bit of messiness is inevitable. There is nothing quite like sitting at the counter enjoying a juicy burger, basket of fries, and a whiskey, beer, or cider from Arsenal Cider House. If you aren't feeling a burger, the wood-fired pizzas are equally as awesome. Additional location: South Side, 1505 E. Carson Street, Pittsburgh, PA 15203; (412) 904-4620.

Landmarks

Grand Concourse, 100 W. Station Square Dr., Pittsburgh, PA 15219; (412) 261-1717; www.muer.com/grand-concourse; Seafood; $$$$ (Gandy Dancer: $$). The Pittsburgh and Lake Erie Railroad Station was built in 1901. Now, a century and some change later, the trains are long gone but the grandeur of an era gone by remains. Since 1978, the Grand Concourse has occupied this ornate space along the Monongahela River and provided Pittsburghers with the opportunity to marvel at truly remarkable architecture while indulging in classic seafood fare. It is one of the only places in town that offers the option of a freshwater lobster tail as a side dish. Can everyone say "fancy"? The Sunday brunch here is particularly epic with everything from salmon Rockefeller to bananas Foster. Take a date here, cozy up in a plush banquette, and, boy howdy, do you mean business! The Grand Concourse's sister restaurant, The Gandy Dancer, is right next door. The old-timey railroad feel extends to the Dancer, but the splendor is traded for a more casual quaintness. It is a good spot for a cocktail, saddled up to the polished-wood bar, or for a hardy fish sandwich.

The Original Oyster House, 20 Market Sq., Pittsburgh, PA 15222; (412) 566-7925; www.originaloysterhousepittsburgh.com; Seafood; $. Some bars and restaurants scream Pittsburgh. They're made up of the fabric of what makes Pittsburgh, Pittsburgh. They smell like Pittsburgh. They look like Pittsburgh. And with walls filled with portraits of our city's heroes and flickering Iron City neons, some just give you the true sense of what it's like to be from the 'Burgh. The Original Oyster House in Market Square is one of those places where you can cozy up to the bar, strike up a conversation, and leave with a full belly and a new friend. It was established in 1870 and is Pittsburgh's oldest bar and restaurant. Films have been made here. Important sports figures, entertainers, and politicians have eaten here. And most importantly, giant fish sandwiches that require a special bun are on the menu here. If that doesn't make you want to join the ranks of its thousands of other customers, then maybe its New England clam chowder, Maryland-style crab cakes, baked scrod, or giant collection of Miss America Pageant contestant photographs will.

Specialty Stores, Markets & Producers

GO Pretzel, 807 Liberty Ave., Pittsburgh, PA 15222; www.gopretzel.com. Close to several main bus lines and the Wood Street T Station, GO Pretzel is the perfect spot for a quick bite before, during, and after an adventure through the city. The tiny storefront space is no nonsense, and so is its menu: pretzels, pretzels, and more pretzels. You have your choice of either sweet or savory knots of goodness and an addition of a dipping sauce, like a sweet glaze or hot mustard, if you feel like a taste twist. Pretzel dogs also make an appearance, but our money is always on the Soft Baked Original pretzel for a fresh, salty snack. As an added bonus, the pretzels contain no trans fats. Go ahead and have two.

The Strip District

Need unlicensed sports apparel? Head to the Strip. Got a hankering for fresh noodles? Get on over to the Strip. Want to people watch like a pro? Trot on down to the Strip.

Desire a true Pittsburgh experience? You guessed it . . . take a trip to the Strip.

The Strip District is the market-filled area from 11th to 33rd Streets sandwiched between Liberty Avenue and Smallman Street. Once populated with factories manufacturing the likes of steel and glass, this bustling stretch of neighborhood now boasts a diverse and fresh selection of ethnic food and the most original Pittsburgh memorabilia in town. Though you can no longer fulfill an order for steel, you can order up some fresh mozzarella and a football stadium snow globe.

The dining scene here, like the retail, offers a bit of everything. A refined palate will have no trouble finding a restaurant that ticks all the boxes of a good meal. While swanky dinner spots abound, the real stars of the Strip are the "this food is sticking to my ribs" places that have become Pittsburgh institutions. If you don't stand in line outside of a restaurant at least once while visiting the neighborhood, you are doing something wrong.

Just remember to follow the crowds for lunch and then get fancy for the late-night meals. But you should always keep your newly purchased black and gold merchandise at the ready.

Foodie Faves

Bar Marco, 2216 Penn Ave., Pittsburgh, PA 15222; (412) 471-1900; www.barmarcopgh.com; Wine Bar; $$. Housed in the former No. 7 Engine Co. building, Bar Marco is a quaint wine bar and tapas restaurant serving small plates with big flavor. The drinks menu has a few specialty cocktails, wine, and champagne. But don't think you can just get fancy cocktails at this place. There are PBR pounders and other cans of beer on the menu. To accompany your glass of wine or can of beer, order a few small plates to share amongst friends. Try the duck BLT and the *patatas bravas*, a dish of potatoes, cubed and drizzled with a slightly spicy red pepper sauce. You can also order a selection of meats, cheeses, and other goodies and craft your own plate of nibbles. Bar Marco is open Wed through Sat from 5 p.m. to 2 a.m. and draws a variety of patrons, making it one of our new favorite places to people watch.

Bella Notte Pizza Pasta & More, 1914 Penn Ave., Pittsburgh, PA 15222; (412) 281-4488; Pizza; $$. Bella Notte is just a short walk from numerous cafes, florists, and specialty markets. You can sit inside and watch pizza dough being tossed with care, or, if weather permits, pull up a seat outside and watch the crowds pass by giving your plate googly eyes. The most important detail to your pizza order will be deciding what toppings to get. The topping list is quite long, including pineapple, hot sausage, artichokes, Canadian bacon, and the list goes on. Our topping of choice at Bella Notte is pepperoni, which is shredded and thrown on the pizza, achieved nowhere else. The shredding seems to allow all of the juices to seep out of the pepperoni and onto the pizza, and we love it. In addition to pizza, there are hoagies and salads and more on the menu, but really, it's all about the pizza here.

Cafe on the Strip, 1814 Penn Ave., Pittsburgh, PA 15222; (412) 288-9895; Italian; $. When you find yourself in the Strip on a cold winter day, looking for warmth is key. One place you can get warm and feed your belly is at Cafe on the Strip, which has a fireplace that will make you want to cuddle up to the person next to you. This small breakfast and lunch spot has Italian specialty dishes, including lasagna, manicotti, ziti, eggplant, and other pastas. Gourmet pizzas and sandwiches are also on the menu. We like breakfast here in the morning. If you aren't an early bird, no worries—breakfast is served all day. The omelets are great as well as the Italian toast that come with them. If the weather is pleasant, sit outside at one of the few sidewalk tables. This is a great spot to take in all of the sensations of the Strip.

Cioppino, 2350 Railroad St., Pittsburgh, PA 15222; (412) 281-6593; www.cioppinoofpittsburgh.com; Steak House; $$$. On the backside of what used to house a small local grocery store is Cioppino, specializing in seafood and steaks. The main dining room is open, breezy, and filled with rich wood tones. Oversize leather chairs and couches, dark lighting, and the rich smell of cigars make for a relaxing atmosphere in the lounge and cigar bar. Can't decide where to sit? Why not experience all three? Start with a drink in the bar, where you can choose from the extensive domestic and import beer list, martinis, single malts, or cognac. Then, enjoy dinner in the main dining area. Starters include shrimp cocktail, lobster risotto, oysters on the half shell, and beef carpaccio. Entrees include seafood options like cioppino, which consists of clams, Dungeness crab, Mediterranean sea bass, mussels, jumbo shrimp, scallops, fennel, and onion, and meat options of filet mignon or New York strip steak. Finish the night with an after-dinner cocktail, a selection of house-made desserts, and a cigar in the cigar bar.

Eleven Contemporary Kitchen, 1150 Smallman St., Pittsburgh, PA 15222; (412) 201-5656; www.bigburrito.com/eleven; American; $$$–$$$$. Eleven Contemporary Kitchen is a member of the big Burrito family of restaurants (see **Mad Mex** [p. 147], **Casbah** [p. 124], **Kaya Island Cuisine** [p. 56], **Soba Lounge** [p. 166], and **Umi** [p. 174]). One of the swankiest big Burrito restaurants is Eleven, which provides an upscale dining experience from its intimate booths to its proclaimed "Contemporary American" cuisine. Waitstaff is assigned to particular tasks, so you will never have an empty water glass or want for bread; the copper menu covers dance under the low light; and the food is presented beautifully with a certain level of comfort cooked right in. Dining at Eleven demands a slower pace and a diner's willingness to feel pampered. While flavorful dishes like the farmhouse chicken resting on a bed of creamy risotto may fill you up, do not skip the sweetness. The chocolate-peanut-pretzel candy bar, a brownie sandwiched between thin chocolate, a peanut butter mousse, with a dollop of chocolate peanut butter ice cream on top is a game changer in the dessert realm. Treats this miraculously delicious are a rare breed. Just like Eleven.

The Enrico Biscotti Co. and Enrico's Cafe, 2022 Penn Ave., Pittsburgh, PA 15222; (412) 281-2602; www.enricobiscotti.com; Italian; $. "I'll take one of each please!" will be your favorite phrase at The Enrico Biscotti Co. You will want to devour every pastry you lay your eyes on, including the handmade Italian biscotti and macaroons. Once you have your bags of biscotti in hand, make an immediate right out of the tiny bakery and walk down the narrow passage to Enrico's Cafe. Serving lunch 6 days a week (Mon through Sat) from 11 a.m. to 3 p.m., and brunch on Sat from 8 until 11 a.m., Enrico's Cafe offers up rustic Italian dishes all prepared in the open-aired kitchen, including a wood-fired oven for the pizza pies. The beans and greens are a must order, as well as the brick oven pizzas. The menu changes daily, and special dinners and cooking classes are held often. Check Enrico's website for more details on these special events.

Pittsburgh Public Market

Inspired by market houses of Pittsburgh past and other metropolitan markets like the Reading Terminal Market in Philadelphia and the West Side Market in Cleveland, the **Pittsburgh Public Market** is a year-round place to pick up fresh food, prepared food, and a select amount of non-food-related fun.

The Market burst onto the scene in 2011 in its current 10,000-square-foot space. Housed in a former produce terminal on Smallman Street, the surrounds are expansive. You can almost imagine the trains pulling up to unload produce and auction off the goods to the hungriest of consumers. With open hours every Friday, Saturday, and Sunday, Pittsburghers and tourists can check out the digs each weekend. All of the vendors are locally owned and operated, and all of the products are locally sourced. Part of the charm of the Market is the vendor and visitor interaction—you can ask the person manning the booth product questions and get some insider tips. The Market has space for 50 vendors and hopes to grow as popularity continues to build.

Some current food-centric vendors, which have been at it since the get-go, are the Crested Duck Charcuterie (www.crestedduck.com) for freshly butchered meat, Gosia's Pierogies (www.gosiaspierogies .com) for pierogies, East End Brewing (www.eastendbrewing.com) for brewskis, and Clarion River Organics (www.clarionriverorganics .com) for farm-fresh produce. Small and new businesses alike are given an opportunity to thrive.

While the Market has its hand on the pulse of deliciousness, it also tries to bring the public a nice experience to go along with their purchases. The Market acts as a gathering place, offering different themed weekends and activities for any curious visitor. You can pick up prepared food and settle in at a collection of tables in the corner to take in all the sights and sounds. Every second Saturday of the month at the Market, visitors are treated to live music by local talented folk. Nothing like downing some pierogies to the sounds of bluegrass (or some other tune-age), we say!

The Market also often partners with nonprofits (think museums and libraries) to have family-friendly crafts and informational booths. You may visit to get a cookie or to fill up a growler and leave with a wreath you crafted with your skilled hands, or lots of help from a friendly neighbor.

For more information on the Pittsburgh Public Market, visit their website at www.pittsburghpublicmarket.org. The Market is owned by the local nonprofit Neighbors in the Strip, www.neighborsinthestrip.com, which champions the Strip District and all it has to offer. Pittsburgh Public Market, Produce Terminal Building, Smallman Street entrance, off 17th Street.

Get down to the Market soon—you'll love what and who you run into!

Kaya Island Cuisine, 2000 Smallman St., Pittsburgh, PA 15222; (412) 261-6565; www.bigburrito.com/kaya; International; $$$. Spice is definitely not lacking in any dish you'll find at Kaya. Don't be afraid to mix and match *tropas* or starters. We recommend the conch fritters, the Kaya chips with mango-tomatillo salsa, or the

Yucatan hot bean dip. If you are feeling an entree, order the crispy fish tacos served with Reyna's tortillas. If you're looking for a unique take on a traditional burger, order the Kaya burger, served with a fried egg, avocado, crispy bacon, Chihuahua cheese, and Kaya's special sauce. Kaya is known for its happy hour, Mon through Fri from 5 to 7 p.m., with half off draft beers and single serving drinks, and Sunday brunch from 11 a.m. to 3 p.m. If you're in the Strip on a Thursday, head to Kaya for fried chicken night, featuring all-natural and locally raised chickens. Eat up, mon!

La Prima Espresso Bar, 205 21st St., Pittsburgh, PA 15222; (412) 281-1922; www.laprima.com; Coffee Shop; $. Getting around the Strip super early on Saturday morning can be quite difficult if you are not an early bird. You need to be alert as you walk, shop, and carry your loads of goods. To help keep your eyes open during your shopping journey is La Prima, both a neighborhood coffee shop and coffee roaster. This is a favorite spot of local 'Burghers and for a good cause. At La Prima, not only are quality coffees and espressos crafted, but the coffee beans are roasted in house. Top-notch quality if you ask us. Other locations: Oakland, Carnegie

Mellon University, Wean Hall, 5000 Forbes Ave., Pittsburgh, PA 15213; (412) 268-2000.

Osteria 2350, 2350 Railroad St., Pittsburgh, PA 15222; (412) 281-6595; www.osteria2350pittsburgh.com; Italian, $. Right next to Cioppino is Osteria 2350, both of which are owned and operated by Chef Greg Alauzen. While Cioppino excels at fine dining, Osteria 2350 takes a rustic, home-style approach to Italian classics. The menu features soups, salads, sandwiches, and pasta. And, it is an excellent choice for lunch or a laid-back dinner. We enjoy pulling up a burlap-covered chair to the stainless steel bar for a quick bite. The antipasti plate is always a good option to start and includes Parma Sausage Products prosciutto, salami rustico, sweet sopressata, coppa secca, mozzarella, and aged provolone. If you're in the mood for a sandwich, two good options to consider are the meatball sub, which is large enough for two, or the prosciutto sandwich made with Parma Sausage Product prosciutto, roasted red peppers, fresh mozzarella, and balsamic. While the sandwiches and pizza are always a great choice, the pasta, most of it made in house, is the way to go. Our favorite is the house-made gnocchi baked with parmigiano reggiano and fontina. The gnocchi is delicate and fluffy, and the sweet red sauce and hearty dose of cheese make it our go-to choice for both lunch and dinner.

Penn Avenue Fish Company, 2208 Penn Ave., Pittsburgh, PA 15222; (412) 434-7200; www.pennavefishcompany.com; Seafood; $–$$. Besides purchasing fresh fish and seafood at the Penn

Avenue Fish Company to take home and cook yourself, you can get killer fish sandwiches for lunch after a morning of shopping. Of course there are a few other places in the Strip where you can get a fish sandwich, but at Penn Avenue Fish Company you can order something more nontraditional. Fish sandwiches come in a plethora of varieties, including salmon, tuna, swordfish, tilapia, and cod. Fish tacos and wraps are also on the menu, as well as specialty seafood soups and pizzas that are a definite must-try. Penn Avenue Fish Company also makes some super sushi, which can also be ordered for special parties and private occasions. You can purchase sushi-grade tuna to take home and make your own, but why bother when Penn Avenue Fish Company can make it for you? Additional location: Downtown; 308 Forbes Ave., Pittsburgh, PA 15222; (412) 562-1710.

Peppi's Old Tyme Sandwich Shop, 1721 Penn Ave., Pittsburgh, PA 15222; (412) 562-0125; www.peppisubs.com; Sandwiches; $. Philadelphia may be known for its cheese steaks, but Pittsburgh can definitely hold its own thanks to Peppi's Old Tyme Sandwich Shop. At Peppi's, you can order up your cheese steak with chicken, steak, sausage, Italian meats, and even veggies. Whichever way you choose, we recommend ordering your sub with onions and peppers, and don't forget fries on the side. All of their sandwiches are served on locally made Mike & Dave's Italian bread. The most famous item on the menu is the "RoethlisBurger," a hot sausage and beef sandwich topped with scrambled eggs and American cheese. The sandwich is named after Steelers quarterback Ben Roethlisberger and can also be ordered as "The #7." At Peppi's, the workers move fast, and it's amazing to watch them slicing, dicing, frying, and wrapping. It's enough to make you work up an appetite, which is good, considering most of Peppi's subs can feed half of the Pittsburgh Steelers. Additional locations: See website.

Pho Van Vietnamese Noodles & Grill, 2120 Penn Ave., Pittsburgh, PA 15222; (412) 281-7999; www.phovan.net; Vietnamese; $$. Pho Van offers fresh and fun Vietnamese food. Pho (pronounced "fuh") is a beef and noodle-based dish that is influenced by both Chinese and French cuisine. At Pho Van you can order your noodles with a variety of cuts of beef including tenderloin, brisket, tips, meatballs, or even get pho chicken. Each order of pho is served with sides of basil, bean sprouts, and lime, flavors that all incorporate well with the beef and noodles. If you aren't sure what you want to go for, you can order off the grill. We recommend the rice noodles and grilled shrimp bowl, which is topped cucumber, carrots, bean sprouts, peanuts, and Pho's homemade chili garlic sauce. It's a great way to experience Vietnamese food without venturing too far out of your comfort zone. We say go "pho" it!

21st Street Coffee and Tea, 50 21st St., Pittsburgh, PA 15222; (412) 281-0809; http://21streetcoffee.com; Coffee Shop; $. A good cup of coffee or tea is a morning essential. Even more essential if you are going shopping for produce before noon. One of our favorite local coffee shops is 21st Street Coffee and Tea. Unlike some coffee shops, 21st Street hand-crafts each pot of coffee and tea to perfection. Intelligentsia coffee beans are used to brew each cup individually, which can take a few more minutes than getting a cup of joe at a standard coffee shop. Be patient and try not to watch the slow drip process, as it won't happen as fast as you may like. Just sit at the high top bar and people watch outside the windows while your coffee is being prepared. Additional location: 225 5th Ave., Pittsburgh, PA 15222; (412) 281-0121.

Landmarks

DeLuca's, 2015 Penn Ave., Pittsburgh, PA 15222; (412) 566-2195; Diner; $. Red and white checkered floors. Green wooden booths from years ago. Grease scents floating through the air from an open kitchen behind the counter. Welcome to DeLuca's, a throwback diner with, what some might argue, Pittsburgh's most perfect breakfast. The menu includes lunch options, but to go to DeLuca's and leave without sampling the morning's best is a crime. The giant, fluffy pancakes are the star of the show at this joint. With a lengthy list of mix-ins like chocolate chips and blueberries, your pancakes can be personalized to your liking. If you have a real sweet tooth, order a pancake (or waffle) sundae, with ice cream and topping combos that will instigate a trip to the dentist. Other solid breakfast items include a big breakfast burrito and omelets that dwarf the plates. Lines form outside every Saturday and Sunday, but don't fear the wait. Once indoors you'll be treated to illogical amounts of food that have been satisfying 'Burghers for decades.

Klavon's Ice Cream Parlor, 2801 Penn Ave., Pittsburgh, PA 15222; (412) 434-0451; www.klavonsicecream.com; Ice Cream; $. Step through the doors at 2801 Penn Ave. and, sure enough, you'll be transported through time. Opened as a pharmacy in the 1920s, Klavon's has since been re-imagined as an ice cream parlor complete with original features, and family ownership, intact. A marble counter runs the length of the shop dotted with metal barstools. Wooden booths provide alternative seating across the brown and beige floor. On display are relics from the pharmacy days. All the nostalgia is as delightful as the ice cream and, good golly, the ice cream is a delight! Klavon's offers all the classic sundaes, deliciously thick milk shakes, and floats an ice cream lover could want. Also on the menu are old-fashioned treats like phosphates (carbonated fountain sodas made from scratch) and ice cream sodas. Flavored whipped cream, created in house, makes a nice topper to any treat. Service here is top-notch with a truly friendly staff who will make you feel right at home, if home were an early-20th-century drugstore. If you need more sugar as you exit, a plethora of penny candy sits by the cash register ready to be devoured. Klavon's also serves coffee and lunch.

P&G Pamela's Diner, 60 21st St., Pittsburgh, PA 15222; (412) 281-6366; www.pamelasdiner.com; Diner; $. P&G Pamela's Diner is a Pittsburgh classic. For out-of-towners the original Strip District location is a must-try although there are five other equally delightful locations. College students. Families. The after church crowd. It seems like everyone heads to Pamela's on Saturday and Sunday mornings for the famous crepe-style pancakes. Even President Barack Obama flipped for the flapjacks back in 2008. He enjoyed them so much that the following Memorial Day those famous break-fast staples were served at the White House for the President, his wife, and 80 veterans. After that how could you not want to stop by and see what all the fuss is about? Our go-to dish is the Morning After, which offers up 2 crepe pancakes, eggs, your choice of bacon or sausage, and toast. We admit we almost always go a step further and order a side of the Lyonnaise potatoes and recommend you do the same as the crispy, perfectly seasoned taters complement the crepes in a way that has us going back morning after morning. Additional locations: See website.

Primanti Bros., 46 18th St., Pittsburgh, PA 15222; (412) 263-2142; www.primantibros.com; Sandwiches; $. The Primanti sandwich is a Pittsburgh staple, and when visiting, you must eat at least one. If you eat more than one in a single day, we won't judge. Started in the early 1930s, Primanti Bros. sold sandwiches to truck drivers delivering goods to the Strip District. Layered on two thick, hand-cut slices of white Italian bread, the Primanti sandwich comes with a meat of your choice (capicola, fish, sirloin steak, roast beef and much more), provolone cheese, fresh-cut french fries, coleslaw, and tomatoes. Onions are extra. One rule of thumb to eating at Primanti Bros.: Order the sandwich as it comes. No substitutions please, or you will be judged. The Strip location is open 24 hours a day, 7 days a week, with 16 other locations throughout Pittsburgh and 3 in Florida. If you make it to one of the suburban locations, try the homemade pizza. Even though you should always get a sandwich at Primanti Bros., the pizza is also quite tasty. Additional locations: See website.

Smallman Street Deli, 2840 Smallman St. #1, Pittsburgh, PA 15222; (412) 434-5800; www.smallmanstreetdeli.com; Deli; $. Smallman Street Deli is one of those places you get excited to visit. The enormous deli board lists out meats and cheeses galore that you can order and take home with you. You can order homemade soups that change daily (try its famous matzo ball or its hearty chili), or make it a complete meal and pair it with a classic Reuben or Rachel. Our favorite part of the meal has to be its famous crunchy kosher dill pickles. Smallman Street Deli is a family-owned and -operated

How to Make
a Primanti Bros. Sandwich N'at
(When You Can't Get the Real Thing)

Sit in a **Primanti Bros.** in the city long enough and you're bound to hear someone say, "I came right here from the airport. The first thing I do when I come to Pittsburgh is get a Primanti Bros. Sandwich N'at!" Its seriously stacked sandwich is almost as legendary to some as Franco's Immaculate Reception. And once a Primanti sandwich craving hits, it's hard to ignore. So while a homemade version might not evoke the same nostalgic feelings, it will at least hold you over until you can find the real thing.

We don't know the secret recipe, but we have eaten enough sandwiches in our day to know what goes into making one. Here is our own recipe for making a Primanti Bros. sandwich of your own, at home.

Step 1: Start with 2 thick slices of Italian bread. Go to your nearest grocery store and pick up a freshly baked Italian loaf and cut it into thick slices. This is the key to having a proper sandwich foundation.

Step 2: Then comes the meat and cheese. Turkey, ham, bacon, whatever your meat of choice, heat it up and top it with a few slices of cheese (we suggest provolone). Layer it on one slice of Italian bread.

Step 3: Next comes a hearty handful of french fries. (You want measurements? Try your hand.) Fresh cut is the way to go.

Step 4: Then add a handful of coleslaw, and not the mayo kind. (Don't be a baby. Leave this off and you just have a sad sandwich.)

Step 5: Next comes 2 slices of tomato.

Step 6: Top it off with a fried egg (okay—this is the only optional step).

Step 7: Slap the other slice of Italian bread on top and cut in half.

Step 8: Enjoy with your favorite beer. We suggest an ice-cold Iron City.

joint, and they sure do make you feel like family when you show up. We challenge you to not want to go back the next day after you experience a deli the way a deli should be. Additional location: Squirrel Hill, 1912 Murray Ave., Pittsburgh, PA 15217; (412) 421-3354.

Specialty Stores, Markets & Producers

Benkovitz Seafood, 2300 Smallman St., Pittsburgh, PA 15222; (412) 263-3016; www.benkovitzseafood.com. If you want really good seafood soups and chowders, Benkovitz is the place to go. The soup selection changes daily and includes shrimp bisque, Manhattan clam chowder, creamy crab, seafood chowder, seafood bisque, and New England clam chowder. You can't really go wrong with any of the choices, but the shrimp bisque is our absolute favorite. It is jam-packed with chunks of shrimp. Beyond soups, Benkovitz's food menu includes fish sandwiches, fish dinners, seafood pastas, seafood salads, crab cakes, and tons of other seafood dishes. There are a few tables to sit and enjoy your seafood, but Benkovitz is known for their stand-up counters with bottles of various sauces to complement your seafood order. In addition to prepared seafood, Benkovitz has a fresh fish counter and frozen seafood section. Benkovitz has been supplying Pittsburghers with seafood since the early 1900s, and the retailer's longevity proves that it has some of the best seafood in town.

Fort Pitt Candy Co., 1642 Penn Ave., Pittsburgh, PA 15222; (412) 281-9016; www.fortpittcandy.com. Looking for Nerds? Pop Rocks? Sugar Babies? Or a simple Tootsie Roll? You are going to want to head to the Fort Pitt Candy Co. Upon walking into the dimly lit storefront, you will literally be surrounded from floor to ceiling with candy. So, watch your step as you walk around the

sugary confections. With seasonal merchandise and candies reminiscent of childhood, like candy cigarettes and flying saucers (at least from our childhoods), this place is sure to satisfy your sugar craving. Candy can be purchased by the box or individually, depending on how intense your sugar craving might be. In addition to sweets, the Fort Pitt Candy Co. carries snack items, such as chips and pretzels, various tobacco products, and is a spot to play your numbers, aka the Pennsylvania Lottery.

The Leaf & Bean Company, 2200 Penn Ave. #1, Pittsburgh, PA 15222; (412) 434-1480; www.leafandbeanstrip.com. Leaves and beans. Beans and leaves. What a concept for a specialty store. The Leaf & Bean Company is a one-stop shop for all your fine tobacco and caffeine needs. Its 2 locations, the Strip District and McMurray, offer a place to sit and enjoy a cup of joe while enjoying a smoke with a bud. Even if you aren't one to indulge, you're not going to want to miss a trip to The Leaf & Bean. During the warmer months, the exterior has seats available for sipping and smoking in the sunshine, and when there's a chill in the air, you can take the party inside and enjoy the mellow atmosphere. You'll be surrounded by flea market finds that would make your grandma and hipster neighbor jealous. The Leaf & Bean has its own humidor, rolls cigars in store, features live music on Saturday, and offers free Wi-Fi. Once you've been, you're definitely going to want to become a regular.

Lotus Food Co., 1649 Penn Ave., Pittsburgh, PA 15222; (412) 281-3050. Lotus Food Co. is a large Asian specialty grocer that fantastically offers fresh tofu sold by the block. The space is also well stocked with additional goodness from snacks to frozen and fresh fish to dumplings. Let's say you have a craving for shrimp puffs. Guess what? You can buy them here, along with soybean drinks, fish sauce, and any other Asian condiment that you won't find at your run-of-the-mill grocery spot. On weekends, Lotus is a particularly popular market, so brace yourself for a bit of a crowd. It will help to have a plan as you navigate the aisles, but it is nice to take your time and examine all of the interesting flavors and spices that will make your meal sparkle.

Mancini's Bread Company, 1717 Penn Ave., Pittsburgh, PA 15222; (412) 765-3545; www.mancinisbreadcompany.com. If you are watching your carbs, I would skip right over this and move to the next listing. Tuscan, Italian, multigrain, baguette, rolls, buns, loaves, and more! It's all about the fresh, crusty bread at Mancini's Bread Company. Upon entering the door, you can smell the aromatics of the fresh bread baking. But if that doesn't 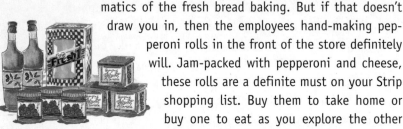 draw you in, then the employees hand-making pepperoni rolls in the front of the store definitely will. Jam-packed with pepperoni and cheese, these rolls are a definite must on your Strip shopping list. Buy them to take home or buy one to eat as you explore the other specialty shops in the Strip. Other gourmet goods sold at Mancini's include homemade pizza sauce, olive oil, bread crumbs, and bruschetta spread, which all make the perfect companion to its breads. Additional locations: Downtown, 440 Market St., Pittsburgh, PA 15222; (412) 281-8116; and 601 Mancini Way, McKees Rocks, PA 15136; (412) 331-8508.

Mon Aimee Chocolat, 2101 Penn Ave., Pittsburgh, PA 15222; (412) 395-0022; www.monaimeechocolat.com. Mon Aimee Chocolat, you say? A specialty shop whose specialty is chocolate, you say? Sign. Us. Up. Mon Aimee Chocolat sells sweet confections from all over the United States as well as 26 countries. You can find chocolate-covered bacon bars, truffles, nostalgic candies like candy cigarettes and Teaberry gum. Plus something that makes Mon Aimee famous: its wide variety of malt balls. You will have between 10 and 12 flavors to choose from on any given day. If you are in search

Shoppin' in the Strip

There's more to shopping for fresh produce, meats, cheeses, and fish in the Strip District. Whether you are turning these fresh ingredients into a lavish dinner party for friends or packing up coolers to head to a tailgating party, you may find yourself in need of wine, beer, cookie sheets, and black and gold decorations. Here are a few spots in the Strip where you can pick up such necessities:

Palate Partners/Dreadnought Wines, 2013 Penn Ave., Pittsburgh, PA 15222; (412) 391-8502; www.palatepartners.com. Your place for specialty wines, wine events, tastings, and wine gifts. Stop by if you need a bottle of wine and look for the Pittsburgh-inspired bottles of Redd Up Red, Yinzer Blanc, or Bubbles N'at.

BeerHive, 2117 Penn Ave., Pittsburgh, PA 15222; (412) 904-4502; http://thebeerhive.com. If beer is what you need, head to the BeerHive for a growler or six-packs of American craft beer, imports, and seasonal brews.

In the Kitchen, 1725 Penn Ave., Pittsburgh, PA 15222; (412) 261-5513; www.shopinthekitchen.com. At In the Kitchen, you can find practically anything you need to cook and serve up a great meal. This independently owned kitchenware store is home to cooking pans, cookie cutters, pepper grinders, cutting boards, juicers, and plenty of other cooking gadgets.

Mike Feinberg Company, 1736 Penn Ave., Pittsburgh, PA 15222; (412) 471-2922; www.mikefeinbergcompany.com. In the 1970s, the Mike Feinberg Company was the original distributor of Myron Cope's Terrible Towel. Today, it still is the destination spot for Pittsburgh and black and gold merchandise and decorations. Shelves filled from the floor to the ceiling are jam-packed with plastic plates, confetti, and decorations for practically any holiday or special occasion. Whether you need party supplies or not, stop by Mike Feinberg's and stroll around the aisles. You are always bound to find something you need.

of a bit of whimsy, choose one (or more) of its unique chocolate molds in shapes like deviled eggs, frogs, and popsicles. Would you rather slurp your sweets? Mon Aimee has a to-die-for hot chocolate, and on a warm day in the 'Burgh, get a scoop of Capogiro Gelato Artisans' gelato.

Parma Sausage Products, Inc., 1734 Penn Ave., Pittsburgh, PA 15222, (412) 391-4238; www.parmasausage.com. Parma Sausage Products, Inc., is a must stop in the Strip District for any occasion, on any kind of day. The small family business specializes in Italian pork products. Downstairs is the deli counter, which is filled with friendly faces and delicious meats. Upstairs is where the real magic happens. Here, Parma makes fresh sausage that is hand trimmed, ground, mixed with spices, and stuffed in natural casings; salami and pepperoni that are aged in its custom-built aging room; coppa secca; prosciutto made from fresh Berkshire Pork ham; and pancetta. It's hard to beat fresh anything—let alone fresh meat. So fresh you can taste the quality, care, and commitment Parma puts into each product available. And lucky for you, Parma offers its products online so you can enjoy them in the comfort of your own home if you can't make it to its home in the Strip.

Pennsylvania Macaroni Company, 2010–12 Penn Ave., Pittsburgh, PA 15222; (412) 471-8330; www.pennmac.com. The Pennsylvania Macaroni Company, known to Pittsburghers as "Penn Mac," is the go-to specialty store in the Strip for Italian goods and cheese. The lively cheese counter at the store sells over 200,000 pounds of cheese each week! And that's no surprise because the store stocks over 400 different varieties of artisanal and imported cheeses, such as Danish Havarti with dill, aged Crotonese, and sticky toffee cheese. Besides cheese, the store has practically any product you may need to cook an Italian feast in the grocery section, including fresh pasta, olive oil, fruits and vegetables, spices, and sauces, to name just a few. If you are from out of town and fall in love with the store, you can shop online and sign up online for the Cheese of the Month Club. See website for details.

Pittsburgh Popcorn Company, 209 21st St., Pittsburgh, PA 15222; (412) 281-5200; www.pghpopcorn.com. Reminiscent of a classic boardwalk shop in terms of branding and feel, the Pittsburgh Popcorn Company offers flavorful popcorn that is far from traditional. These popped kernels get extra-special treatment. Everyday offerings include crunchy caramel, sweet and salty kettle, Wisconsin cheddar, and cheddar/caramel mix, among others. Things get really crazy and seriously delicious for the flavors of the week. Thin Mint-flavored popcorn. Buffalo wing-flavored popcorn. Dill pickle-flavored popcorn. Each week brings different choices of way-above-average kernel creations. Popcorn is sold by the bag or tin. The special weekly flavors can sometimes carry a higher price tag, but also a higher payoff on the delightful-ness scale. The Pittsburgh Popcorn Company sells its goods online, but the weekly flavors are only found in stores. Other places to get poppin': Oakland, 3710 5th

Ave., Pittsburgh, PA 15213; (412) 605-0444; and Downtown, 822 Liberty Ave., Pittsburgh, PA 15222; (412) 281-2499.

Prestogeorge Coffee & Tea, 1719 Penn Ave., Pittsburgh, PA 15222; (412) 471-0133; www.prestogeorge.com. If the coffee and tea don't draw you into Prestogeorge, then the roasted peanuts will. Peanuts are roasted outside the front door in an antique roaster and sold by the brown bagful inside. Just as the shop's name says, coffee and tea are the prime products sold. The walls are stocked with glass containers of coffee beans and loose-leaf teas with enough flavors to please all of the coffee and tea lovers in your life. Flavors are seriously out the wazoo. Think Scottish breakfast tea, jasmine flowering tea, sticky bun coffee, and apricot cream coffee, just to name a few. If you don't want to carry coffee beans around the Strip with you (because they can be quite heavy), you can order a cup of joe, tea, latte, smoothie, or other specialty coffee drink at the inside coffee bar.

Reyna Foods, 2031 Penn Ave., Pittsburgh, PA 15222; (412) 261-2606; www.reynafoods.com. Reyna Foods has been supplying Pittsburgh with Latin American and Caribbean food and products for over 20 years. A wholesale supplier and retail store, Reyna Foods carries a wide variety of Latin American brands as well as its own homemade products. Reyna makes blue, white, red, and yellow corn tortilla chips that are available by the bag or in bulk. Also, you can find black and gold chips for all your Pittsburgh sports parties.

You can purchase a variety of freshly made salsas, seasonings, empanadas, and tamales as well. In the back of the market, fresh corn and flour tortillas are made daily. When you're done shopping, make a pit stop at the taco stand out front. There, you can get soft corn tortilla tacos made with your choice of meat, topped with sour cream, lettuce, cheese, tomato, onions, and cilantro. We suggest getting at least two tacos, because these babies are so good you'll regret only getting one.

Robert Wholey Market, 1711 Penn Ave., Pittsburgh, PA 15222; (412) 391-3737; www.wholey.com. Robert Wholey Market is the place to get fresh seafood in Pittsburgh. Though the market also sells fresh meats and poultry, it's all about the seafood here. When walking through the chilled fish market, you will encounter fresh lobsters, cooked and raw shrimp, crabs, oysters, mussels, clams, fish, and much more, all of which are available at Wholey's to take home for your own personal cooking. Wholey's also has a produce and grocery section and a fudge counter with several homemade flavors like creamy cappuccino and coconut bon bon. If cooking isn't your forte, visit Andy's Sushi Bar for some sushi-grade action. Don't like sushi? Stop by the fish kitchen and pick up a fresh breaded fish sandwich, such as the Wholey Whaler (1 pound of fried fish goodness on a bun), a lobster roll, crab cakes, or lobster macaroni and cheese, and chow down. On your way out, stop by the huge brass piggy bank and drop in a coin or two, which will get donated to charity.

North

The North Shore and North Side, accessed quite easily by the Three Sisters Bridges (the three bright yellow bridges that could be triplets), are in close proximity to one another but vastly different. Each distinct area is worth a visit and a long stay.

Heinz Field, PNC Park, Carnegie Science Center, Rivers Casino, and The Andy Warhol Museum dominate the shore region of the Allegheny and the Ohio Rivers. A riverfront trail provides opportunity for a scenic stroll, especially during active boating seasons. Not surprisingly, the North Shore boasts good locations to catch a bite to eat before catching a foul ball or to hang out and watch any sort of sport on TV.

Just beyond the Shore lies old Allegheny City, or the North Side, one of the most architecturally stunning areas in Pittsburgh. Sections like the Mexican War Streets and Deutschtown are lined with gorgeous row houses and hundreds of years of history. Here, the restaurants are all intimate spaces that fit within the historic surroundings. Food offerings are diverse, creative, and unexpected in the best way possible.

Pittsburgh to the North is more than a collage of old and new; it is a fascinating slice of the city that tastes as good as it looks.

Foodie Faves

Bistro To Go & Bistro Soul, 415 E. Ohio St., Pittsburgh, PA 15212; (412) 231-0218; http://bistroandcompany.com; Bistro; $$. Bistro To Go and Bistro Soul are sister restaurants located right next door to each other. Though they share a common space, their menus are quite different. Bistro To Go offers a weekly, seasonally inspired menu that includes several entrees, such as chicken, salmon, and pasta, a few side dishes, and soups. These items can be taken on the run or can be enjoyed at one of the few small tables in front of Bistro To Go and in the outside courtyard. Next door, at Bistro Soul, spicy barbecue sauces, country-style chicken, gumbo, cobblers, and beans and rice are all made from scratch. A fun fact about Bistro Soul is that no deep fryer is used in preparing the food! The chicken is oven-baked! Nontraditional, but easy on the arteries. Enjoy your Southern meal in the large dining room located behind the ordering counter at Bistro Soul, which also turns into a breakfast buffet on Sunday from 11 a.m. to 2 p.m.; french toast, scrambled eggs, bacon, and made-to-order omelets are all-you-can-eat.

Carmi Family Restaurant, 917 Western Ave., Pittsburgh, PA 15233; (412) 231-0100; www.carmirestaurant.com; Southern; $–$$.

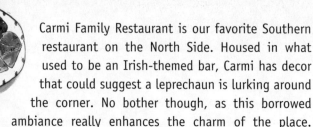

Carmi Family Restaurant is our favorite Southern restaurant on the North Side. Housed in what used to be an Irish-themed bar, Carmi has decor that could suggest a leprechaun is lurking around the corner. No bother though, as this borrowed ambiance really enhances the charm of the place. Plus, you will absolutely feel lucky once your food arrives and you experience Southern cooking at its finest. Order the chicken and waffles—the fried chicken is seasoned to perfection and crisp as can be. The baked macaroni and cheese will make you rue the day you ever ate the boxed variety. And the chicken and dumpling soup is comfort in a cup! It certainly helps that the service here is beyond outstanding. The waitstaff is attentive, but not intrusive, and incredibly friendly. You will feel like part of the family the moment you sit down. Maybe that leprechaun needs a roommate? See Owner Carleen Kenney's recipe for **Candied Yams** on p. 254.

Legends of the North Shore, 500 E. North Ave., Pittsburgh, PA 15212; (412) 321-8000; www.legendsatthenorthshore.com; Italian; $$. Legends of the North Shore is worth a trip if only for the home-made focaccia that makes its way to each table to start the meal. These crispy, nicely seasoned carb sticks are perhaps what put the "legend" in Legends. And even though the bar is set high from the get-go, you won't be disappointed with what comes next. Legends offers comforting Italian favorites, crafted lovingly in the open kitchen swallowing half of the cozy restaurant space. Homemade spaghetti noodles, smothered in "Mama's Gravy" (Legend's own chunky tomato marinara), topped with a giant meatball that falls apart at the touch of a fork, is a classic, and perfect, choice for lunch or dinner. If pasta just won't do, a portion of the menu is dedicated to sandwiches prepared with rustic Italian flair. Prepare to be floored by combos like zucchini and goat cheese (again, on that legendary focaccia). Legends has promotional deals often, including a standing 10 percent off your meal with any same-day theater ticket. Get cultured, then get carbed. Nothing better.

Monterey Pub, 1227 Monterey St., Pittsburgh, PA 15212; (412) 322-6535; www.montereypub.com; Irish; $$. Nestled amongst row houses in the historic Mexican War Streets district, Monterey Pub is a warm, neighborhood joint with traditional bar food as well as distinctive Irish dishes. You can seat yourself along the bar in a cozy, wooden booth, or head to the (slightly) larger dining area in the back, complete with fireplace. The decor here makes certain that you are aware of the Guinness on tap. This brew also makes a good showing in the absolutely delicious Irish fare offered on the menu. Try the pub-style shepherd's pie, an outstanding taste of Ireland with a layer of Guinness-marinated shredded meat, vegetables, and cheddar-topped mashed potatoes. Other Irish tastes include bangers and mash and fish-and-chips. Be sure to ask about the desserts of the day. The homemade concoctions like chocolate butter cake are sweet meal endings and will allow you to linger a little longer in the charming surrounds.

Wheel Deliver

Sometimes, the "perfect" meal doesn't always come from one restaurant, but consists of several items from different restaurants. On a hungry night, you may be feeling like eating a taco (or two), a piece of lasagna, side of french fries, fried rice, and key lime pie to finish off your smorgasbord meal. We have definitely been in the same boat. There are very few restaurants that have everything you want all in one place, but in Pittsburgh, we have something even better.

Wheel Deliver (412-421-9346; http://wheeldeliver.net) is a take-out service providing hungry Pittsburghers with the options of ordering from multiple restaurants and having all of the glorious food delivered to their homes, hotel rooms, and college dorms. A genius idea if you ask us.

About 30 restaurants participate in this food delivery service, and many of the menus are located on Wheel Deliver's website. Cuisine type varies from pizza joints, bar food, and sandwiches to Chinese, Italian, Mexican, Indian, Thai, and Middle Eastern, just

Nicky's Thai Kitchen, 856 Western Ave., Pittsburgh, PA 15233; (412) 321-8424; www.nickysthaikitchen.com; Thai; $$. Nicky's Thai Kitchen is small. Like 18 tables small. And it's loud. It gets significantly larger and quieter in the warmer months though when the back patio opens up. Despite the cramped quarters, Pittsburghers still flock to this North Side staple for quality Thai cuisine. The menu is extensive and even standard Thai dishes like phad Thai and green curry are special here. It also offers chef to name a few. Wheel Deliver also has you covered with desserts and beverages. Mouth watering yet?

To order, simply view the menus online. Once you decide on the restaurants and menu items, either call Wheel Deliver or order online. Wheel Deliver will charge you a 15 percent deliver fee in addition to the menu price of each item, really a nominal fee to eat a variety of food items from multiple restaurants in the comfort of your pajamas. There is a minimum order amount and an additional delivery charge if Wheel Delivery is traveling to certain neighborhoods. See website for details. Wheel Deliver accepts cash, credit cards, and student funds from Carnegie Mellon University and the University of Pittsburgh. Follow Wheel Deliver on Twitter (@Wheel_Deliver) for new restaurants and special offers.

If you are visiting Pittsburgh and you want to try a number of restaurants, but can't get to them all, Wheel Deliver is at your service. Just remember to tip your driver. He was buzzing all over town picking up your goods and deserves a tip for not eating them on his way to you.

specials like a sweet and tangy shrimp red chili and *gaprow lad kao*, or stir-fried meat (pork, chicken, or beef) in a spicy brown sauce with bell pepper, basil, and a fried egg on top for good measure. Jasmine rice accompanies dishes, but opt for the nuttier brown rice for a small up-charge. As far as appetizers, fresh spring rolls come sliced and oozing with color, and the crab rangoons come delicately crisp and served with an intoxicating pineapple sauce. Nicky's is BYOB but only charges a corkage fee on Friday and Saturday. We recommend making a reservation for weekends unless you want to spend time gazing into the eyes of the large Garuda statue in the entrance. Additional location: 321 South Ave., Verona, PA 15147; (412) 828-0339.

Priory Fine Pastries, 528 E. Ohio St., Pittsburgh, PA 15212; (412) 321-7270; www.prioryfinepastries.com; Bakery; $. Priory Fine Pastries is announced on East Ohio Street with a colorful wooden sign jutting out into the North Side air. The cheerful shop is owned and operated by the Graf family, who run the nearby Priory Hotel and Pittsburgh's Grand Hall. The bakery occupies the site of the first D.L. Clark Candy Company (think Clark bars and the like). The history here is fascinating, but it takes a backseat to the current confection magic. You may enter the bakery to buy  cookies or cupcakes, but you should probably eat a doughnut while you are here too. Doughnuts that are as fresh as the Priory's are uncommon, and it is always breakfast some-where, right? Fill up the rest of your bakery box with any combination of treats—they are really all delicious. Some suggestions if you get overwhelmed while pondering your sugar high: the burnt almond torte cupcake (truly moist yellow cake with an airy cream frosting), the chocolate crackle cookie, and the lady locks (as close to a grandma-made cookie as you can get).

Redfin Blues, 100 Waterfront Dr., Pittsburgh, PA 15212; (412) 322-5837; www.redfinblues.com; Seafood; $$. Redfin Blues at Washington's Landing has a lovely view of the Allegheny River and offers patrons the option to arrive via boat! A great place for summertime dining because of its large patio and outdoor bar, Redfin Blues is the closest Pittsburghers get to a beach bum's paradise. With such enticements as all-you-can-eat crab clusters every day and menu items like the shrimp and crab pizza, grilled ahi tuna sandwich, and Chilean salmon entree, Redfin Blues might give you the false illusion that you're not in western Pennsylvania. Kick back, enjoy an iced tea and one or two pounds of peel-and-eat shrimp while watching the boats float past. We're fans of the big crab cakes and never eat there without ordering a bowl of the Redfin bisque, the perfect combo of lobster, shrimp, and crab.

Rivers Casino, 777 Casino Dr., Pittsburgh, PA 15212; (412) 231-7777; www.theriverscasino.com; Speciality; $–$$$. If you have hundreds of nickels burning a hole in your pocket, there is only one solution: Get your jingle-jangling self to the Rivers Casino. Time for some gambling and, perhaps, a trip through a buffet of epic proportions. Rivers Casino has five distinct dining locales throughout the space. Grand View Buffet is the only all-you-can-eat option of the bunch, and it is a doozie. Buffet stations include Asian, Italian, and barbecue, among others. We personally fill up at the dessert station that includes surprisingly elegant treats. Grand View Buffet also lives up to its name and offers quite the pretty river picture through the expansive windows. For a quick bite, try the West End Cafe or Ciao on the main casino floor. We like to dine on chicken tenders at the West End Cafe then head to Ciao for gelato. For sit-down service get your (hopefully) lucky self to the Wheelhouse Bar and Grill or Andrew's Steak & Seafood. The Wheelhouse has quality burgers and enormous televisions for all your sports-watching needs. Andrew's Steak & Seafood has, you guessed it, steak and seafood, and is the fanciest spot to use your winnings on tastiness.

Landmarks

Max's Allegheny Tavern, 537 Suismon St., Pittsburgh, PA 15212; (412) 231-1899; www.maxsalleghenytavern.com; German; $$. If you are looking for authentic German fare, head to Max's Allegheny Tavern, the site of a former hotel in the early 1900s and a well-known speakeasy during Prohibition. Whether enjoying a few brews during happy hour or a full meal in one of the dining rooms, you must try the Bavarian soft pretzels, which come three per order. These deep-fried goodies are accompanied by a side of honey mustard sauce, and you can even order them stuffed with cheese. As for German fare, it may be hard to pinpoint what exactly you want on the extensive menu. Have no fear! Get your fill of wursts and other German delicacies with the Max's Sampler Platter, in which you

can choose three of Max's entrees, ranging from bratwurst and kielbasa to various schnitzels and roast pork. Be sure to save room for dessert because 1) there should always be room, and 2) Max's has apple strudel, served with or without vanilla ice cream.

The Park House, 403 E. Ohio St., Pittsburgh, PA 15212; (412) 224-2273; http://parkhousepgh.com; Neighborhood Bar; $. The Park House is touted as Pittsburgh's oldest tavern (apparently, The Park House was the 'Burgh's first licensed bar at the completion of Prohibition). The building dates back to 1889, and not much has changed decor wise so it seems. Rich, dark wood paneling and the narrow space create a warm atmosphere. You'll feel even more welcome as you help yourself to all the free popcorn and peanuts you can handle. Try not to fill up on the snacks; the food at The Park House is not the typical bar fare. Really delicious hummus, falafel, and grilled lamb pita give the menu a Middle Eastern tilt. It is a great and delightful departure from barroom standards. Make sure to ask about the special, as it could be something crazy awesome like a peanut butter and bacon sandwich. The Park House also has a nice selection of craft beers on draft, live music multiple days a week, and always a Wednesday night bluegrass jam.

BreadWorks Bakery, 2110 Brighton Rd., Pittsburgh, PA 15212; (412) 231-7555; www.breadworkspgh.com. If you are dining out in one of the city's restaurants and fall in love with the bread that is included in the bread basket, it is likely that it came from BreadWorks Bakery if it wasn't made in house. This well-known Pittsburgh bread company supplies many local restaurants and specialty stores with its products, and Pittsburghers buy them like hotcakes. If you can't find these products in one of the specialty markets (they sell out fast), you can still carb up by heading to the retail location housed within the bakery. You can purchase rolls, loaves, and buns straight from the oven 7 days a week. Hopefully the bread you purchase makes it back to your house or other intended location, because once your car starts to smell like a bakery, you may find yourself tearing off pieces of goodness until just an empty white bag is left.

South

Pittsburgh's South Side has stunning Victorian row houses, and Mount Washington has magnificent views. The South is also home to many 'Burghers in the residential neighborhoods of Banksville, Beechview, and Brookline.

The South Side is bursting at the seams with hidden gems in the old architecture, like small storefront restaurants, happening boutiques, and parlors of the tattoo variety. You have probably heard some crazy-time stories about this section of the 'Burgh. Most of them are probably true. East Carson Street runs through the heart of the South Side flats and is home to the most bars on one street, in Pittsburgh proper. While the conditions of the sidewalks on a Sunday morning can often be suspect, the South Side is one of the most enchanting areas to get a bite to eat. Restaurants here are intimate, by virtue of their architectural location, and eclectic in choice. You can find any flavor you desire and then pop around the corner for a cocktail.

Mount Washington is a short trip up a tall hill by car or, more purely Pittsburgh, by incline. While the area is mainly residential, the neighborhood has the best views of the city, and restaurants have capitalized. Romance hovers in the air here, as it is hard to not be totally taken with the 'Burgh and its sparkling lights below.

Foodie Faves

Beehive Coffee House, 1327 E. Carson St., Pittsburgh, PA 15203; (412) 488-4483; www.beehivebuzz.com; Coffee Shop; $. Beehive Coffee House is by far one of the coolest and quirkiest cafes you might ever come across. Re-purposed and recycled items have been transformed from trash into treasure and have found new homes on the walls of the Beehive as funk-a-delic art. Once you place an order for one of its famous hand-squeezed lemonades, specialty teas, or a classic latte and a rice krispy treat, grab a seat at one of the many tables with mismatched chairs and funky lamps. The Beehive has free Wi-Fi so if you get hungry while surfing the web, order one of its specialty sandwiches, wraps, soft pretzels, or soups. The Beehive Coffee House has Pittsburgh citizens and visitors fawning over its awesomeness day after day.

Beto's Pizza, 1473 Banksville Rd., Pittsburgh, PA 15216; (412) 561-0121; Pizza; $. At Beto's, you are either going to absolutely fall madly in love with its thick, square pizza slices, or you will never ever want to eat a slice of it again. Why? The toppings are cold. Yes, cold. Cold cheese, cold banana peppers. Cold. The thick square crusts are crispy, piping hot, and topped with crushed tomato sauce and cold toppings of your choice. You may think it's very weird (we did), but the pizza is seriously excellent. You can order in and take a seat in the small dine-in room or take the pizza to go. No matter where you choose to eat your cold-topping pizza, the line to order will be long and most likely out the door. Pizza is ordered by the slice ($1.25 each) with toppings at additional charge (50 cents per slice). The toppings are piled so high, you might just breathe an olive up your nose when you take a bite. Besides pizza, Beto's also serves up hoagies, sandwiches, salads, and a long list of fried side dishes.

Big Dog Coffee, 2717 Sarah St., Pittsburgh, PA 15203; (412) 586-7306; www.bigdogcoffee.net; Coffee Shop; $. Neighborhood coffee shops are just as prevalent as neighborhood bars in Pittsburgh. They're in most neighborhoods, tucked among row houses and store-lined streets. The best ones provide more than just coffee and snacks. They provide a creative space for learning and dreaming like only a coffee house can. Originally a bakery, Big Dog Coffee, off East Carson Street, has all the charm you'd expect from a building that's been around since 1889. A fireplace, two bay window nooks, a twinkling chandelier, and a large built-in wooden bar make the inside feel more like a cozy house than a coffee shop. Big Dog serves Intelligentsia Coffee products made by baristas that know how to make a great cup of joe. From lattes,

Grow Pittsburgh

Locally sourced produce is all the rage in the Pittsburgh restaurant scene. We totally dig it, but who is growing it?

Leading the charge for ultra-local, urban farming is the nonprofit organization **Grow Pittsburgh.** Grow Pittsburgh offers resources to residents who are interested in urban vegetable gardens and teaches citizens how to farm responsibly. Along with workshops and classes for adults and children, Grow Pittsburgh works with communities to start gardens that eventually provide fresh produce for the neighborhood. A renewed community spirit is often harvested as well, as neighbors are working together toward a shared goal. Community gardening = community happy times.

Grow Pittsburgh also manages two farms and an urban greenhouse: Braddock Farms, The Frick Art and Historical Center Greenhouse, and Shiloh Peace Garden, adjacent to The Frick. Braddock Farms occupies two abandoned lots, equivalent to an acre, on Braddock and 10th Street in the borough of Braddock. The organization partners with the Braddock Youth Project, which allows

students to intern on the farm and become familiar with all steps of urban agriculture. Interns farm and manage the farm stand for 8 weeks during the growing season. The Frick Greenhouse allows for year-round organic growing and enables Grow Pittsburgh to grow seedlings for their community gardens. Fresh produce from each of the farms is sold to the community through farm stands, typically active from mid-June until the end of October, and through restaurant distribution. Pittsburgh chefs are able to reap the benefits of a truly local produce supplier. Let's be real, it doesn't get more fresh than picking the produce and putting it on the plate several short hours later! Since the farms are small, an attitude of experimentation is prevalent, so more unique crops like cardamom leaves and ginger can be produced, affording chefs more creativity.

You can support the efforts of Grow Pittsburgh in a number of different ways. Perhaps the most fun (and delicious) way to offer support is by dining out during the organization's Let Us Eat! events. Let Us Eat! is hosted by fabulous restaurants throughout the city the second Thursday of each month. Ten percent of every diner's bill goes to Grow Pittsburgh. Previous restaurant partners have included **Salt of the Earth** (p. 162), **Avenue B** (p. 118), and **Elements Contemporary Cuisine** (p. 28). Grow Pittsburgh also has a partnership with La Prima Coffee. La Prima produces a Grow Pittsburgh coffee blend, with a dollar of every pound sold benefiting the organization. Annual membership at Grow Pittsburgh is also an option that comes with a whole host of awesomeness like vegetable discounts.

To learn more about Grow Pittsburgh events and how the organization is changing the urban produce landscape, visit their website at www.growpittsburgh.org.

mochas, espresso, tea, and more, Big Dog has all the coffee shop basics covered. To accompany its tasty robust coffee, Big Dog serves pies, cookies, and breads from local pastry chefs; homemade soups; gelato from **Mercurio's** (p. 146) in Shadyside, and organic oatmeal with lots of fix-ins'.

Caffe Davio, 2516 E. Carson St., Pittsburgh, PA 15203; (412) 431-1119; Italian; $ (Dinner; $$$). When entering Caffe Davio, you are not going to be impressed with the interior, but you will be impressed with the food. The walls have a few pictures hanging on them, and the tables and chairs are basic. You can see directly into the kitchen, hearing the pots and pans sizzle with flavor. Breakfast, lunch, and dinner are all good options when going to Caffe Davio. By day, the teeny-tiny less-than-10-table restaurant cooks up diner-style food for breakfast and lunch. We're talking omelets, pancakes, french toast, home fries, breakfast sandwiches, wraps, salads, and sandwiches. We like that Caffe Davio serves up fresh-cut french fries and homemade potato chips during lunch. At night, this neighborhood restaurant turns into a BYOB Italian restaurant with home-style food, including veal, filet mignon, and fish entrees. Of course there are fresh and homemade pasta dishes too. A definite must-try if you can get a reservation.

Cambod-Ican Kitchen, 1701 E. Carson St., Pittsburgh, PA 15203; (412) 381-6199; www.cambodicankitchen.com; Cambodian; $. Character: Not all restaurants have it, but the ones that do leave a lasting impression long beyond their food. Cambod-Ican has character and tons of it. What was once a tiny street truck sandwiched between two buildings in the South Side has become a full-fledged restaurant. Some remnants of the street vendor life remains: handwritten menus and humorous notes that line the walls, a friendly and speedy staff, and a window to place your order. Upon inspection of the menu you'll see it holds several items with high regard. The fried wontons are a favorite and the shish kabob platter comes with two "world-famous" chicken kabobs, rice, and Cambod-Ican's special "Moon" sauce. You'll probably want to order extra "Moon" sauce. Trust us. If you're in the mood for a little spice, try the curried vegetable bowl with a bevy of fresh vegetables and your choice of meat. Don't forget to send a friend to the bathroom while you're there. We know it sounds weird but it will provide a hearty chuckle when you see the bathroom keys.

Carson Street Deli, 1507 E. Carson St., Pittsburgh, PA 15203; (412) 381-5335; www.carsonstreetdeliandcraftbeer.com; Deli; $$. The Donnie Brasco at Carson Street Deli is one of our favorite sandwiches in the 'Burgh, forget about it. For less than a 10 spot you get buffalo chicken, hot pepper cheese, banana pepper rings, lettuce, red onion, tomato, and egg salad piled high on fresh baked BreadWorks Italian bread drenched in bleu cheese dressing. Okay, you can order ranch if you're one of those people, but we recommend its more delicious counterpart. Carson Street Deli has a ridiculous number of other delightful

sandwich combinations including the Balboa, a French baguette filled with imported Dilusso Genoa salami, sopressata, prosciutto, hard salami, spicy capicola, provolone, oil and oregano, and roasted red peppers on a French baguette. Or you can build a sandwich and eat a legacy that is all your own. One of the best delis in Pittsburgh, Carson Street Deli also boasts over 300 craft beers that you can crack open whilst in the deli or beer garden, or mix and match a six-pack and take home with you.

DISH Osteria and Bar, 128 S. 17th St., Pittsburgh, PA 15203; (412) 390-2012; www.dishosteria.com; Italian; $$$. Tucked away off the main path of East Carson Street, you will find DISH Osteria and Bar located on the first floor of an old house. The bar has a South Side neighborhood feel, but with a touch of European flair. Don't let the homely green-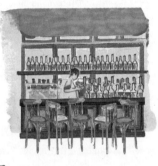
and-white exterior fool you. Inside is a lively bar and a small dining room with amazing Italian food. We suggest visiting DISH for at least a cocktail or glass of wine, or three, in the evening hours. If you do have time to dine at DISH, be sure to call and make a reservation way in advance. The dishes are prepared in the small kitchen and consist of house-made antipasti, handmade pasta dishes, and main entrees of fresh seafood and steak. We are always big fans of ordering what's on the daily special menu, so ask what the chef is cooking up special the day you go.

Double Wide Grill, 2339 E. Carson St., Pittsburgh, PA 15203; (412) 390-1111; www.doublewidegrill.com; Barbecue; $$. Once a gas station, Double Wide Grill specializes in barbecue and vegetarian diner food. Its character shines through in both its decor and menu. A large vintage pickup truck sits above the full-size bar, where you can enjoy one of the 30-plus drafts. One of the most creative food features at Double Wide is the "Build Your Own TV Dinner" option. Choose from "On Tráys" including half rack of barbecue ribs, brisket, pulled pork, and coconut rum tilapia, and sides like hubcap potatoes, garlic vinegar coleslaw, or caramelized onion and cilantro rice. You can also get several varieties of wood-grilled burgers like the breakfast burger, your choice of burger (beef, turkey, chicken breast, lentil, or portobello) on thick Texas toast and finished with bacon, a fried egg, and cheddar cheese, or the Rebel Yell Jalapeño burger with pickled and fresh jalapeños, sautéed onions, and Swiss cheese. Double Wide is also one of the few locations along East Carson Street with a large outdoor patio, so be sure to visit during the summer months and join in a game of cornhole.

Fiori's Pizza, 103 Capital Ave., Pittsburgh, PA 15226; (412) 343-7788; www.fiorispizzaria.com; Pizza; $. Fiori's is a Pittsburgh pizza staple. The small shop cranks out pies like it's their job. Oh, well, we guess it is! Call in an order for pickup or take one of the few seats for a dine-in experience. Either way, you're going to fall in love with the cheesy goodness that is placed before you. Something that makes a slice of Fiori's different from other slices is the sweet sauce. We like ours loaded up with pepperoni, black olives, and hot pepper rings. The service is fast and friendly but the parking is like that at many other Pittsburgh establishments: almost nonexistent. Order a side of onion rings and maybe some buffalo wings to go with your pizza. One of our favorite things about Fiori's is the fact that they're open late, and we mean late, especially on the weekends. So when those late-night pizza cravings hit around 2 a.m., you know where to go!

Gypsy Cafe, 1330 Bingham St., Pittsburgh, PA 15203; (412) 381-4977; www.gypsycafe.net; International; $$–$$$. Gypsy Cafe is tucked away in an old church along a quiet road in the South Side. The outside is rather unassuming, but inside, the tall gold columns, religious relics, worn church pews, and woven carpets suggest that an interesting dining experience is afoot. Here, you can sample the customer-favorite Hungarian goulash under the many portraits of the Virgin Mary. Here, you can sit amongst old-world diners and diners of the plaid-shirted and mustached variety. Here, you can have your cards read, again in the sight-line of some patron saints. The Gypsy Cafe is indeed a study of contradictions, with marvelous results. Awesomely, the entrees are as satisfying as the quirky, warm atmosphere. Expect comforting, noodle-heavy dishes with a Hungarian, Eastern European, and Mediterranean lean, like Szekely goulash made with pork shoulder, onions, bacon, paprika, egg noodles, and sour cream. Try to visit on a Thursday after 8 p.m. so you can be treated to live music by the Bingham Street Tamburitzans. Make your reservations today. We see a good time in your future.

Ibiza Spanish Tapas & Wine Bar, 2224 E. Carson St., Pittsburgh, PA 15203; (412) 325-2227; www.ibizatapasrestaurant.com; Spanish; $$–$$$. Ibiza is known for making tasty tapas and one of the best sangrias in town (along with its sister restaurant **Mallorca** (p. 98), located next door). When making a reservation, be sure to request seating on the back patio. At night, the patio is lit with candlelight and the light that comes in from the floor-to-ceiling window dividing the inside restaurant from the outside. The menu is seasonal, and the tapas reflect flavors from across the globe, mostly hitting Spanish notes. We suggest ordering a few tapas plates, like the scallops in mango sauce (*vieras a la parrilla en salsa de mango*), an entree, such as the grilled meat platter (*parrillada Argentina con chimichurri*), and a pitcher of sangria to share with your dinner guests. The tapas plates come out as prepared, so there is no rush when dining here. Also, don't worry about finding parking in the South Side because Ibiza has valet.

Isabela on Grandview, 1318 Grandview Ave., Pittsburgh, PA 15211; (412) 431-5882; www.isabelaongrandview.com; International; $$$$. Isabela on Grandview is an intimate restaurant with ridiculously expansive views of Pittsburgh. With seating upstairs for about 2 dozen, and windows for days, no diner will be in want for the show-stopping scene of the Golden Triangle and our dazzling cityscape. Equally as enthralling is the open kitchen in the back of the dining room. The husband-and-wife chef team,

Dan and Sherri Leiphart, can be seen assembling all of the plates off the menu, which is constantly in flux. A pre-fixe Chef Tasting Menu of 7 courses is offered every day for diners who want to get a good sample of the elegant fare. Steak here is a good bet, but more interesting flavor combinations like lobster and grits can make appearances on the menu as well. You will be treated like a rock star from the moment you arrive until the moment you leave. Chances are you'll even get a photo snapped by the owner, George Merrick, as he makes his rounds. Your smile will come easy, thanks to the good meal, excellent service, and one heck of a backdrop.

La Tavola Italiana, 1 Boggs Ave., Pittsburgh, PA 15211; (412) 481-6627; www.latavolaitalianarestaurant.com; Italian; $$$. High atop scenic Mount Washington sits La Tavola Italiana. If you're looking for a quick Italian dinner, this is not the spot. Life slows once you're seated as La Tavola's seasoned waitstaff recites the specials of the day. For the main course the menu covers all the basics: traditional pasta dishes, chicken, veal, seafood, and steak.

We suggest a chef's special: tortellini with giant lumps of crab meat and shrimp bathed in a spicy yet not overpowering roasted red pepper cream sauce. Whichever dish you choose comes with a salad lightly tossed in the house dressing and accompanied by crunchy garlic bread. Since you're not being rushed out the door, you'll have room for one of the homemade desserts like cannoli or tiramisú. La Tavola is BYOB so bring a bottle of wine (or two) and enjoy a relaxing homemade Italian dinner.

The Library, 2302 E. Carson St., Pittsburgh, PA 15203; (412) 381-0517; www.thelibrary-pgh.com; Neighborhood Bar; $$. Best known for their happy hour special, The Library offers half off appetizers and has sides under $5 so you can try the Arabian Nights (Cajun black bean and chickpea hummus served with pita and veggies), The Fellowship of the Ring (onion rings with smoked jalapeño aioli), and Marco Polo (pepperoni rolls made with homemade pizza sauce) all for less than the cost of a hardback book. If you opt for a sandwich or wrap, we suggest the sweet potato fries on the side, and to help combat the fear of a pending book report, grab a drink. The specialty cocktails have literary references as well, like James and the Giant Peach (Long Island made with Absolut Peach) and Inferno (Jim Beam Bourbon, Triple Sec, sweet and sour mix, and orange juice) plus beer and wine. The Library has indoor and outdoor dining, and we promise you won't be sssssh'd.

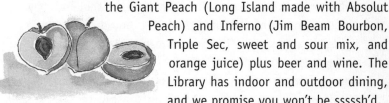

Local Bar + Kitchen, 1515 E. Carson St., Pittsburgh, PA 15203; (412) 431-1125; www.localpgh.com; Neighborhood Bar; $$. Local Bar + Kitchen is one of the best-looking bars in the South Side and has a large rooftop deck for outdoor dining. It's equipped with heat so you can dine outdoors well into the fall months. The chicken wings, pierogies from Pierogies Plus in McKees Rocks, and cinnamon sweet potato wedges are exceptionally good. And if you smell fresh baked pizza, you might want to get some—it's wood fired! The Plain Jane Street pie is served with house-made red sauce or white garlic sauce topped with mozzarella cheese. Here's something else that rocks about Local: They offer a 10 percent discount per party for anyone who shows up before or after a show and presents their ticket for Diesel Club, which is right next door. That should take some of the stress out of where to go for a pre-concert drink or a post-concert side of fries.

Mallorca Restaurant, 2228 E. Carson St., Pittsburgh, PA 15203; (412) 488-1818; www.mallorcarestaurant.com; Spanish; $$$. Mallorca serves traditional Spanish cuisine in the heart of the South Side. The cozy, main dining area is reminiscent of a library, but instead of books, wine lines the shelves. Candlelit tables set the mood, even during the afternoon. A second dining room is a little lighter in atmosphere. The hosts, wearing suits, offer service with a smile and an appropriate "señor" or "señorita" greeting. The menu heavily favors seafood, with shrimp, lobster, and clams as specialties. The *paella valencia* is a traditional dish with Spanish sausage, rice, chicken, and the aforementioned seafood. For non-sea-excavated food, try the *pollo Mallorca*, chicken in a creamy red sauce stuffed with spinach, pine nuts, and raisins. Every table receives a plate of crisp vegetables, rice, and thick-cut potato chips to share. Eating everything from your packed plate will be an impossibility, and taking a siesta after will be a necessity.

Mario's South Side Saloon, 1514 E. Carson St., Pittsburgh, PA 15203; (412) 381-5610; www.mariospgh.com; Neighborhood Bar; $. In the South Side and want to watch a football game? You can go to

any of the bars, but Mario's is always a good call. Mario's attracts a crowd of all ages: college kids looking for beer specials and cable television to watch a football game to their parents looking for the same thing. Who doesn't love a beer special and a football game? Among your drafts and bottles of beers is a menu of delicious bar food, including pastas, ribs, sandwiches, and burgers. And of course, traditional Pittsburgh bar food like Yinzerogies (pierogies) and buffalo chicken dip. If you really want to become a Yinzer, try our city's brew, an Iron City, or I.C. Light if you are watching your calories. If you don't like drinking beer, you can still order an Iron City, but in your sandwich. The Iron City Reuben has all the traditional fixings of a Reuben, but the sauerkraut is marinated in Iron City. Additional location: Shadyside, 5442 Walnut St., Pittsburgh, PA 15232; (412) 681-3713.

Mike and Tony's Gyros, 1414 E. Carson St., Pittsburgh, PA 15203; (412) 431-2299; www.mikeandtonysgyros.com; Mediterranean; $. In Pittsburgh, the bars close at 2 a.m. And, if you find yourself in a South Side bar when the lights are turned on and you're being escorted out by the "bar cops," you probably need to know what to do next. Answer: You find yourself some late-night grub. There are a few quality post-drinking places to eat, and Mike and Tony's is one of the crowded eateries where Pittsburghers line up. Open until 3 a.m. on Thursday, Friday, and Saturday, Mike and Tony's is just the place to get a nice greasy meal to cure an unwanted hangover.

A gyro with a side of french fries will hit just the right spot. If not, other Greek specialties are offered, including souvlaki, spinach pies, and baklava. Additional location: Downtown, 927 Liberty Ave., Pittsburgh, PA 15222; (412) 391-4077. (Note: The Downtown location is not open for the late crowd. See website for details.)

Nakama Japanese Steakhouse and Sushi Bar, 1611 E. Carson St., Pittsburgh, PA 15203; (412) 381-6000; www.eatatnakama.com; Japanese (Hibachi: $$$–$$$$; Sushi: $–$$). If you want to eat and drink where all the cool kids do, then trendy Nakama is the spot. Since its opening in 2003, Nakama has been packed with patrons, and the popularity doesn't seem to be quieting down anytime soon. You can enjoy sit-down hibachi in the back of the restaurant, where the chefs are always eager to please while they flip their spatulas cooking scallops, filet mignon, and sesame chicken. If you are just looking for sushi, the small sushi bar in the front is the perfect spot to post up and watch your meal made in front of you. Just want to grab a drink? The large bar overlooking East Carson Street is always a hot spot among patrons. Reservations are a definite must if you want to sit hibachi style, and there are a variety of specials offered during the week. See website for all the details.

OTB Bicycle Cafe, 2518 E. Carson St., Pittsburgh, PA 15203, (412) 381-3698; www.otbbicyclecafe.com; Neighborhood Bar; $$.

OTB Bicycle Cafe is a bike-friendly bar and restaurant. OTB is the place to go if you are looking for quirky menu items, or if you have a fierce craving for a burger slathered in peanut butter. Yes, you read that right. That would be The Hybrid, a half-pound burger with lots of bacon and a healthy serving of Wholey's homemade peanut butter. It's delish. Just trust us, okay? All the menu items are cleverly named after bike parts or bike lingo, like the Clipless Pedal, sesame-encrusted ahi tuna, and the Tandem, an old-fashioned grilled cheese sandwich paired with a bowl of tomato soup. You can have your pick of burgers, paninis, salads, and it's a bar after all, so lots and lots of beer. It might be enough to even make you want to take a bike ride afterward.

Pi Coal Fired Pizza, 1707 E. Carson St., Pittsburgh, PA 15203; (412) 431-5095; www.picoalfired.com; Pizza; $$. Pi Coal Fired Pizza is pizza done right. Its pizzas are coal fired, which is a nice change of pace from the big, greasy (but delicious) slices found at other pizza shops along Carson Street. Pi has several pizzas on the menu that are fan favorites, but we prefer the "create your own" option. First, your dough will take a bath in San Marzano tomato sauce, and then it gets to say hi to some very important pieces of fresh mozzarella and basil leaves. Now it's up to you to choose the perfect toppings to make this pizza really rock. Our toppings of choice are the cherry tomatoes, capers, and sausage. Wish your pie good luck as it gets baked, and watch in awe as it comes out with thin, crispy crust. You may feel such a connection to this pizza, this work of art, that you don't want to eat it, but go ahead, it won't mind.

Would You Like a Side of Live Music with That?

If there's something we love as much as food, it might be beer. If there's something we love as much as beer, it might be live music. Put those three together and it's a trifecta of utter awesomeness. Luckily, we live in this super sweet town, the king of trifectas, Pittsburgh.

The 'Burgh is home to many a musical talent, and nothing beats a beat like an accompanying beer and burger, right? Here's the lowdown: **New Amsterdam** (p. 147) in Lawrenceville has the best fish tacos in the city, so we say, not to mention some seriously tasty craft beers on tap so pair that with an acoustic set on a Saturday night and you've got yourself one heck of an outing.

There are days when we crave bluegrass. Those days are Wednesday, and our Wednesdays are reserved for **The Park House** (p. 83) in the North Side. The Park House not only has craft brews and microbrews on tap but also gives away peanuts and popcorn for free. Plus there are games on the table for your amusement. This is in addition to the sweet tunes. Be still our beating hearts.

If there is one place you must go to listen to live music in the city, it's **Brillobox** (p. 121) in Bloomfield. Part restaurant/bar and

Piper's Pub, 1828 E. Carson St., Pittsburgh, PA 15203; (412) 381-3977; http://piperspub.com; International; $$. In Pittsburgh, we love our Pittsburgh Steelers and we love watching them even more. It is a given that any time a game is on, bars all over the city are

part musical mecca, Brillobox brings in local and national acts alike. Music makers like The Low Anthem, Donora, and 1,2,3 have graced the second-floor stage at Brillobox, and we thank them. Another hip spot is **The Thunderbird Cafe** (p. 172) in Lawrenceville. Here you can rock out to local bands and eat sandwiches, wraps, quesadillas, and an assortment of appetizers, all under 10 bucks.

Pittsburgh truly runs the gamut of musical amazingness. If jazz and blues are more your speed, you're going to want to stop by **NOLA on the Square** (p. 36) in Market Square Downtown. You'll feast on New Orleans–style Cajun food while toe tapping to airy trumpet and saxophone tune-age. Before heading to the theater in the Cultural District, drop by **Backstage Bar** (p. 24) to indulge in a glass of wine and the tunes of many local musical talents, including one of our favorites, Joy Ike.

Get transported to an Eastern European village on Thursday nights at the **Gypsy Cafe** (p. 94) in the South Side. Here, you can find the Bingham Street Tamburitzans, who stroll from table to table, serenading guests with Eastern European melodies. Dancing, singing, and requests are welcomed by the Tamburitzans.

Be sure to check out "Live Entertainment" in Appendix B for more local spots with live music.

broadcasting. Piper's Pub loves football too, but this place really loves the kind of football that we call soccer in America. Piper's is Pittsburgh's place to get traditional fare from across the pond in the British Isles and the place to watch football games from across the

Atlantic. The place even opens up in the early morning hours if soccer games are on the telly. The menu is full of bangers, corned beef, cabbage, shepherd's pie, Guinness stew, and fish-and-chips. You can also get a perfectly grilled Reuben or Rachel too. To wash down your meal, you must try one of Piper's Scotches or a draft from the beer list. Be sure to check out brunch on Saturday and Sunday.

Pittsburgh BBQ Company, 1000 Banksville Ave., Pittsburgh, PA 15216; (412) 563-1005; www.pghbbq.com; Barbeque; $$. Get your barbecue on all year long at Pittsburgh BBQ Company. You'll need to set your own table though because Pittsburgh BBQ is carry-out only. We like that though, because when we have a hankerin' for barbecue on our way home we stop by and grab a combo. Our favorite combos are the pulled pork and pulled chicken sandwiches. They're both smoked and smeared in homemade barbecue sauce. You have your choice of hickory baked beans, coleslaw, baked apples, corn bread, macaroni and cheese, or macaroni salad as sides. The tough part is choosing the two lucky sides that will accompany you and your pulled pork sandwich and 20-ounce soft drink home. Here's a tip: We usually pick the corn bread because it goes perfectly with barbecue sauce (and is a rare menu item at other restaurants) and the coleslaw because we like to pile it on top of our pulled pork sandwich. Additional location: US 22, Delmont, PA 15626.

Pizza Sola, 1417 E. Carson St., Pittsburgh, PA 15203; (412) 481-3888; www.pizzasola.com; Pizza; $. If you find yourself wandering along East Carson Street after a long night of bar-hopping, Pizza Sola should be one of your final destinations. Don't let the long serpentine line snaking its way out of the door deter you. A giant slice of New York–style pizza is exactly what you need. Plus, overhearing the already legendary tales of college students will provide a hearty dose of entertainment while you wait. Once you make it to the counter comes the tricky part: What pizza to enjoy? Yes, Pizza Sola has other menu items, but its pizza is belle of the ball. Each pie is hand-tossed and topped with its own homemade tomato sauce, and 100 percent whole milk mozzarella. You can also choose from a variety of classic and gourmet toppings to create your own pizza or choose from red sauce, white sauce, or "always famous pizza" premade options by either the slice or whole pie. And don't forget to add a locally made Red Ribbon flavored pop to your order. Once you've paid, grab a stool, several napkins, and take in the sounds and shenanigans of the South Side at night. Additional locations: See website.

Redbeard's Bar & Grill, 201 Shiloh St., Pittsburgh, PA 15211; (412) 431-3730; www.redbeardspgh.com; Neighborhood Bar; $$. Redbeard's Bar & Grill is an authentic Pittsburgh neighborhood bar. The walls are lined with murals of Pittsburgh sports heroes and signed jerseys of current superstars. The folks on the barstools are regulars. And the good times are yours to be had. It might look cramped from the outside, but once inside it opens up and offers three areas to sit: the bar, dining room, or patio (there is a heated tent for the winter months). With 12 high-def TVs, it's the perfect spot up on the Mount (that's Mount Washington for you non-locals) to watch a Steelers or Penguins game. The menu is largely standard bar food with a few hidden gems like deep-fried pickles and stuffed banana peppers. Tuesday nights are all about tacos and Wednesday nights are all about wings at Redbeard's, so be sure stop by early on either night to grab a table.

17th Street Cafe, 75 S. 17th St., Pittsburgh, PA 15203; (412) 381-4566; www.17thstreetcafe.com; Italian; $$. 17th Street Cafe off East Carson Street feels like home. The quaint restaurant is as cozy and warm as the owner himself, who often visits tables to say hello. The menu consists of mostly Italian favorites with a 17th Street Cafe twist. Starters like greens and beans can be spiced up a bit by adding portobello mushrooms and asiago cheese. Main courses include dishes like wild mushroom ravioli, stuffed with woody crimini mushrooms and drizzled with truffle oil, and horse-radish-encrusted salmon finished with a honey- and roasted-shallot cream sauce. Pay attention to the specials of the day because they are equal parts comfort and unique flavor combinations. The main attraction and a must-try are the asiago cheese stuffed pillows. These can be substituted for any of the pasta dishes, and we recommend doing so. The pillows are so delicate and packed with flavor that they'll instantly push your dish to the next level. We especially enjoy them with pesto, which is a rich green color and has a hearty fresh flavor.

Shiloh Grill, 123 Shiloh St., Pittsburgh, PA 15211; (412) 431-4000; www.theshilohgrill.com; Neighborhood Bar; $$. Personality must run in the family because the "older sister" of **Harris Grill** (p. 137) in Shadyside has just as much spunk and sarcastic attitude as its younger sibling. Shiloh Grill offers a similar drink and food menu as Harris Grill, just in a more majestically elevated location. Order up Polish Church Basement Pierogies and The Baby Burghers Platter of sliders. Open weekdays at 3:59 p.m. and Saturday at 10:59 a.m., Shiloh has a small dining area and bar as well as a deck for warmer non-raining Pittsburgh days or nights. Good luck with that last part. Shiloh also has a Sunday brunch buffet starting promptly at 10:01 a.m. The prix-fixe menu with "over one million different things" includes a frozen mimosa or hair of the dog Bloody Mary as the perfect cure for those hangover blues. In addition to the buffet choices, omelets are also available for brunch. And don't forget, Tuesday is Bacon Night here too!

The Smiling Moose, 1306 E. Carson St., Pittsburgh, PA 15203; (412) 431-4668; www.smiling-moose.com; Neighborhood Bar; $$. Maybe best known as a Pittsburgh punk rock hot spot, The Smiling Moose has started flexing its culinary muscles. The downstairs bar looks like it was decorated by a college student, complete with cult movie posters and classic arcade games. The menu on the other hand is far from rebelling with youth angst. It features soups, snacks, salads, sandwiches, and sliders. While menu items like crostini of rosemary and basil, topped with fresh and lively tomato salsa and farmer's cheese, and the grilled cheese sandwich with three cheeses (cheddar, pepper jack, and mozzarella), bacon, and tomato are delicious, the sliders are a must. Choose from options like the Chinese five-spice burger topped with peanut cilantro and sweet chili mayo or hot pastrami with grilled pepper, kraut pepper jack, and horseradish mayo. Sliders come three to an order and are hopefully accompanied by a flavorful yet light pasta salad with peas, sunflower seeds, and farmer's cheese. The Smiling Moose also has 20 beers on draft and a cooler full of bottles to go with whatever you choose off the menu. See Owner Mike Scarlatelli's recipe for **The Captain Spaulding** on p. 267.

Stagioni, 2104 E. Carson St., Pittsburgh, PA 15203; (412) 586-4738; www.stagionipgh.com; Italian; $$. Stagioni relocated from its tiny storefront in the Bloomfield neighborhood to a charmingly redone, two-floor space on the South Side in 2012. The new location allows for more people to experience the rotating  Italian menu full of homemade pastas and additional Italian treats. Waiters are well informed about the entree choices and are happy to explain your options. While the menu changes frequently, one staple is always right on top: Made to Order Mozzarella. Here's the deal: you order the mozzarella; the chefs make it on command. As fresh as it gets, folks, and an easy choice for best dish night in and night out. The mozzarella comes with proscuitto, olives, and roasted red peppers, and is bathed in a light balsamic reduction. Once your mozzarella plate has been licked clean, try the gnocchi dish of the evening. The light and airy (really!) gnocchi is prepared in house, along with the other pastas. As the bustling energy of the South Side zips past the windows, you'll hardly notice; you'll be too busy finding room for dessert and cooing, "Delizioso!"

Yo Rita, 1120 E. Carson St., Pittsburgh, PA 15203; (412) 904-3557; www.yoritasouthside.com; Eclectic; $. The sexy pin-up girl on the window might make you think you're walking into a tattoo shop. Don't worry, the only regret you'll have after leaving Yo Rita is failing to try one of every gourmet taco on the menu. Upon being seated you'll be given a basket of perfectly salted tortilla chips and two kinds of salsa, mild and hot. While you're perusing the short menu, be sure to take the chalkboard specials into consideration. The ceviche and soup rotate on a daily basis, and there's always a specialty taco available. As far as appetizers go, it doesn't get any better than the *albondigas*, bison meatballs delicately placed in a smoky tomato sauce, drizzled with piri piri and cotija cheese, and finished with crispy plantains. If you don't succumb to their tender deliciousness, then we suggest trying a few tacos. These finely crafted soft tacos are filled to the gills with quality ingredients. It might seem pricey for a lone taco, but you'll forget about the sting once you sink your teeth into the first bite. All are served in a flour tortilla with shredded cabbage. A few of our favorites include the Velvet Underground (red and golden beets, scallion, aged cheddar, sweet potatoes, and *aji amarillo crema*) and the braised chicken, chipotle barbecue, crispy tortilla strips, and queso fresco.

The Zenith, 86 S. 26th St., Pittsburgh, PA 15203; (412) 481-4833; www.zenithpgh.com; Vegetarian; $$. Part vegetarian restaurant, part art gallery, part antiques store. The Zenith is a hidden gem on the South Side. Just as eclectic as the antiques store part of The Zenith is the restaurant, complete with mix-matched antique furniture, dishes, and wall art that is all for sale. The Zenith has an extensive menu of teas sold by the pot, and a weekly menu of soups, appetizers, salads, entrees, and sandwiches that will even please meat eaters. The restaurant is open for lunch and dinner on Thursday, Friday, and Saturday, and for brunch on Sunday. By far one of the most unique places in the city, The Zenith allows you to fill up your belly with tea and eats, fill your closet with vintage clothing, and fill your house with antique treasures.

Landmarks

Fat Head's Saloon, 1805 E. Carson St., Pittsburgh, PA 15203; (412) 431-7433; http://fatheadspittsburgh.com; Sandwiches; $. Beer and sandwiches. That's what you are going to get when you go to Fat Head's. Known for sandwiches as big as your head, aka Headwiches, this landmark is the place to go to in the South Side. 'Burghers and non-'Burghers agree. *Maxim Magazine* voted Fat Head's The Southside Slopes Headwich the #5 best sandwich in the U.S.A! That may be because this Headwich comes with kielbasa, grilled onions, fried pierogies, American cheese, and a zesty horseradish sauce. If you can't finish a Headwich, it's okay because most folks can't conquer it. Other delish options include wings, salads, sandwiches, wraps, and burgers. Whatever you order, you must accompany it with a beer. Fat Head's serves up an impressive beer menu complete with beer from its own brewery in Cleveland. (Gasp, Cleveland! There is a Fat Head's Saloon there too, but let's not talk about it.)

LeMont, 1114 Grandview Ave., Pittsburgh, PA 15211; (412) 431-3100; www.lemontpittsburgh.com; American; $$$$. The most quintessential Pittsburgh dining experience is sitting at one of the upscale restaurants on Grandview Avenue on Mount Washington and looking out over the breathtaking Pittsburgh skyline. LeMont delivers the view and more. The prices aren't cheap, but you will have million-dollar views. If you are watching your pocketbook, have a drink and bite to eat in the swanky lounge, which has live music every night. If you want to impress your dinner guest, make a reservation (by phone) for the dining room and have your dinner prepared tableside, choosing from either steak Diane or chateaubriand for two. Not every entree is prepared tableside;

there is a full kitchen serving up poultry, steak, veal, and a selection of appetizers and a-la-carte side dishes. The only other element that would make your trip to the LeMont even more quintessentially Pittsburgh is to take a trip up and down one of the Inclines.

Specialty Stores, Markets & Producers

The Milk Shake Factory by Edward Marc Chocolatier, 1705 E. Carson St., Pittsburgh, PA 15203; (412) 488-1808; www .themilkshakefactory.com. The Milk Shake Factory? Make that the DREAM factory! The cutest little shop along East Carson Street, The Milk Shake Factory by Edward Marc Chocolatier has a menu of over 55 flavors of milk shakes, an assortment   o f sundaes, and old-fashioned floats and sodas. Don't see anything you like on the menu? The milk shake magicians will whip you up something wonderful. The best thing about these shakes is the Factory's commitment to hardy milk and real ingredients. If you choose a shake with cake, you better believe you will be drinking up real cake crumbs through your straw! After making the tough flavor choice, enjoy your iced confection at one of the old-fashioned soda shop tables. Old-timey-ness extends throughout this gem, from the tin ceilings to the checkered floor.

The Milk Shake Factory by Edward Marc Chocolatier is under the ownership of the Edward Marc Chocolatier, a fourth-generation gourmet chocolate business almost a century strong. Try to resist the chocolates sold here; it will not happen (nor should it!). See The Milk Shake Factory's recipe for **PB & J Milk Shake** on p. 264.

The Pretzel Shop, 2316 E. Carson St., Pittsburgh, PA 15203; (412) 431-2574. The Pretzel Shop is a cash-only specialty store, open 6 days a week and closed on Sunday. The shop sells soft pretzels and caters to college kids, vintage deal seekers, and outdoor enthusiasts who are looking for a quick bite to eat between meals. Pretzel sandwiches are available for breakfast and lunch, and we count them as a meal. For breakfast you can order a hot sausage, egg, and cheese, and for lunch you have your choice of a pizza pretzel, a ham and cheese pretzel, a chicken salad pretzel, and more. To satisfy your pretzel craving and your sweet tooth, what is better than a twisted mound of salty, carby goodness? We're referring to their cinnamon and sugar pretzel. Pretzels might just become the universal meal. The Pretzel Shop even shares its twisted knots with local area eateries, so you can find them in a variety of unique dishes throughout the city.

East

You will see that the East chapter is the largest, and rightfully so. The East boasts thriving communities chock-full of hipsters, academics, artists, and families. Universities, boutiques, galleries, and bars fill the streets. Each neighborhood has a distinct character, from the artful Lawrenceville to the Victorian, swanky Shadyside. There is literally something for everyone in the area and the dining scene proves equally as fruitful.

It helps that this large cross section of town is experiencing a culinary renaissance. Innovative chefs are bringing their exciting, experimental cuisines to the neighborhoods (East Liberty and Garfield are especially heating up). Restaurants here are revitalizing communities and reinvigorating the Pittsburgh dining scene. New, interesting spots are popping up alongside old favorites, and our tummies could not be more pleased.

Abay Ethiopian Cuisine, 130 S. Highland Ave., East Liberty, Pittsburgh, PA 15206; (412) 661-9736; www.abayrestaurant.com; Ethiopian; $$. Abay offers Pittsburghers a one-of-a-kind dining experience, and it's just that, an experience. You can take the common road once you've entered through the bright blue foyer and pull up a chair at a familiar table or take the road less traveled and request one of the backless stools seated at a *mesob* (a table with a basket-like woven top) and settle in for lots of dunking, dipping, and deliciousness. Abay, Pittsburgh's first Ethiopian restaurant, focuses on communal dining, so you'll be sharing—keep that in mind as you peruse the menu. You'll also want to note that instead of utensils you'll receive *injera*, a flatbread, which you'll use to scoop up your food. We recommend the *kay sir dinich* (potatoes and beets), *azifah* (lentils with spices and lime juice), *ayib be gomen* (collard greens and Abay's homemade cheese), and *tikil gomen* (spiced cabbage, carrots, onions, and tomatoes). Abay also offers beef and chicken entrees. Can't decide what to order? Ask the friendly wait staff for their recommendations.

Aiello's Pizza, 2112 Murray Ave., Squirrel Hill, Pittsburgh, PA 15217; (412) 521-9973; www.aiellospizza.com; Pizza; $$. Aiello's has been serving up Italian favorites to the Squirrel Hill neighborhood since 1978. Traditional pasta and deli-style hoagies are on the menu, but the main attraction here is the pizza. The sauce is a bit on the sweet side, the cheese is plentiful, and the crust has a nice crunch. (Insider tip: It is best to let this pizza cool down a bit before diving in. Due to the generous cheese amount, slices can easily fall victim to the cheese slide-off. Plus, the pies taste their best lukewarm.) Plain cheese pizza is always a hit, allowing you to appreciate the overall, no-nonsense pizza quality without any distracting toppings. But if you are feeling fancy, try one of the gourmet choices like the Murray Avenue with bacon, mushrooms, and four cheeses. Aiello's is family owned and operated, so seeing a familiar face kneading dough is not uncommon—especially once the number is on your speed dial. This eat-in or take-out joint is cash only. An ATM is on-site for those who forget their dollar bills while pizza is on their brains.

Alchemy N'Ale, 5147 Butler St., Lawrenceville, Pittsburgh, PA 15201; (412) 252-2156; Gastropub; $$. One of the area's true gastropubs, Alchemy N'Ale is brimming with personality outside and in. The large retro-looking sign outside makes it easy to spot on the far end of Butler Street, and the interior is warm and inviting with exposed brick and tables made of reclaimed barn wood. The

 rotating menu consists of high-end bar food with several British-inspired selections. Start off with the lobster deviled eggs made with mustard crème fraiche, whipped yolks, roasted horse-radish, celery sea salt, and butter poached lobster, or P.E.I. mussels prepared in two sauces (fennel, red pepper flakes, white wine,

tomato sauce, preserved lemons, and garlic butter or speck, hard cider, garlic, and scallions). Next try the classic fish-and-chips with mushy peas or one of the burgers. We suggest adding an over-easy egg on top or Rogue Smokey Blue cheese on whichever burger you choose. It also has a well-rounded drink selection with over 2 dozen bottled beers. Can't find a beer? Try one of its signature drinks like the Moscow Mule, which consists of vodka and ginger beer garnished with crushed mint and lime.

Alma Pan-Latin Kitchen, 7600 and 7606 Forbes Ave., Regent Square, Pittsburgh, PA 15221; (412) 727-6320; http://almapgh .com; Latin American; $$. Alma Pan-Latin Kitchen's menu focuses on African-influenced cuisine from several Latin American countries like Peru, Dominican Republic, Chile, and Argentina. The kitchen also whips up a few signature dishes of its own, incorporating several cultures into one seamless dish. The Pan-Latin fusion at Alma is not only apparent with the diverse menu but also its atmosphere through its artwork and music. The menu is short but the waitstaff is knowledgeable, friendly, and will kindly offer a few recommendations. The *papitas rellenas*, light, fluffy Peruvian-inspired yuca and potato pillows filled with seasoned beef or the empanadas whose fillings change on a regular basis are excellent starter choices. Both will ignite your taste buds and get them ready for the main course. Main dishes include choices like *bife* steak chimichurri (marinated grilled skirt steak and topped with chimichurri and served atop rice and black beans), *chuletas*, (grilled pork loin topped with pineapple and served with white sweet potato puree) or *sándwich de pollo* *chiludo* (pulled chicken and avocado sandwich). There are also several vegetarian offerings of fish if meat isn't your thing. And don't forget to save room for flan or tres leches for dessert.

Avenue B, 5501 Centre Ave., Friendship, Pittsburgh, PA 15232; (412) 683-3663; www.avenueb-pgh.com; American; $$$. Chef and Owner Chris Bonfili creates a beautifully eclectic, yet familiar, menu that elegantly displays his prowess in the kitchen. It features traditional American-style fare like Kobe meat loaf with goat cheese and chive whipped potatoes, crispy onions, and tomato jam, and dishes subtly influenced by a range of other cultures. In addition to the seasonal menu, Avenue B offers daily chalkboard specials for each course. Creative beginning dishes like rosemary butternut squash soup with maple crème fraîche and main events like ginger barbecue swordfish with spicy scallop fried rice, carrot ginger bisque, and sesame beurre blanc are the norm here. Save room for dessert at Avenue B because the dessert comes architecturally plated, pretty enough to save. But, we advise you to dive right in. Be sure to bring a bottle of wine with you because Avenue B is BYOB.

Bangkok Balcony, 5846 Forbes Ave., Squirrel Hill, Pittsburgh, PA 15217; (412) 521-0728; www.bangkokbalconypgh.com; Thai; $$. Bangkok Balcony sits on a second floor above Forbes Avenue. The small entrance can be easily missed from the sidewalk, but the discovery is worth it. Bangkok Balcony specializes in authentic Thai cuisine and does it quite well. The menu features traditional curries, noodle dishes, and house specialties. We like to start off with the

Thai spring roll, but if you are a mussel appreciator, several appetizers like the Bangkok Balcony mussel fritter, featuring sautéed mussels with bean sprouts, will be a nice beginning. The pad Thai here is top-notch. Being big on noodle dishes, we also like the See-You Noodles, with your choice of meat, broccoli, and egg. Dishes can be customized on a spiciness level of 1 to 10. Depending on your mood,  you could eat a mild entree or just have the fire department on standby to hose down your mouth after a level 10. Bangkok Balcony's sister restaurant, **Silk Elephant** (p. 164), is close by on Murray Avenue.

Big Jim's Restaurant & Bar, 201 Saline St., Greenfield, Pittsburgh, PA 15207; (412) 421-0532; www.bigjimsrestaurant.com; Neighborhood Bar; $–$$. Big Jim's in Lower Greenfield, aka "The Run," looks like a typical neighborhood bar from the outside. And on the inside, it looks like a typical neighborhood bar too, complete with wall-to-wall wood paneling, dim lighting, and tacky decor. Big Jim's attracts regulars, college students from Oakland, and folks wanting to taste the amazing food after hearing about the bar on Food Network's *Diners, Drive-ins and Dives*. Everything on the menu is recommended by the friendly staff, but when you go here, you must get a sandwich. Big Jim's Specialty Sandwiches are huge and the veal cutlet ala Parmigiana is served on half a loaf of bread. Half a loaf of bread! If you don't see a Signature Sandwich you like, you can create your own half-pound sandwich. The homemade wedding soup is the perfect complement to a large sandwich—that is, if your stomach has the room. Pizza, calzones, pasta, and salads are also on the menu, but we repeat: get a sandwich. Your stomach won't be sorry.

Bloomfield Bridge Tavern, 4412 Liberty Ave., Bloomfield, Pittsburgh, PA 15224; (412) 682-8611; http://bloomfieldbridge tavern.com; Neighborhood Bar; $$. Pierogie and kielbasa and potato pancakes! Oh, my! *Haluski* (cabbage and noodles), *kluski* (homemade noodles and cottage cheese), and *gotabki* (stuffed cabbage) too! If you're a die-hard fan of Polish cuisine, and we mean die-hard, don't forget to get a bowl of the *czarnina*, Polish duck soup. While it seems like someone's Polish grandmother rules the roost, don't worry; if you're craving something other than carbs, Bloomfield Bridge Tavern offers a variety of other menu items. Choose from Pittsburgh bar standards like Bridge wings, Bridge fries covered in mozzarella and American cheese, grilled chicken salad with fries and cheese, or a hot sausage sandwich. Bloomfield Bridge Tavern also has a hearty draft and bottle beer selection and live music featuring national and local talent on the weekends. Plus every Wednesday, BBT turns into "The Polish Party House" for Drum and Bass Night, a must-go-to event to truly appreciate the uniqueness this tavern has to offer.

BRGR, 5997 Penn Circle South, East Liberty, Pittsburgh, PA 15206; (412) 362-2333; http://brgrpgh.com; Burgers; $$. One of the most

perfect meals in the world: a juicy burger and a thick milk shake. You can find this perfect meal and much more at BRGR. The burgers come gourmet, with fancy toppings and combinations of ingredients beyond the traditional mustard, ketchup, and pickles. Try the Double Yoi, a beef burger topped with pastrami, fried egg, Swiss cheese, coleslaw, and Thousand Island
dressing. If beef isn't your meat of choice, you can still enjoy a burger (and even a hot dog). The non-beef gourmet burgers include salmon, turkey, black bean falafel, lamb, and crabcake. With your burger, order a side of the BRGR Fries with truffle cheese whiz (who says cheese whiz isn't gourmet?) or the house-made chips with crack dip. We did not make this up. BRGR denotes its cheese dip as so good, it may become addictive like a drug, though legal in this case. To top your meal off, order a spiked milkshake or float. Additional location: 20111 Rt. 19 and Freedom Rd., Cranberry, PA 16066; (724) 742-2333.

Brillobox, 4104 Penn Ave., Bloomfield, Pittsburgh, PA 15224; (412) 621-4900; www.brillobox.net; Neighborhood Bar; $$. Half watering hole, half cultural catchall, Brillobox is a creative space used for concerts, special events, and socializing. Downstairs houses a hipster bar complete with eclectic artwork, a killer jukebox, mustaches, and pants tighter than an 80s glam rocker. It also has a deliciously diverse big bottle and draft beer selection and food menu. While Brillobox has a full menu, we suggest hitting this place for appetizers. You can't go wrong with any app here, but the *pommes frites* are nicely seasoned and come piled high in a cone accompanied by awesome dipping sauces (curry ketchup, spicy red pepper mayo, and garlic dijon aioli). The fried seitan skewers are also tasty and come prepared either buffalo style or Korean barbecue style. Upstairs plays home to an events venue where concerts from artists like Neon Indian, Tapes n' Tapes, and Handsome Furs are a regular occurrence. If you're lucky, you might be there for a dance party, community event, or some of the hardest trivia around. If you have a hipster hankering on a Sunday, stop by after brunch for the Starving Artist Vegetarian Supper, where the chef prepares a different healthy and cheap vegetarian meal each week.

The Cafe at the Frick, 7227 Reynolds St., Point Breeze, Pittsburgh, PA 15208; (412) 371-0600; www.thefrickpittsburgh .org/start/cafe.php; Eclectic; $$–$$$. Located on the grounds of the beautiful Frick Art and Historical Center, or quite simply, The Frick, The Cafe at the Frick soars above typical museum-quality

eateries. Windows wrap around the small space, which allows diners to gaze upon the illustrious former dwellings of industrialist Henry Clay Frick. The setting makes one feel fancy, and the food served continues the trend. The Cafe prepares inspired lunch and brunch dishes that use fresh produce grown at the on-site greenhouse. Therefore, the menu changes with the growing seasons and, sometimes, the art exhibitions inside (i.e., a Faberge show produced Russian centric meal choices). The house-made desserts are also top-notch and baked fresh daily. Afternoon tea is offered every day after 2:30 p.m., so you can feel like a coal magnate taking a leisurely break. It is important to make a reservation here as the limited tables fill up fast. Trust us, you don't want to be turned away!

Cafe Phipps, 1 Schenley Park, Oakland, Pittsburgh, PA 15213; (412) 622-6914; http://phipps.conservatory.org; International; $. Phipps Conservatory and Botanical Gardens is a quiet place to escape the hustle and bustle of the city. Whether you walk through the gardens or grab a bite to eat at Cafe Phipps,  nature will surround you and provide ecofriendly inspiration. Cafe Phipps is a Green Restaurant Certified eating establishment committed to providing fresh and healthy food that is good for both its patrons and the environment. The Cafe is open for lunch Monday through Sunday and for dinner on Friday nights. Many of the food items on the menu are vegan or vegetarian, and are made from in-season local and organic produce. Salads, paninis, sandwiches, wraps, flatbreads, and soups fill the chalkboard menu. You can't go wrong with one of the paninis, such as the prosciutto apple panini, which comes paired with the side salad of the day. In addition to the food, the Cafe makes a huge effort to be sustainable. The coffee is fair-trade and organic, the water is filtered on-site, the beer and wine are organic, and the take-out containers and serviceware are compostable. We give Phipps' and Cafe Phipps two green thumbs up!

Cafe Zinho, 238 Spahr St., Shadyside, Pittsburgh 15232; (412) 363-1500; International; $$$. Cafe Zinho is a small space that actually feels like you are eating in someone's living room. You are, in fact, eating in a converted garage, but the space is so warm, eclectic, and welcoming, you'll feel like an invited guest at an old friend's. Just as any good dinner guest would, bring a bottle of wine; this place is BYOB! The menu features just  about every meat in the book—lamb, pork, duck—and our favorite cheeses: goat, feta, gorgonzola. Goat cheese in puff pastry appetizer, you have our hearts. Dishes like chicken stuffed with gorgonzola and wild mushroom ravioli are generous and satisfying. The menu does get altered every so often, but the cuisine remains hearty. If you end up being hungry for dessert, the Cafe has changing, daily selections to choose from that should cap off your meal nicely. Cafe Zinho also sets up several sidewalk tables in good Pittsburgh weather.

Casbah, 229 S. Highland Ave., Shadyside, Pittsburgh, PA 15206; (412) 661-5656; www.bigburrito.com/casbah; Mediterranean; $$$–$$$$. If you want to dine in a Mediterranean-inspired outdoor patio surrounded by plants, flowers, and Greek-esque sculptures, then Casbah is the place to go. Warning: Mediterranean Sea not included. The inside of the restaurant houses a few tables and a large bar and lounge, but the outside front patio is where you want to be seated to enjoy your meal. The patio is covered and open all-year long. Many of the dishes are prepared with local ingredients, celebrating the farm-to-table concept done in many local restaurants. Our favorite dishes include the orecchiette pasta, mixed with dried cranberries and grilled chicken, and tossed in a sage and goat cheese sauce. Rich and heavenly enough to share with your dinner guest. If pasta isn't for you, there are a variety of entrees of lamb, chicken, pork, filet, and fish to choose from, though it may be hard to choose just one.

Crazy Mocha Coffee Company, 5830 Ellsworth Ave., Shadyside, Pittsburgh, PA 15232; (412) 441-9344; www.crazymocha.com; Coffee Shop; $. In just about any part of this city, you can find a Crazy Mocha Coffee Company shop to satisfy your cravings for coffee and desserts. Located in many neighborhoods, local hospitals, and in the main branch of the Carnegie Library of Pittsburgh in Oakland, the Crazy Mocha Coffee Company continues to expand around the city, with plans in the works to move up I-79 to Erie. At Crazy Mocha you can find specialty coffee and espresso drinks, a counter full of pastries, and images of goats drinking coffee. Yeah, there is a house blend coffee, a specialty flavored coffee, and a decaf brewing, but here it's all about the specialty creations. Try the caramel latte, chai latte, or Italian soda. And, of course, a hot chocolate. To accompany your coffee drink of choice, a pastry is in order. Cookies large enough to fill small plates and huge brownies are up for grabs, as well as muffins, pound cakes, and biscotti in a variety of flavors, including our faves: coconut lemon and macadamia nut and red velvet. Tons of additional locations: See website.

Crêpes Parisiennes, 732 Filbert St., Shadyside, Pittsburgh, PA 15232; (412) 683-2333; French; $. Reminiscent of a Parisian cafe and crêpe stand is Crepes Parisiennes in Shadyside, located in the basement of a house. Crêpes Parisiennes always has a line out the door on the weekends and is cash only. You can choose from savory or sweet crêpes, or both, and enjoy a *cafe au lait* while you wait for your crêpe to be made on one of the two crêpemakers. The savory crêpes such as egg and cheese, smoked salmon, and mixed vegetables and cheese come with your choice of one of four sauces inside (Asian-inspired soytang, béchamel, crème fraîche, and garlic olive oil) and a side salad with house-made champagne vinaigrette. The vinaigrette is so tasty you might want to order a second side salad to enjoy. For the sweet crêpes, you can never go wrong with a crêpe stuffed with Nutella or mandarin oranges and chocolate. Additional location: Oakland, 207 S. Craig St., Pittsburgh, PA 15213; (412) 683-1912.

Cure, 5336 Butler St., Lawrenceville, Pittsburgh, PA 15201; (412) 252-2595; www.curepittsburgh.com; Eclectic; $$–$$$. The scent of smoked meat will greet your nostrils the moment you enter Cure. The scent will stay with you even after leaving, which acts as a welcome reminder of a meal well done. Cure is an intimate space with wood-lined walls, a long banquette, and clear vision lines all the way back to the kitchen. The handwritten menu, which is an ever-evolving organism, is presented on a wood block. Options are limited, but the selections are sure to please your palate. Cure calls its food "extra local urban Mediterranean," but we just call it delicious. You can expect creative preparations and combinations of flavors. Pistachios and duck? Apple cider and beef cheeks? Sure, why not? You can also expect the meat (of any kind) on your plate to be perfect. A place with a heavy meat smell and a pig logo cannot disappoint in that department. Executive Chef and Butcher Justin Severino makes sure of it. Remember your beverage of choice, as this spot is BYOB.

D's SixPax and Dogz, 1118 S. Braddock Ave., Swissvale, Pittsburgh, PA 15218; (412) 241-4666; www.ds6pax.com; Neighborhood Bar; $. As the name suggests, at D's you can find six-packs and hot dogs. Perhaps rather unexpected is the sheer volume of brews that can fill your pack and the downright gourmet options for your dog. D's boasts a microbrew selection that is unrivaled in the area. Step into the beer cave behind the main room and prepare to have your mind blown. The menu choices may be more limited than the brewskies, but this neighborhood bar serves up truly satisfying, and most often deep-fried, snacks. The fries, which can be ordered by the handful, are a good start or nice to share. You will need to save room for a hot dog, be it all beef, turkey, or veggie. After choosing your dog, pick from a variety of preselected topping combos including the likes of the Bacon Cheddar (more, please!) or the Mason Dixon (chili and coleslaw), or make your own powerhouse compilation. Additional location: 4320 Northern Pike, Monroeville, PA 15146; (412) 856-5666.

Deli on Butler Street, 4034 Butler St., Lawrenceville, Pittsburgh, PA 15201; (412) 682-6866; www.delionbutler.com; Deli; $. It's all about family at the Deli on Butler Street. So much so, you will feel like a member of the family after just one visit. Owner Gary Gigliotti opened the family-run deli in 2008 after the passing of his late father, Pasquale, who told him at a young age that he should own a deli. Honoring his father, a menu item is named after him, the Pasquale specialty sandwich that features ham, turkey, roast beef, red onion, two kinds of cheese (provolone and colby), and the deli's special sauce. All specialty sandwiches are served on either Italian, marble rye, or whole wheat bread, and with lettuce, tomato, and a pickle spear. We love pickle spears! Other items on the menu include salads, soups, paninis, and wraps. Also, you can order sliced lunch meat and cheeses by the pound. There is no seating, so grab your order to go. Additional location: Deli on North Avenue, North Side, 4 E. North Ave., Pittsburgh, PA 15212; (412) 322-3354.

Del's Bar and Ristorante DelPizzo, 4428 Liberty Ave., Bloomfield, Pittsburgh, PA 15224; (412) 683-1448; www.delsrest .com; Italian; $$. Del's is officially listed as Italian in this book because of the cuisine, but in our eyes, it is definitely a neighborhood gathering spot and watering hole. At Del's, you feel like you are a part of a large, extended family with the staff and other patrons. The tables are close together, but the closeness is welcomed. If you are up for it, chat with your neighbors and ask them about Pittsburgh. They are sure to be filled with a story or three to tell you. Ask the staff their dish recommendations, history of the joint, and their appearance on Food Network's show *Restaurant: Impossible*. They received a cosmetic face-lift, but Del's is still Del's. The menu is lengthy and includes all things Italian, such as pastas, pizzas, chicken, veal, and seafood dishes. We are talking a seriously huge menu. The portions are just as huge, giving you practically two meals for the price of one. You will definitely need a doggie bag for your leftover Alfredo penne or lasagna.

Dinette, 5996 Penn Circle S, Shadyside, Pittsburgh, PA 15206; (412) 362-0202; http://dinette-pgh.com; Pizza; $$. The large windows create an open breeziness. The simple decor and table settings give it a minimalist swagger. The garden on the roof where the chef's father, Seth, grows ingredients like tomatoes, arugula, shishito peppers, figs, and herbs makes it pretty darn cool. And that's all before we've even talked about the menu. The daily rotating menu at Dinette, located on the second level of the East Side plaza, is only open for dinner and focuses largely on thin-crust pizza. Yes, there are several starter course selections that will make your mouth water at the description alone, but you go to Dinette to experience gourmet pizza. Pizza with salt-cured anchovies, jalapeños, capers, fresh mozzarella, and tomato or portobello mushrooms, radicchio, belletoile triple cream, and hazelnuts. This is not your average pepperoni pizza here, folks. This is innovative pizza from Chef-Owner Sonja Finn, who finds inspiration for her menu through using seasonal ingredients. The pizzas are perfect for sharing and allow room to sample dessert. We suggest whatever Arborio Rice Pudding is available. Visit Dinette's website for more information about the rooftop garden.

Dozen Bake Shop, 3511 Butler St., Lawrenceville, Pittsburgh, PA 15201; (412) 683-2327; www.dozenbakeshop.com; Neighborhood Cafe; $$. Dozen Bake Shop's light blue logo helps brighten up Butler Street. The moment you enter, you will feel like you're walking into a friend's kitchen for tea. Pull up a chair and make yourself at home, because it is time for . . . *brunch!* We love brunch. It combines the best meal of the day, breakfast, with lunch and what could be bad about that? Homemade cinnamon rolls, vegetable turnovers, eggs this way and eggs that way, soups, sandwiches, teas, and coffees. Dozen also serves cupcakes. They always have a vanilla and a chocolate cupcake on the menu but check daily for special flavors. They even spruce things up seasonally so there's always something new, like using a local brew to make the East End chocolate stout cupcake. Cupcakes and beer? We love it! And vegans can get their cupcake fill too, with options like the vegan ginger lemon cake. Additional location: Oakland, 417 S. Craig St., Pittsburgh, PA 15213; (412) 682-1718.

E2, 5904 Bryant St., Highland Park, Pittsburgh, PA 15206; (412) 441-1200; http://e2pgh.com; Italian; $$$. Kate Romane, chef and

CONFLICT KITCHEN

We don't usually mix dinner with politics, but Pittsburgh's **Conflict Kitchen** isn't afraid to stir the pot. This restaurant doubles as a public art project headed by Carnegie Mellon University assistant professor of art Jon Rubin and artist Dawn Weleski, serving up dishes from countries that the United States is in conflict with. Conflict Kitchen takes on a new country's identity and has created Iranian, Afghan, Cuban, North Korean, and Venezuelan dishes, which have never been found in Pittsburgh before now.

For less than 10 dollars, some past dishes have included: turnovers from Afghan (*bolani pazi*) stuffed with lentils, leeks, pumpkin, or potatoes; Iranian *kubideh* with spiced ground beef, onion, mint, and basil; and corn cake sandwiches with chicken, avocado, cheese, and beans. If you're looking to school your taste buds, we recommend you stop by for a bite to eat and an open discussion about the people and culture of these conflicting countries. Be sure not to throw your food wrapper away when finished eating. On it you will find interviews, ranging from popular culture to politics, from both people in the conflicting country and the diaspora in the United States.

Visit the Conflict Kitchen website, www.conflictkitchen .org, for location.

owner of E2 in Highland Park, creates dishes you wish you could make. They're simple, rustic, and full of flavors that blend together seamlessly. E2 serves dinner, but your first experience should be brunch. The vibe is casual and cozy, and the chalkboard menu is filled with rustic, sweet, and savory Italian-influenced choices. From simple one- or two-ingredient items to the more complex, E2 completes each dish with sincerity and heart. And you can tell. Start your brunch off sweetly with a bag of doughnuts, lightly fried pieces of sourdough that are tossed with ginger and sugar; beignets, airy fried dough with a sprinkling of powdered sugar; or zeppoli rolled in Parmesan cheese and black pepper and stuffed with anchovy (the anchovy is optional). For $5 each, why not try all three? As for your main brunch entree, recommendations get a little tricky. The menu is constantly changing, but any version of the polenta, frittata, or fried egg hoagie won't steer you wrong. See Chef Kate Romane's recipe for **Spaghetti Carbonara** on p. 260.

Eat Unique, 305 S. Craig St., Oakland, Pittsburgh, PA 15213; (412) 683-9993; www.eatuniquecafe.com; Neighborhood Cafe; $. Tired of the same old chain lunch spot? Eat Unique. With a long list of created on-the-spot sandwiches and salads, Eat Unique adds some much-needed flavor to the lunchtime routine. Vegetarians and healthy food addicts can find some solace here with options packed full of veggies and freshness. The Summer Sandwich, a take on mozzarella, tomato, and pesto, is a standout choice; the classic BLT is a favorite for those who require bacon on

seriously delicious farm bread; and the tomato soup sprinkled with feta is a nice introduction to some of Oakland's best homemade potage. Be sure to expect a bit of a wait for your food, especially during the lunchtime rush; crafting quality meals takes time. You can always call and order ahead if you are in a hurry. An important note: Even if you are trying to keep things healthy, don't forgo the sea salt chocolate chip cookies. Those puppies are life-changing on the delicious scale and are the size of your face—which will be smiling after your lunch.

Eden, 735 Copeland St., Shadyside, Pittsburgh, PA 15232; (412) 802-7070; www.edenpitt.com; Neighborhood Cafe; $$. Eden is the type of place you feel healthier just by walking inside. Dedicated to fresh ingredients and gluten-free *everything*, Eden's menu is vegetable heavy (you can order veggie fries and raw ketchup, for instance) and one of the most interesting in the city. Many of the items are also vegan friendly, like vegan waffles for Sunday brunch. Meat is on the menu too, which changes seasonally, but the stars here are absolutely the twists on the veggies. If you are feeling adventurous, take a shot . . . of kale or spinach, with hints of lemon or lime and ginger. Healthy shots not your thing? Bring your liquor; this joint is BYOB. As a fun touch, the food here isn't the only thing that is locally sourced; regional artists' work graces the white walls and pairs nicely with the otherwise minimalist interior.

The Elbow Room, 5533 Walnut St., Shadyside, Pittsburgh, PA 15232; (412) 441-5222; www.elbowroompittsburgh.com; Neighborhood Bar; $$. After outgrowing its former space that now houses **1947 Tavern** (p. 148), The Elbow Room moved to busy Walnut Street in a huge space above a shoe store and a women's boutique. In its new and improved location, The Elbow Room has a large dining area with tables and booths and a long bar. If you want the best seat in the house, ask to be seated at one of the high-top tables near the windows overlooking Walnut Street for ample people watching. As for the food, small and large plates of traditional neighborhood bar fare fill the menu. We recommend trying one of the burgers, such as The Johnny Apple Burger topped with brie, bacon, and apples. Any of the burgers on the menu can be made with either fresh ground turkey, chicken, ground beef, salmon, or as a veggie burger. And you cannot go wrong with one of the salad bowls, some of which come with fries, Pittsburgh style. Get here during happy hour, which unlike other happy hours, lasts from 9 to 11 p.m. and offers signature martinis for a $5 bill.

Fuel & Fuddle, 212 Oakland Ave., Oakland, Pittsburgh, PA 15213; (412) 682-3473; www.fuelandfuddle.com; Neighborhood Bar; $–$$. At Fuel & Fuddle the seating is tight, but the food is definitely worth sitting awkwardly close to your unknown dining neighbors. The Kick-Gas Nachos are a kick-gas start to a meal or an accompaniment to a beer. The nachos are topped with the house-made Rosa's chicken chili that is just as delicious solo. Make use of the brick oven and order one of the quirky-named individual pizza pies, such as the Smoking Hen, a barbecue-style pizza topped with zesty barbecue sauce, chicken, smoked mozzarella, red onion, grilled corn, and sprinkled on top with cilantro. Unique to Fuel & Fuddle are the sandwiches and burgers served on long, twisted rolls, as opposed to round buns. It's odd, but they come with mixed fries of regular and sweet potatoes. Fuel & Fuddle also serves its own beer, crafted for the restaurant by the Smuttynose Brewing Company in New Hampshire.

Gluuteny, 1923 Murray Ave., Squirrel Hill, Pittsburgh, PA 15217; (412) 521-4890; www.gluuteny.com; Bakery; $. Gluuteny looks a lot like other bakeries you may have visited. It has a classic black-and-white-checkered floor, it smells like Grandma's kitchen, and has a display case full of mouthwatering sweet and savory treats. The difference: Everything inside is gluten and casein free. Gluuteny began in 2005 after founder Mojca Pipus's daughter was diagnosed with autistic spectrum disorder. After extensive research, Mojca discovered her daughter could benefit from completely changing her diet. So Mojca began creating tasty gluten- and casein-free items loved by kids and adults alike. The menu at Gluuteny features cupcakes, cookies, brownies, tarts, whoopee pies, and breads. A must-purchase is the pumpkin pound cake. It's moist, delicately soft, and smells like a perfect fall day with hints of pumpkin and allspice. If you're more of a chocolate fan, we suggest a brownie or chocolate chip cookie. It's so rich we bet you won't even know it's gluten and casein free. Want to know one of the best parts about Gluuteny (besides everything it bakes, of course)? It ships its dry baking mixes anywhere in the world. So even when you're far away you can have a little bit of gluten- and casein-free Pittsburgh with you.

The Green Mango, 1109 S. Braddock Ave., Swissvale, Pittsburgh, PA 15218; (412) 244-3310; www.thegreenmango.com; Thai; $$. The Green Mango serves up their share of spice. We recommend the shrimp Summer roll: it's fresh, light, and loaded with lots of greenery (lettuce, mint, cilantro, and basil), shrimp, and vermicelli and is wrapped in thin rice paper and served with homemade dipping sauce. It's often hard to follow such a great appetizer, but their entrees are equally fresh. They are filling though, so sometimes we like to reserve a bit for a midnight snack. You can't go wrong with spicy drunken noodles or spicy pineapple curry with chicken. Another fan favorite is the spicy Thai beef salad. The Green Mango serves several dishes with mango, so make that a must-try while you're visiting! Even if you need a to-go box for half your dinner, order the homemade Thai custard at the end of your meal. We hope you'll love the friendly service and energy at The Green Mango as much as we do! Additional locations: See website.

Gullifty's, 1922 Murray Ave., Squirrel Hill, Pittsburgh, PA 15217; (412) 521-8222; www.gulliftys.us; American; $–$$. First thing you will notice upon entering Gullifty's: the dessert case. You have to walk by it to get to the laid-back dining room or bar. Desserts here cannot be avoided, nor should they be avoided. Enormous cakes (try the 5th Dimension: chocolate cake, cheesecake, chocolate chunks, and chocolate sauce). Out-of-control sundaes (try the Killer Kookie: warm chocolate chip cookie covered in ice cream and bananas). Pies for days (try the Ten Pound Apple Pie: self-explanatory, friends!). Gullifty's has the mantra of "Pittsburgh's best desserts," and it is hard to argue otherwise, as it certainly has an exorbitant amount of desserts and an option for every taste. The food on the menu  is as wide-ranging as the dessert selections. There is barbecue, sandwiches, seafood, pasta, pizza, soups—you name it, Gullifty's most likely has it. Just remember that whatever you order shouldn't be too filling; you must save room for dessert.

Harris Grill, 5747 Ellsworth Ave., Shadyside, Pittsburgh, PA 15232; (412) 362-5273; www.harrisgrill.com; Neighborhood Bar; $$. Harris Grill would easily win the "Class Clown" title in your high school's yearbook superlative contest. The owners have a sense of humor, so be sure to pay attention when you're dining, drinking, or recovering from drinking here. Harris is best in the summer. The front patio is the perfect spot to people watch as you sip on its famous frozen pink cosmo (add a shot of Chambord for only $2). Try to not fill up on those stiff frozen treats though. Harris has quite the extensive menu. With items like fresh fried cheesy balls (gently fried Arsenal cheese curds served with sweet and spicy gold sauce), *macaronis et fromage de langoustine* (macaroni and cheese with Atlantic lobster and lump crab meat), and Aw, You're Pullin' My Pork (slow-cooked pork shoulder with its Big Gay Al's Strawberry Chipotle Barbecue Sauce), how could you not want to sample something? Even if you don't have room for dessert you should try The Wrongest Dessert Ever. As the menu says, it's "pleasing to both the eye and the palate." Bacon Night happens every Tuesday at Harris, where baskets of bacon are complimentary at the bar and only a dollar at the tables, so get there early if you want free bacon.

Hemingway's Cafe, 3911 Forbes Ave., Oakland, Pittsburgh, PA 15213; (412) 621-4100; www.hemingways-cafe.com; Neighborhood Bar; $. In Oakland, the place to go for a cheap lunch is Hemingway's Cafe. To receive the half-off lunchtime special, you must have your order placed between 11 and 11:45 a.m. (Warning: Not all items are half-off during this time period, though many are.) The menu consists of your standard neighborhood bar food: appetizers, sandwiches and wraps, burgers, pastas, and pizza. Our must-eat menu item is the pita chips appetizer, though it could be a full meal on its own. These are deep-fried pieces of pita bread topped with a spicy cream cheese artichoke spread. Holy yum. Another good choice: the Philly chicken or Philly steak wraps with a side of mayo. And maybe by far the best item on the menu, the grilled cheese made with your choice of cheese (American, cheddar, pepper jack, provolone, or Swiss) and thick slices of Italian bread. When asked what side to accompany your lunch selection, order the seasoned curly fries. The half-price menu is pulled back out from 9 p.m. until midnight in case you want your second grilled cheese and fries of the day.

Joe's Dog House, Carnegie Mellon University Campus, Tech Street and Margaret Morrison Street, Oakland, Pittsburgh, PA 15213; www .joesdoghousepgh.com; Hot Dogs; $. Monday through Friday on the Carnegie Mellon University Campus, you can find Joe's Dog House, a hot dog cart with red-and-white umbrella, serving up gourmet hot dogs. No mystery meat dogs at this cart. You can find all-beef dogs, kielbasa, chicken sausage, soy dogs, tofu sausage, and a few burgers, all priced under $5. Perfect for students on a budget. For an extra dollar, you can make your dog a meal with the addition of a pop (aka soda) or water and a bag of chips. On Saturday, the cart moves to Walnut Street in Shadyside and attracts the shoppers looking for a hunger fix. The lines get long, but a perfectly charred dog from Joe's is worth the wait. Additional location: Shadyside, Walnut Street (typically across the street from the Apple Store) Pittsburgh, PA 15232.

Joseph Tambellini Restaurant, 5701 Bryant St., Highland Park, Pittsburgh, PA 15206; (412) 665-9000; http://josephtambellini .com; Italian; $$$–$$$$. If you are looking for a classy place with classy food, head to Joseph Tambellini's in Highland Park. Run by Chef Joseph Tambellini and his wife, Melissa (who serves as hostess), the restaurant has the feel of dining in an elegant parlor, especially in the first-floor dining room and bar. When making a reservation, which we recommend, ask for seating on the first floor. Each day, there is a list of five to six entree specials prepared by Chef Joseph and his staff including fresh fish, lamb, and beef. Since this is an Italian place, you must try the fresh handmade pasta. We highly recommend the tomato basil cream sauce with whichever fresh pasta shape you choose off the menu. If you order a non-pasta entree, such as the fresh fish of the day or the jumbo lump crab cakes, a pasta course will come with your meal. In addition, a house salad comes with every entree, dressed with fancy curled carrot strings, garbanzo beans, and couscous. Yes, couscous on a salad is divine. At Tambellini's, you are sure to have an elegant meal that will fill your stomach right up.

Jozsa Corner Hungarian Restaurant, 4800 2nd Ave., Hazelwood, Pittsburgh, PA 15207; (412) 422-1886; International; $. Alexander Jozsa Bodnar, the restaurant's owner, opened Jozsa's in 1988 and has been single-handedly churning out authentic Hungarian food ever since. First things first: If you want to experience Jozsa Corner Hungarian, you're going to have to call and make a reservation. Groups of diners (four-person minimum) can visit during the week or weekend for a one-of-a-kind multicourse meal. We suggest making a reservation for the "Hungarian Night" on the second Friday of each month. Alexander serves his guests family-style in a cozy dining space full of tchotchkes and memories. Don't look for a menu because there isn't one. Expect dishes like traditional *haluska*, cabbage and egg noodles; Transylvanian goulash, with sweet cabbage and meat; and chicken paprikash, chicken simmered with onions and paprika and dolloped in sour cream. Dining at Jozsa Corner Hungarian Restaurant is one of the most unique dining experiences in the 'Burgh. Don't forget to sign the guestbook before you leave.

Kelly's Bar & Lounge, 6012 Penn Circle S, East Liberty, Pittsburgh, PA 15206; (412) 363-6012; Neighborhood Bar; $$. Dive bars run rampant in Pittsburgh. Most follow a similar structure: dark nooks, lingering smoke, kitschy decor, and regulars. While that may be the norm, not all are of the same caliber, and Kelly's Bar & Lounge elevates the game. Surprisingly well lit, Kelly's smoke has long lifted, as has its kitschy decor. Regulars still rule the roost, but what makes it a standout is its classic cocktail list and "good food" menu. In the mood for a Pimm's Cup, Fire Fly, Harvey Wallbanger, or Pink Squirrel? You can get it here along with a host of other cocktails long forgotten by the masses. Plus what other dive bar has grilled haloumi and olives on its menu? Not many. You can also get Pittsburgh Bites, big chunks of either tofu or chicken in a mild or hot sauce; Cajun meat loaf with mashed sweet potatoes; or a PLT sandwich (pancetta, lettuce, and tomato). If you want to really experience Kelly's at its finest though, get the macaroni and cheese, which arrives at the table bubbling and lightly crusted with bread crumbs. And if all else fails, the jukebox is filled with punk, rock 'n roll, and soul classics that will make your night an instant hit.

Kevin's Deli, 101 N. Dithridge St., Suite 120, Oakland, Pittsburgh, PA 15213; (412) 621-6368; http://kevinsdeli.com; Deli; $. Want to know a secret only the locals know? Kevin's Deli in Webster Hall. Tucked away on the ground floor in the back of this residential building is Kevin's Deli, where Kevin and a few others whip up sandwiches in an extremely tiny kitchen. If you have ever wanted to know what it feels like to work in a kitchen without doing actual work, go to Kevin's and wait for your order. As you wait, you can hear the phone ring with callers placing take-out orders. Then you can witness one of Kevin's workers scribble down the orders on pieces of scrap paper. As needed, ingredients are passed back and forth across the small deli case from the coolers by the entrance to the small cooking area that includes a tiny sink, tiny grill top, and deep fryer located behind the counter. The menu is filled with sandwiches, ranging from cold deli-style to hot hoagies, tuna melts, and reubens. Breakfast sandwiches are served all day, as well as omelets and hash browns. Seating is limited to a few tables located outside the building, so takeout is your best bet.

Khalil's II Restaurant, 4757 Baum Blvd., Bloomfield, Pittsburgh, PA 15213; (412) 683-4757; www.khalils.biz; Middle Eastern; $$. You will not leave Khalil's hungry. When we go we settle in for the long haul and begin with the mazza appetizer, a combo of its house-made hummus, baba ghanoush, medamas, tabouli, feta, and olives and accompanied by warm pita. Then we move onto a bowl of its hearty lentil soup. Next up is the main course, usually a lamb shish kabob (chicken or shrimp is also available). All main dishes are served with a salad topped with Khalil's special dressing and steamed rice with pine nuts. Okay, so sometimes we end up taking enough food home to last a week, but what's wrong with that? We never leave Khalil's without witnessing someone breaking out into song and dance, which we happily watch and secretly wish we could join in. Oh, and we never forget the baklava.

La Casa Wine and Tapas Bar, 5884 Ellsworth Ave., Shadyside, Pittsburgh, PA 15232; (412) 441-3090; www.casablanca212.com; Moroccan; Tapas $-$$; Entrees $$-$$$. Looking to take a pretty lady out to dinner in Shadyside? Let us suggest La Casa, where you can make great conversation over Moroccan small plates and glasses of wine. In addition to a dining room with a bar, this wine and tapas bar has outside dining on the sidewalk alongside Ellsworth Avenue and on the back patio. The tapas come either hot or cold and are made to please a variety of palates, including vegetarians, meat eaters, and seafood lovers. Some of our faves to share are the *queso manchego*, baked manchego cheese with tomato dip, and *gambas al ajillio*, sautéed shrimp in a white wine and garlic sauce. You are definitely going to want to dip a piece of bread from the complimentary bread basket into this sauce. Trust us. Though you may think these small plates are not large enough for sharing, they are at La Casa. In case the small plates don't fill you up, salads and traditional Moroccan entree dishes, including chicken tagine and vegetarian couscous, are offered. La Casa is open for dinner every day of the week and also for lunch on Saturday. Reservations are strongly recommended.

La Gourmandine Bakery and Pastry Shop, 4605 Butler St., Lawrenceville, Pittsburgh, PA 15201; (412) 682-2210; www.lagour mandinebakery.com; Bakery; $. La Gourmandine's husband-and-wife owner team of Fabien and Lisanne Moreau both hail from France; we are sure glad they moved to Pittsburgh and brought the baked goods with them! La Gourmandine offers French pastries that are visually stunning and absurdly delicious. You will want to order one of everything just to stare at each delicate confection for longer 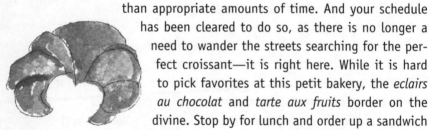 than appropriate amounts of time. And your schedule has been cleared to do so, as there is no longer a need to wander the streets searching for the perfect croissant—it is right here. While it is hard to pick favorites at this petit bakery, the *eclairs au chocolat* and *tarte aux fruits* border on the divine. Stop by for lunch and order up a sandwich on a baguette or a helping of quiche. The hand-written chalkboards on the exposed-brick wall and baskets of bread behind the bakery glass all make for a charming scene. In warm weather, small tables appear out front on the sidewalk, adding to this Lawrenceville spot's certain *je ne sais quoi.*

Legume, 214 N. Craig St., Oakland, Pittsburgh, PA 15213; (412) 621-2700; http://legumebistro.com; Eclectic; $$$–$$$$. Legume has a sleek space on North Craig Street. While the interior is vast, it still manages to feel cozy at each table. The very low light and flickering candles can take the credit for that loveliness. While the name of Legume might suggest a vegetable-heavy offering, this is not the case. Vegetarians will be pleased, but there is indeed meat to eat! The menu here is inventive and always changing. You can find the daily menu online, or just take the chance that whatever is offered will be great (it will be). Starter salads that feature the likes of curly endive and pears will literally melt in your mouth. We didn't know it was possible for salad to actually do that, but we learn something new every day! Entrees are perfectly portioned and, again, melt in your mouth-able. Splurge on one of the desserts created in house. Legume's truffle chocolate cake is easily one of the greatest cakes in the history of ever. For a fixed price and the adventurous diner, try the chef's tasting menus, which offer a hearty sampling of menu goodness. Valet parking is available across the street for a very reasonable $2.

Lot 17, 4617 Liberty Ave., Bloomfield, Pittsburgh, PA 15224; (412) 687-8117; www.lot17.net; Neighborhood Bar; $$. You can find sweet potato dishes in restaurants all over the city, but few serve them as well as Lot 17. Lot 17 in Bloomfield serves its fries to perfection with a side of sweet, buttery goodness. Usually it takes some persuading to get us to order something besides 12 orders of sweet potato fries, but luckily they have lots of menu items that pair well with the taters. The grilled salmon BLT, the stuffed burger, and the tuna wrap with grilled tuna steak would all be happy to share a plate with crispy, saucy sweetness (oh man, we're starting to name our fries), but you can also just get a side order if you go for the sea scallop kabob or the vegetable stir-fry. It's always abuzz with soccer game watchers, beer drinkers, and like we said . . . sometimes four girls with a table full of fries.

Mercurio's, 5523 Walnut St., Shadyside, Pittsburgh, PA 15232; (412) 621-6220; www.mercuriosgelatopizza.com; Ice Cream; $. Sometimes strolling along the three rivers of the 'Burgh feels like strolling along the canals of Venice. OK, it actually doesn't feel like that at all. The 'Burgh is one thousand times more romantic—lies! Anyway, just because we aren't in Italy doesn't mean we can't indulge in one of the boot-shaped country's finest treasures: gelato! This creamy, frozen treat gets us every time. With less butterfat than ice cream, you can even eat more with less guilt, or at least that is what we tell ourselves. Mercurio's in Shadyside is the perfect place to indulge, with 30 daily flavors and additional tastes on rotation. We love a cup of Birthday Cake (actual cake is mixed in, you guys!) and the Stracciatella (essentially a fancy chocolate chip). Payment per cup or cone is based on weight. Mercurio's also has several beers on tap and an assortment of Italian snacks like paninis and pizza. Nothing like pizza, beer, and a heaping cup of gelato to get the heart racing. Perhaps Pittsburgh does have Venice beat in the ways of love!

Mad Mex, 370 Atwood St., Oakland, Pittsburgh, PA 15213; (412) 681-5656; www.madmex.com; Mexican; $$. The original Mad Mex location opened in the collegiate neighborhood of Oakland and locations have been popping up over the city and 'Burbs ever since. You can down a Big Azz 22-ounce margarita in five fruity flavors or go traditional. You can choose from original, strawberry, mango, or one of their many seasonal flavors, such as cranberry during Thanksgiving. During their infamous happy hours, these monster margs are half off, so prepare yourself accordingly. Some of our favorite menu items include the Wing-O-Rito, boneless buffalo chicken burrito, served with waffle fries. We also recommend their loaded nachos grande, blue corn bread, and Black Beanie Quesadeenie, loaded with Kaya Yucatan black bean dip, cheese, and pineapple—a strange but delicious combination. We are suckers for their home-made bleu cheese dressing. We use the term "dressing" loosely as you'll have the best luck eating it with a fork rather than drizzling it anywhere. Seriously, it does a bang-up job of making you want to order an extra side so you can dunk the contents of your pockets in it. Additional locations: See website.

New Amsterdam, 4421 Butler St., Lawrenceville, Pittsburgh, PA 15201; (412) 904-2915; www.newamsterdam412.com; Neighborhood Bar; $$. If you're on the hunt for killer fish tacos in Pittsburgh, look no further than New Amsterdam. Located in the newly revamped and ultra-cool Lawrenceville neighborhood, New Amsterdam is a haven for good music, microbrews, and, like we said . . . super rad fish tacos. If you're enjoying the 'Burgh in the summer months, and you stop by New Amsterdam, you'll feel rad sitting at a high-top table with the garage-style door lifted to allow for welcome warm breezes. Kick back and enjoy a cold East End beer and munch on seasoned fries. It caters to our vegetarian friends and offers appetizers and entrees delectable enough to make a carnivore think twice. The cauliflower nugs and the macaroni and cheese, with provolone, goat, and Parmesan cheeses, are a must-try. If you feel like being a true Pittsburgher, you can chow down on pierogies and kraut. New Amsterdam is known for its live music events and support of local artists. The musical talent almost rivals the food.

1947 Tavern, 5744½ Ellsworth Ave., Shadyside, Pittsburgh, PA 15232; (412) 363-1947; www.1947tavern.com; Gastropub; $$–$$$. 1947 Tavern is not your typical neighborhood bar. Yes it's quaint, comfortable, dimly lit, and a touch upscale. But it's a bit more upscale than that. Jazz music fills the speakers as specialty cocktails are handcrafted behind the bar with diligence and elegant food is prepared in the kitchen. The menu features swanky starters, such as scallops wrapped in prosciutto and served with rainbow Swiss chard and a bourbon glaze, tavern fries with a house-made creamy pimento cheese sauce, and a cheese and pâté du jour plate. Macaroni and cheese is also on the menu a few times, twice as a starter (traditional or with bacon, because everything is better with bacon) and as a main dish with lobster. Sandwiches, burgers, pastas, and main entrees also fill the menu. Whatever you choose, be sure to save room for cake or pie because 1947 Tavern donates $1 of every piece sold to the Shadyside Boys & Girls Club.

Oh Yeah! Ice Cream & Coffee Co., 232 S. Highland Ave., Shadyside, Pittsburgh, PA 15206; (412) 200-5574; Ice Cream; $. Squirrel meat, marshmallow fluff, bee pollen, Cookie Crisp, Nutella, peanut butter, figs, walnuts, peach cobbler, brown sugar, gummy bears, and mango. And that's not even half of the mix-ins you can choose from at Oh Yeah! Ice Cream & Coffee Co. Okay, you can't really get squirrel meat, but it's on the list! We swear! Here's the drill: first decide on a base flavor. These vary, but vanilla, chocolate, sweet cream, birthday cake, and a few others are pretty regular flavors. Insiders tip: Several of the base flavors come in soy as well. Next, pick your mix-ins. Let your imagination run wild and evoke your inner mad scientist. Construct your perfect ice cream concoction like peanut butter and grape jelly. Finally, choose a size and give them your order. The staff then makes ice cream magic happen with a specially designed machine that combines all the ingredients together into an ice cream frenzy. You can even put your whole creation on top of a waffle if you want.

Paris 66, 6018 Penn Circle S, East Liberty, Pittsburgh, PA 15206; (412) 404-8166; www.paris66bistro.com; French; $$. The distance between Pittsburgh and Paris is about 4,000 miles. Paris 66 just happens to have the feel of a cafe that could be a stone's throw from the Champs-Élysées, without all of the flight time. This quaint bistro, with limited seating, an all-season patio, and a "bonjour!" greeting as you enter, offers food that fits its tagline: "Everyday French cuisine." Savory crêpes, traditional quiches, and classic croques headline the menu. Thursday through Saturday, *plats du jour* are created for dinner that range from *beouf bourgignon* to mussels. Brunch on Sunday features our favorite fare, eggs Provençal:

 scrambled eggs, feta, tomatoes, herbs . . . *j'adore*! After your meal, try one of the many flavors of homemade French macarons with equal parts taste and prettiness. Bring your favorite travel reading, order up a *pan au chocolat* and a warm brew, and settle in under the decorative Metropolitan sign posts; you'll be in Paris in a heartbeat.

Park Bruges, 5801 Bryant St., Highland Park, Pittsburgh, PA 15206; (412) 661-3334; www.pointbrugge.com; Bistro; $$. Park Bruges is the sister restaurant to the Point Breeze-located **Point Brugge Cafe** (p. 156). With a similar menu and a shared, relaxed ambiance to its relative, Park Bruges is an inviting place for a bite to eat. The cozy booths, rich color palette for the decor, and the table layout around the bar make it easy to spend hours here enjoying good conversation and a Merlot or two. The menu has a French influence with choices like the *tarte flambées,* which start with crust baked at the local **Enrico Biscotti** (p. 53), or the Montreal favorite of *poutine* (gravy and cheese curds on fries). Not all the plates are French, but they do all inspire a bit of "ooo la la." Park

Bruges holds a Jazz Monday the first Monday of every month. From 7:30 to 10:30 p.m., pay a $5 cover, enjoy live music, and order from a special menu.

People's Indian Restaurant, 5147 Penn Ave., Garfield, Pittsburgh, PA 15224; (412) 661-3160; Indian; $$. People's Indian Restaurant serves up some seriously sensational authentic Indian food. It may look closed from the outside, but have no fear, it's open six days a week (closed Sunday). The quiet, dimly lit interior sets the mood for some serious naan munching. The extensive menu is filled with various kabobs, curries, peneer, and pakora dishes. Stop by for lunch and sample a bevy of dishes from the lunch buffet. Dinner is great anytime at People's, but if you're there from 5 to 6 p.m. or 9 to 10 p.m., you'll receive a special offer: Buy one entree get one at 50 percent off. One of our favorite dishes is the chicken tikki masala: generous chunks of tender chicken bathed in a smoky, creamy tomato sauce. If you're looking for a vegetarian option, our go-to is the Aloo Mattar: peas and potatoes cooked to perfection in a curry sauce. You can choose your spiciness level, but be warned, People's is not afraid of spice. Be sure to take a spoonful of the colorful Mukhwas, an after-dinner breath freshener and digestive aid, at the counter on your way out.

Piccolo Forno, 3801 Butler St., Lawrenceville, Pittsburgh, PA 15201; (412) 622-0111; www.piccolo-forno.com; Italian; $$. While Piccolo Forno is a great spot for dinner, we suggest stopping by for lunch. The menu covers all the Italian basics: antipasti, *insalate*

Farmers' Markets & Community Supported Agriculture

There is something extra fantastic about fresh, local produce. We love it. You love it. Let's get it! Locally grown veggies and fruit are ours to be had at the many farmers' markets in town. Residents who want a hearty dose of the good stuff on a weekly basis can also participate in a Community Supported Agriculture (CSA) program through a local farm or farm alliance.

Listed here are a few resources that can get you on the fast track to farm freshness:

Penn's Corner Farm Alliance
www.pennscorner.com
Penn's Corner Farm Alliance is a farmer cooperative in western Pennsylvania that has a robust CSA program and an online farm stand. How 21st century!

Pittsburgh CitiParks Farmers Markets
www.city.pittsburgh.pa.us/parks/farmers_market.htm Pittsburgh CitiParks hosts farmers' markets in 7 locations throughout the city during the summer and fall. Check them out online to see the specific locations to get your goods.

Farmers@Firehouse
www.farmersatfirehouse.com
The vendors at Farmers@Firehouse in the Strip District are either Certified Organic or Certified Naturally Grown. Get your *au naturel* eats and other locally produced products like maple syrup and artisan breads.

The Farmer's Market Cooperative of East Liberty
www.farmersmarketcooperativeofeastliberty.com
The Farmer's Market Cooperative of East Liberty is an indoor market that is open every Saturday, year-round. In operation since 1941, this oldie is a goodie. In addition to produce and products straight from the farm, you can pick up the likes of pastas and doughnuts.

Buy Local PA
www.buylocalpa.org
Buy Local PA is the ultimate resource for finding local food sources. Type in your zip code in the search bar, and like magic, see all the farms and farm stands in the area.

Grow Pittsburgh
www.growpittsburgh.org
Grow Pittsburgh is dedicated to urban agriculture. Their website is especially helpful in locating all of the farms in the region, so you officially have no excuse for not getting your daily serving of veggies (p. 88).

Pittsburgh Public Market
www.pittsburghpublicmarket.org
Pittsburgh Public Market is a year-round, indoor market in the Strip. Farmers tend to show up in the summer. Find out more about the Market in our swell profile on page 54.

(salad), *zuppe del giorno* (soup), *pizze* (pizza), pasta, and panini, which means you'll probably be having a long bountiful lunch—  bring friends! Start your lunch extravaganza off with the crostini di polenta that's baked and topped with gorgonzola, mushroom spread, and marinated roasted cherry tomatoes or the *affettati*, which is an assortment of local meats from Parma Sausage Products, Inc. and imported cheeses. You may also want to try one of the *insalate*, all large enough to share. We like the *insalata di farro* made from Tuscan wheat grain with grape tomatoes, onion, radicchio, arugula, and basil. Piccolo Forno also has pasta and panini on the menu, but the pizza is too good to pass up. A classic margherita or bianca pizza is always a safe bet. If you're looking to kick it up a notch though, consider the capricciosa with crushed tomatoes, artichokes, mushrooms, olives, fresh mozzarella, mushroom, prosciutto cotto, and an egg, or the *speck e mascarpone* with crushed tomatoes, fresh mozzarella, mascarpone, and speck.

Pittsburgh Pretzel Sandwich Shop, 3531 Forbes Ave., Oakland, Pittsburgh, PA 15213; (412) 235-7807; www.pittsburghpretzel .com; Sandwiches; $. Pittsburgh has a love for soft pretzels it seems, doesn't it? We love them. For breakfast, lunch, dinner, or as a snack, a soft pretzel is always a great idea. This knotted goodness is even better as a sandwich. The Pittsburgh Pretzel Sandwich Shop serves up a traditional twisted pretzel that comes either salted or cinnamon-sugared, and also as bite-size poppers. Many dipping sauces are up for grabs, such as cheddar cheese sauce or berry cream cheese, but at a small price. And of course, there are sandwiches. Breakfast sandwiches made with bacon, ham, sausage, eggs, and cheese are served all day long. Other sandwiches better suited for lunch and dinner are available, including buffalo chicken, BLT, ham and cheese, and the list goes on. You can make your sandwich a meal by adding the daily soup or try your soup served in a pretzel bread bowl. Genius! Our favorite sandwich at this shop is the grilled cheese. Try the jalapeño grilled cheese if you are feeling spicy. Cheese and pretzels are always a perfect combo.

Plum Pan-Asian Kitchen, 5996 Penn Circle S, Shadyside, Pittsburgh, PA 15206; (412) 363-7586; http://plumpanasiankitchen .com; Pan-Asian; $$. Plum is nestled at the bottom of the East Side plaza bordering Penn Circle South. From the street you can see the large, colorful light fixtures and the sleek banquette running the length of the windows. It creates a seductive dining scene that will lure you in with its swank and promise of quality eats. Inside, the sushi bar is right in the center of the dining room. You can watch as the sushi chef masterfully crafts the special plum rolls like the Elvis roll (shrimp tempura, cucumber, and tuna) and other divine sushi creations. On the cooked side of things, the pan-fried vegetable dumplings with savory brown sauce are pan-fried fantasticness. Entrees include curries, noodles and rice, vegetarian, and house specialties like Thai spicy duck. We personally cannot get enough of the simple dry sautéed string beans (with choice of meat, of course), again in that crazy good brown sauce.

Point Brugge Cafe, 401 Hastings St., Point Breeze, Pittsburgh, PA 15206; (412) 441-3334; http://pointbrugge.com; Bistro; $$. You can't make a reservation at Point Brugge Cafe so we suggest going before 6 p.m. If you can't, try grabbing a seat at the bar. You'll be treated to the same quality service, but you'll be a part of the ebb and flow of the restaurant. The menu is made up of Belgian-inspired cuisine and has a decent selection of wine and beer. If it is your first time visiting Point Brugge, order yourself the *moules frites* and a good Belgian beer. All the sauces are excellent, but we suggest the classic white wine sauce, which is rich and velvety. Here's a tip: Take the crusty bread that accompanies the dish and let it soak up the sauce for a good minute, then place a mussel (or two) on the soggy bread, and enjoy. When you wake up from that food coma, you can thank us.

The Porch at Schenley, 221 Schenley Dr., Oakland, Pittsburgh, PA 15213; (412) 687-6724; www.theporchatschenley.com; Neighborhood Cafe; $–$$. The Porch at Schenley celebrates the concept of outside-in. Located in Schenley Plaza, a bustling parklet usually full of collegiate fresh air seekers, The Porch has walls of windows that deliver plenty of outdoor scenery. A rooftop garden provides ingredients for the chef to use, in season, for the dishes on the menu with options ranging from sandwiches to rib eye. Fortunately, the waitstaff is very knowledgeable about the meals and can help you make the right choice. Atypical to most dining establishments, the starters on the menu are quite cheap and provide enough to share. The crispy taters and farm bread with apple butter are starters that will provoke a thumbs up from everyone at the table. Colorful and flavorful pizzas arrive on a cookie sheet, right from the oven. Reservations are not accepted at The Porch, but you can put yourself on the waitlist prior to arrival by visiting the website. The Porch also has a take-out window that provides for a very nice picnic in the Plaza.

Pusadee's Garden, 5321 Butler St., Lawrenceville. Pittsburgh, PA 15201; (412) 781-8724; www.pusadeesgarden.com; Thai; $$. Family-owned and operated, Pusadee's Garden is a lush oasis in Upper Lawrenceville. There is an actual garden at Pusadee's Garden, in which you can sit and eat on warm days. The garden is quite lovely and the perfect tranquil spot to enjoy quality Thai cuisine. Inside the small restaurant, peace is achieved through soft lighting extended from the tin ceilings and the white table linens. The menu includes noodle dishes, rice dishes, curries, soup, salads, and a good assortment of apps. To start, we really love the tempura vegetables served with a peanut sauce for dipping. We are never ones to pass on large flat noodles, so the see yew noodle entree, with egg, broccoli, and sweet soy sauce, gets our seal of approval. The house specialties here include crispy tilapia and Thai yellow rice, solid choices for eating in one of the nicest urban gardens in the 412. BYOB and also bring your own dessert—for $1 per glass/person.

Quiet Storm, 5430 Penn Ave., Friendship, Pittsburgh, PA 15206; (412) 661-9355; www.qspgh.com; Neighborhood Cafe; $$. **The Quiet Storm is a favorite spot for Pittsburgh's artists and musicians. The Quiet Storm also caters to vegetarians and vegans who are looking for foods that don't skimp on flavor. Inside is filled with local art, knickknacks, bookshelves with books and games (for ample fun times), and something we love: bright red, vinyl barstools. Who doesn't love to spin on those? Best of all, Quiet Storm has some  of the nicest servers in the city. They make you feel welcome, and they get you excited about what you're about to eat! We always get excited about the milk shakes, particularly the espresso milk shake, which combines the best of both worlds—coffee and ice cream! Another must-try is the apple panini, with Granny Smith apples, cream and cheddar cheeses, homemade seisage, and apple butter. The Quiet Storm has one of the most popular Sunday brunches in the city, where you can feast upon your brunch basics but also their brunch burritos and the East Ender, a salad piled high with veggies, tofu, TVP bacon, and taters. Plus, you'll get your caffeine fix with bottomless coffee.**

Razzy Fresh, 1717 Murray Ave., Squirrel Hill, Pittsburgh, PA 15217; (412) 521-3145; www.razzyfresh.com; Ice Cream; $. **Razzy Fresh, we love you so hard. Razzy Fresh is a frozen yogurt emporium that is often equated to a desirable substitute for actual human romantic relationships. Who needs sweet nothings whispered in his or her ear**

when you can eat heaps of frozen yogurt that taste like dreams? Upon entering, grab a cup (only two sizes: large and bucket), fill said cup with whatever frozen yogurt suits your fancy (Razzy has 12 flavors daily, which rotate throughout the week, including original tangy yogurt and a long list of sweet options), and then pile on toppings from cookie crumbles to fresh berries. D.I.Y. magic! Pay for your creation by the ounce and then dig in! The whole process has us twitter-pated just thinking about it. Two more spots to get your Razz on in Oakland: 300 S. Craig St., Pittsburgh 15213; (412) 681-0515; and 3533 Forbes Ave., Pittsburgh 15213; (412) 586-5270.

Red Oak Cafe, 3610 Forbes Ave., Oakland, Pittsburgh, PA 15213; (412) 621-2221; Neighborhood Cafe; $. Healthy and fresh food is what Red Oak Cafe is all about. The Cafe's signature menu item is the OTY (oatmeal, tea, and yogurt), a smoothie packed  with healthy good stuff and served warm. Besides this drinkable goodness, Red Oak Cafe serves breakfast all day long, including egg scrambles named after Pittsburgh neighborhoods, breakfast sandwiches, and pancakes. Though you can never have too much breakfast, salads and sandwiches are also on the menu. One of our favorites is the buffalo chicken wrap, made with shaved, grilled chicken breast, roasted red cabbage, buffalo sauce, lettuce, tomato, and bleu cheese crumbles. It is no longer on the "official" menu, but ask for it when you order. When ordering a sandwich, you will be prompted to choose a side. You have to order the house-made chips, even two or three orders. The "chips" are actually fried strips of tortilla shells dusted with a Cajun seasoning that are out-of-this-world good. More hearty, but still healthy, entrees are the daily blue plate specials, including fish, brisket, and jambalaya, available Monday through Friday.

Root 174, 1113 S. Braddock Ave., Swissvale, Pittsburgh, PA 15218; (412) 243-4348; www.root174.com; Eclectic; $$–$$$. Root 174 gives taste buds of the vegan, vegetarian, and meat-eating variety a reason to dance. The always-changing menu, which can be found daily online, focuses on creative preparations of fresh and local ingredients. A chalkboard on the back wall calls out the specials of the day, and your server will be happy to offer advice on selections. Flavors here toe the line between risky and comfortable. An adventurous eater could pick a dish like bone marrow crème brûlée, while one seeking a nice twist on an old favorite could choose the likes of pork with a touch of barbecue sauce. Each plate is unique and proves that Root 174 Chef Keith Fuller is a genius. Really, anyone that can make us pine for another slice of vegan chocolate cake has kitchen brilliance on lockdown. Be sure to make a reservation—the space is incredibly cozy. See Chef Keith's recipe for **Falafel** on p. 255.

Rose Tea Cafe, 5874½ Forbes Ave., Squirrel Hill, Pittsburgh, PA 15217; (412) 421-2238; Taiwanese; $$. Rose Tea Cafe is a popular Taiwanese restaurant known for its bubble teas; even the sign outside boasts a drawing of the famed, tapioca drop filled drinks. If bubble tea doesn't push your delight button, try a mango, mung bean, or papaya milk shake. Along with the creative drink selection, the Taiwanese cuisine also keeps diners pouring through the door. For starters, the steamed or fried dumplings here rank among the best in town. The entree side of the menu is lengthy and full of excellent choices. In fact, the menu is overwhelming in its depth. We know folks who have this spot on their regular dining rotation, and they could easily dine here weekly without meal repeats. Kim chi and hot pot options are aplenty, and unique proteins like pork intestines and squid pop up more than once. For less adventurous eaters, entrees like chicken with mixed vegetables in a savory brown sauce will appease. Anticipate quick service and plenty of food left over for tomorrow's lunch. Takeout is also available.

Round Corner Cantina, 3720 Butler St., Lawrenceville, Pittsburgh, PA 15201; (412) 904-2279; www.roundcornercantina.com; Mexican; $. Set in a building with a legit round corner (hooray architecture impacting restaurant names!), the Round Corner Cantina is a super-hip Lawrenceville haunt. An impressive amount of tequila, brews, sangria, and Micheladas for days, Round Corner Cantina could survive as a bar alone, but the food here is worth a stop-in. In the mood for some gourmet tacos? Cantina has you covered. Made with a variety of meats like pork, hanger steak, and house-made chorizo, the taco flavors provide a good complement to your margarita or basil julep. We give a solid score to the *tacos de carnitas*, slow-roasted pork, onion, cucumber, radish, and cilantro. The chips and salsa and an order of the guacamole are a good table share. Try to get to the Cantina in the spring and summer, so you can sit in the rustic outdoor space, reminiscent of the Wild West and south of the border combined. Brunch is served on Sunday with Bloody Marys and breakfast burritos among other Latin-infused delights.

Salt of the Earth, 5523 Penn Ave., Garfield, Pittsburgh, PA 15206; (412) 441-7258; www.saltpgh.com; Eclectic; $$$$. No detail is overlooked at Salt of the Earth. From the floor-to-ceiling chalkboard menu to the presentation of dishes, Salt of the Earth is excellently executed. The modern design aesthetic might make you temporarily forget you're at a restaurant. That is until your sense of smell kicks in. The mastermind behind the experience is Chef Kevin Sousa, a born-and-bred Pittsburgher and an award-winning chef with an eye for innovation. Forego the reservations and try snagging a seat at the kitchen bar or one of the three long wood communal tables. If you wait for a bar seat, you can watch Chef Kevin and his talented staff work their magic as you dine. The menu consists of several regular items as well as rotating seasonal options. We won't make any dinner recommendations though as the menu is fluent and forever evolving each day. The only tip we'll offer is to get to Salt of the Earth fast and sample as much from the menu as humanly possible.

Sausalido, 4621 Liberty Ave., Bloomfield, Pittsburgh, PA 15224;

(412) 683-4575; www.sausalido.net; Bistro; $$$. Sausalido is a neighborhood bistro open on Monday, and it is BYOB, both sometimes rare gems to find when dining out. When arriving at Sausalido, don't mind the drop ceiling and the tiled floors; the food is where it's at. Upon sitting at one of the 15-ish tables, you will be greeted by fresh, crusty bread and a white bean and olive oil dipping sauce. The menu is seasonal, so items change up often. But what you must get when you visit Sausalido is the daily risotto, which is some of the best in town. In addition to the risotto, there are a handful of starters, including arancini (risotto balls) and roasted "Brousel" sprouts and pancetta, a few salads, and about 10 entree items ranging from pastas and crab cakes to pork and steak. Each entree comes with a side salad served before your meal. We like that the waitstaff paces your meal. You will have time to finish each portion of your meal before receiving the next bit. A relaxed dining experience rules, and Sausalido's got it.

Shady Grove, 5500 Walnut St., Shadyside, Pittsburgh, PA 15232; (412) 697-0909; http://eatshady.com; Neighborhood Bar; $–$$. If you want consistently satisfying bar food in Shadyside, head to Shady Grove. The menu is vast and you may find yourself wanting to order one of everything. It's okay, we often feel that way too. We are here to help. For starters or even as a main meal, get the Shady Sticks. They are by far the best thing on the menu, hands down; pizza dough covered in multiple cheeses and served with marinara sauce. Insiders hint: Ask for a side of ranch dressing to dip these sticks in. Simply salivating. Really, any pizza will satisfy your taste buds. The slightly sweet dough is great topped with practically anything. As for sandwiches, the California BLT is where it's at, sided with fries, and all of the salads are large and in charge, served in stainless steel bowls. Shady Grove always serves up great food and quality drinks, whether you go for happy hour or any hour. Be sure to stop by on Wednesday for half-price bottles of wine. Sit outside if you can. Great spot for people watching.

Silk Elephant, 1712 Murray Ave., Squirrel Hill, Pittsburgh, PA 15217; (412) 421-8801; www.silkelephant.net; Thai; $$. Norraset Nareedokmai is the chef and inspirational force behind the authentic Thai restaurant Silk Elephant. He strives to create an interplay of flavors, ingredients, and textures each time he creates a menu item. The menu at Silk Elephant is extensive. One notable feature of the menu is the variety of tapas options. Various rolls and dumplings (try the salmon!) are available as well as several meat (marinated lamb ribs, chicken kabobs) and vegetarian selections (taro crunch and corn fritters). If you haven't filled up on small plates, we suggest trying the pumpkin curry with grilled chicken. The chicken spends some time marinating in a blend of Thai herbs and spices then takes a swim in the rich pumpkin curry and is finally finished with sweet basil and bell peppers. While you may want to be more adventurous, the pad Thai at Silk Elephant won't let you down. And if the food doesn't blow you away, maybe the entertainment will. Every Thursday and Sunday two young ladies perform traditional Thai dances throughout the restaurant complete with commentary explaining what each dance means.

Silky's Pub, 5135 Liberty Ave., Bloomfield, Pittsburgh, PA 15224; (412) 683-6141; Neighborhood Bar; $$. Located on the corner of Liberty Avenue and South Evaline Street is Silky's Pub. It's your classic neighborhood bar and a great place to watch Pittsburgh sport events, especially if you're a Penguins' fan. The bar is typically filled with people in Malkin, Crosby, and Letang jerseys swigging beers and cheering on the black and gold. It's only slightly less crowded if there isn't a game on, which is an ideal time to get in a game of shuffleboard. The long, well-worn board is a welcome change from the typical pool tables and dartboards found in most bars. In between the cheering and fierce shuffleboard competition, sample something from Silky's standard or special menu. Both are sprinkled with typical bar favorites and unexpected dishes like lobster ravioli. The zucchini planks are always a great choice to start things off. The thinly sliced planks are lightly breaded and especially delicious dipped in Pittsburgh's favorite condiment, second to ketchup: ranch dressing. Burgers are also a great choice at Silky's Pub. Our standard go-to is the bleu burger. It's topped with creamy bleu cheese dressing, bacon, lettuce, and tomato and come served with your choice of a side like waffle fries, coleslaw, or potato salad. Additional locations: Silky's, 1731 Murray Ave., Pittsburgh, PA 15217; (412) 421-9222; and Silky's Crow's Nest, 19th and River Road, Sharpsburg, PA 15215; (412) 782-3707.

Smiling Banana Leaf, 5901 Bryant St., Highland Park, Pittsburgh, PA 15206; (412) 362-3200; http://smilingbananaleaf.com; Thai; $$. Great for lunch or dinner, Smiling Banana Leaf offers classic Thai favorites. Choose from curries, fried rice, noodles, noodle curries, and noodle soups. The interior of the restaurant is cheerful yet relatively small so if you can't get a table, try takeout and head to Highland Park for an impromptu picnic. One great dish to consider, which constantly delivers flavor and a bounty of veggies, is the green curry. The sauce is not as thick as some other green curries around town but still packs a rich, spicy flavor punch. It comes with your choice of meat (choose from chicken, pork, or tofu and vegetables), eggplant, basil leaves, broccoli, green beans, and bell peppers. The spicy green bean entree is also a favorite among diners. Green beans, carrots, and your choice of meat come served in a spicy and tangy chili sauce. Most dishes at Smiling Banana Leaf come served with perfectly cooked white jasmine rice that is delicate and only slightly sticky, which makes it an excellent accompaniment for your meal. Don't forget—Smiling Banana Leaf is BYOB!

Soba Lounge, 5847 Ellsworth Ave., Shadyside, Pittsburgh, PA 15232; (412) 362-5656; www.bigburrito.com/soba; Pan-Asian; $$$. Sleek, swanky, and sexy are all words that describe Soba Lounge in Shadyside. The dark, intimate setting is a perfect spot to take a date and indulge in late-night cocktails and dinner. Reservations are recommended for any night, but don't worry if you find yourself with a short wait at the bar. The cocktail and wine list is extensive (over 10 pages at the moment), the drinks are strong, and the bartenders are very attentive. Toted as "Pittsburgh's premiere example of Pan-Asian cuisine," Soba is known for dishes that exemplify creativity. Start your meal off with the Burmese tea leaf salad. Napa cabbage, peanuts, tomato, cucumber, yellow split peas, sesame seed, cilantro, and crispy

shallot seamlessly blend to create a uniquely fresh flavor unmatched elsewhere. Blue Bay mussels arrive in a deep bowl and submerged in a decadent aioli with Thai sausage and crispy soba noodles that soften once mixed. For entrees we recommend the seared rare tuna, encrusted with white and black sesame seeds gently placed in a sweet and tangy Korean barbecue sauce and served with house-made kim chi and ginger-fried rice. Watch its website for upcoming tasting menus that usually feature four courses and the option to add wine pairings. See Soba's recipe for **Bangkok Tea** on p. 266.

Spak Bros., 5107 Penn Ave., Garfield, Pittsburgh, PA 15224; (412) 362-7725; www.spakbrothers.com; Pizza; $. Vegans and vegetarians rejoice! Plenty of tasty options await you at neighborhood pizza shop Spak Bros. The menu features over 10 vegan options like the ever-popular seitan wings covered in your choice of wing sauce (the barbecue sauce is vegan) or the seitan Pittsburgh "steak" filled with shaved seitan, fries, mushrooms, hot peppers, green peppers, grilled onions, egg, provolone, and mayo. If you're not into meat substitutes, Spak Bros. can still feed a hungry belly. Hoagie options are available and come packed with local ingredients. The Philly steak or hot sausage, made with local sausage, is always a good place to start. Spak Bros. also makes a mean pizza. The topping selections are enough to keep your pie interesting without getting too zany. We suggest going with spinach, mushrooms, and feta cheese. The salty cheese slightly melted tangles perfectly with the spinach and mushroom. It makes a near perfect pizza every time. Spak Bros. only has a short counter so order your food to go and play a round of pinball while you wait.

Spice Island Tea House, 253 Atwood St., Oakland, Pittsburgh, PA 15213; (412) 687-8821; www.spiceislandteahouse.com; Asian; $$. Spice Island Tea House is a favorite among college students. There isn't much that its menu doesn't offer. It's named a tea house for a reason; one full page of their menu lists their many tea varieties available via small or large pots. It offers green teas, black teas, and spiced teas. The teas are all very reasonably priced so you can sample several kinds during the course of one meal. After you've made the tea decision, time to eat. Some of our favorite menu items include the squash fritters appetizer, lemongrass beef, and the ever-famous pad Thai. If you're a fan of curries, coconut, jasmine, and the other strong and spicy flavors infused into Asian cooking, you're going to love dining at the Spice Island Tea House.

Spoon, 134 S. Highland Ave., East Liberty, Pittsburgh, PA 15206; (412) 362-6001; www.spoonpgh.com; American; $$$. Sister restaurant to the next-door **BRGR** (p. 120), Spoon offers beautifully presented American cuisine. The restaurant is committed to using ingredients that are sourced from western Pennsylvania farms and purveyors, whenever available. When at Spoon, dine in the lounge on large leather couches and chairs. Sure, you can have a seat at the bar or at a table, but the lounge is a lot more cozy and relaxed. And the full dinner menu is served in the lounge. Start off with a glass of wine, house cocktail, or share a pitcher of sangria with your dining guests. For dinner, we enjoy sharing a few appetizers, but order whatever tickles your fancy on the menu. The descriptions of the pork, lamb, chicken, pasta, and seafood entrees may have you ordering a few of these as well. A bread basket will accompany whatever you order and it is quite impressive, including a variety of breads. If you can't get a table at BRGR, no worries. Spoon offers its own burger, the Spoon burger, made of Kobe beef and served with truffle fries.

Square Cafe, 1137 S. Braddock Ave., Swissvale, Pittsburgh, PA 15218; (412) 244-8002; www.square-cafe.com; Breakfast and Lunch; $–$$. Square Cafe is a happy morning or afternoon eatery. Bright blue and orange walls, vinyl retro-ish seating, and artwork by local creatives create sunny surroundings. On days when the sun is shining for real, lucky patrons can grab seats on the sidewalk. The staff here also add to the friendly, welcoming atmosphere. Get a milk shake, even at 8 a.m., and then choose from a solid variety of breakfast and lunch options. We tend to order breakfast when we visit here. The omelette ranchero (ham, Amish cheddar, and locally made salsa) and the Brussel sprouts and bacon hash can start the day off right. Might as well get a pancake (perhaps a cinnamon bun or lemon ricotta pancake?) or french toast on the side while you're at it! Lunch here is tasty too, with crepes, wraps, and burgers rounding out the menu. While its logo may be a circle, entrees are served on square plates and bottomless coffee is served in square mugs. We sure do love a theme and think it really is hip to be square.

Station Street Hot Dogs, 6290 Broad St., East Liberty, Pittsburgh, PA 15206; (412) 365-2121; http://stationstreetpgh.com; Hot Dogs; $. Station Street Hot Dogs isn't located on Station Street, but back in 1915, it was. Today, this hot dog shop is located on Broad Street in East Liberty and features gourmet dogs priced under $10. In February 2012, the locally celebrated chef, Kevin Sousa and his brother, Tom Sousa, gave the menu a face-lift with flavorful, 100 percent beef, natural casing dogs. The devil dog comes topped with egg salad, Tabasco sauce, potato chips, and scallions. The chili cheese dog has smoked brisket chili, Arsenal cheese curds, and onions stacked high. The buns are substantial; think more of a roll, preventing sogginess. Just one hot dog will fill you right up, but you best save room for the Duck Fat Fries, fresh-cut fries cooked in duck fat, and you better top them with Heinz ketchup, because in this town, there isn't any other substitute. At Station Street, you order your fries, dog, and Coke in a glass bottle at the register and post up along one of the counter seats and wait for your order to be called. Once you pick up your order, ketchup, yellow mustard, salt, pepper, and sriracha sauce are all up for grabs around the counter so you can top your dogs and fries with extra flavors.

Tamari Restaurant and Lounge, 3519 Butler St., Lawrenceville, Pittsburgh, PA 15201; (412) 325-3435; www.tamaripgh.com; Asian Latin Fusion; $$$. Did someone say outdoor dining? Tamari has some of the best! Tamari also happens to have much more than just a killer spot to eat in the sight-line of the Steel City; cocktails, tapas, and sushi should bring you through the door over and over again. If the weather isn't up for outdoor dining, inside Tamari is classy times. The long bar and open kitchen extend from the front to the back. After you settle in, choose from a variety of beauti- fully presented, Asian-Latin fused dishes to get the sampling going. The lobster macaroni and cheese with truffle aioli is pretty bomb, as are any maki choices. Tamari also features a robata grill, which is a Japanese technique of charcoal grilling, for items like hanger steak and quail egg. Tamari is a fun place to bring a group, because sharing is caring, guys. Order up a bunch of tapas and get the party started. Tamari shares the love with a second location, 701 Warrendale Village Dr., Warrendale, PA 15086; (724) 933-3155.

Tazza D'Oro Cafe & Espresso Bar, 1125 N. Highland Ave., Highland Park, Pittsburgh, PA 15206; (412) 362-3676; www.tazza doro.net; Coffee Shop; $. Tazza D'Oro is by far one of our favorite places to grab a coffee and do some writing in Pittsburgh. Located on the busy North Highland Avenue in Highland Park, the cafe is surrounded by large trees, which almost makes it unnoticeable from the road. But once you visit the cafe, you will never miss it again. The coffee beverages at Tazza D'Oro are made by expert baristas who are trained to make you the perfect cup of coffee. Also, the coffee beans are of the highest quality, again ensuring that you get a perfectly made and tasting cup of joe. Tazza D'Oro has a variety of pastries and paninis to accompany your coffee drink of choice. Like many Pittsburgh restaurants and cafes, Tazza D'Oro sources its food and other ingredients from local, western Pennsylvania farms and independent businesses. Additional location: Carnegie Mellon University, Gates Center, 3rd Floor, Computer Science Building, Forbes Ave., Pittsburgh, PA 15213; (412) 268-2139.

The Thunderbird Cafe, 4023 Butler St., Lawrenceville, Pittsburgh, PA 15201; (412) 682-0177; www.thunderbirdcafe.net; Neighborhood Bar; $$. The Thunderbird Cafe is one of the premier venues to see rockin' live music in the city. Local acts are at The Thunderbird daily, and the joint is almost always packed to capacity. It may just be a neighborhood bar, but do your neighborhood bars have indoor balconies that are perfect for band watching? Whether you're there fist bumping to a local band, like Backstabbing Good People, on a Thursday evening or toe tapping along to blues on a Saturday night, you are going to get hungry. We recommend you grab a few friends who aren't afraid to have a good time, order up a few local craft beers, and head to the second floor of The Thunderbird Cafe. The menu items are inexpensive so we don't feel guilty when we can't make up our minds. A few of our favorite choices include the black and blue burger (because bleu cheese and beef just belong together), the Cajun fries, and the pierogies (you are in Pittsburgh, remember!). We do our fair share of eating out, but eating out is especially fun when you can also be rocking out!

Toast! Kitchen & Wine Bar, 5102 Baum Blvd., Bloomfield, Pittsburgh, PA 15224; (412) 224-2579; www.toastpittsburgh.com; Eclectic, $$$. Contrary to what its name might suggest, Toast! Kitchen & Wine Bar has more than varieties of toast on its menu. The daily rotating menu features locally sourced items that influence the features of the day. Along with the food menu, the wine menu rotates based on availability. The portion sizes at Toast! are ideal for sampling something for each course. Try the sweet onion bisque if it's available for a warm start to your meal. Onions are cooked down and pureed releasing a sweet, mild flavor that even non-onion lovers will enjoy. Plus it's topped with a few pieces of braised duck that complement the sweetness nicely. A popular main course menu item is the stuffed poblano pepper. The pepper is slightly charred and stuffed with a flavorful mushroom quinoa, topped with well-seasoned wilted spinach, and placed in a bath of corn cream. Dessert is a must, especially if you can get the pumpkin french toast. A thick piece of Italian bread is soaked in pumpkin and then topped with a rich scoop of pumpkin ice cream. Breakfast for dessert never felt so right.

Umi, 5849 Ellsworth Ave., Shadyside, Pittsburgh, PA 15232; (412) 362-6198; www.bigburrito.com/umi; Japanese; $$$. Follow the sea dragon up the stairs to the Japanese restaurant Umi. Here you can savor menu items hard to find elsewhere in Pittsburgh. While the space above **Soba** (p. 166) is half the size, it serves equally inventive and delicate dishes. Sit at the sushi bar and watch the chef prepare maki handrolls, sushi, and sashimi with seasoned ease. Tables and tatami tables (traditional Japanese-style low tables) are also available for your dining pleasure. The knowledgeable waitstaff welcomes you with a warm hand towel as you peruse the menu. Once your menu is open, your eyes should go directly to the multicourse *omakase* meal. It's recommended as the best way to thoroughly experience Umi. Choose from 7 or 11 course plus dessert options. If you're celebrating a special occasion or feeling adventurous, go with the "Trust Mr. Shu" option. Whichever option you choose, you'll receive masterpieces presented like pieces of minimalistic art made from the freshest ingredients available. A two-person minimum is required, so be sure to bring a friend for the food adventure.

Union Grill, 413 S. Craig St., Oakland, Pittsburgh, PA 15213; (412) 681-8620; American; $$. Union Grill is an ideal collegiate lunch, dinner, and after-exam hangout spot. It is rare to find the place not hopping. Thankfully, there are plenty of seating options either at the bar or in the larger-than-it-appears-from-the-street dining area. During the warmer months, the front opens up onto the always bustlin' Craig Street, and a handful of diners can bask in the urban outdoors. The portions at this joint are incredibly hardy. If you order the fish taco, you will wind up with what looks to be more like a whale taco. Not that we are complaining—the more good food the merrier! Choose a burger or a sandwich from the menu (and choose the waffle fries—always the waffle fries), and you can't miss. The turkey burger in particular gets a serious "heck yes!" in our book, as its deliciousness sometimes haunts our dreams. Perhaps the most important feature of the Union Grill is on the drink side of the menu: Union Grill has a $10 wine list. We repeat: $10. Bottles. Of. Wine. Enough said.

Vanilla Pastry Studio, 6014 Penn Circle S, East Liberty, Pittsburgh, PA 15206; (412) 361-2306; www.vanillapastry.com; Bakery; $. CUPCAKES! You'll feel like shouting with joy too after trying a cupcake from Vanilla Pastry Studio on Penn Circle South. A giant cupcake marks the spot out front the tiny shop. Filled with bright, cheerful colors and cute nooks to enjoy your sweets, Vanilla Pastry Studio is more chic boutique than traditional bakery inside. The display case is filled with treats just like Mom made, only a little less lopsided. Once you get past the intoxicating smells, it's time to get down to business and choose your cupcake.  The cake is moist and the butter cream or chocolate fudge icing they're topped with won't send you into a sugar coma. They're also just the right size to keep you craving more. The cupcake list varies depending on the day, but if the chocolate/peanut butter, vanilla/dulce de leche, or mango-passionfruit is available, try one, or two. Vanilla Pastry does specialize in other sugary confections like lollys (dessert on a stick), whimsical custom cakes, and wedding cakes as well as decadent goodies like brownies, cookies, and whoopee pies.

Verde Mexican Kitchen & Cantina, 5491 Penn Ave., Garfield, Pittsburgh, PA 15206; (412) 404-8487; www.verdepgh.com; Mexican; $$. If you like tequila, then Verde Mexican Kitchen & Cantina is the place for you. With over 160 varieties made of 100 percent blue agave, Verde Mexican Kitchen & Cantina has one of the largest selections around. Try one of 160 plus varieties in a seasonal or flavored margarita or a tequila flight. If you choose one of those flights, it will be accompanied by a shot of traditional sangrita. The

menu features traditional Mexican flavors and authentic ingredients with a modern flair. Try the guacamole made fresh with your choice of ingredients and spice level. And if you're in the mood for a show, you can have the guacamole made tableside. The *tacos de camote* are worth a try for a main course.

These soft tacos come stuffed with roasted sweet potatoes, fried chickpeas, and lightly dressed with a Mexican-style *tzatziki*. If your meal doesn't come with red rice and black beans, be sure to get them as a side.

Landmarks

The Church Brew Works, 3525 Liberty Ave., Lawrenceville, Pittsburgh, PA 15201; (412) 688-8200; www.churchbrew.com; Gastropub; $$$. Some say visiting The Church Brew Works is somewhat of a religious experience. That could be because the restaurant and microbrewery is located inside a restored Catholic church. The Church Brew Works has been serving up one-of-a-kind brews and dishes for almost 20 years and, in 2001, received National Historic Landmark status, so it's definitely a must-visit while in Pittsburgh. Where else in the city can you get rattlesnake pierogies and free parking? Don't miss the beautifully restored interior of the church, complete with stained-glass windows and altar, which is now home to the copper brewing equipment. The exterior is just as beautiful. Church Brew Works offers a peaceful patio where you can enjoy a rotating menu of starters, pasta, steak, seafood, or one of its many wood-fired pizzas. And of course, grab a pint of the in-house brewed Pious Monk. If you're looking for a nonalcoholic beverage, try the homemade ginger ale and root beer. Read more about the brews here in the "Local Drink Scene" section.

Coca Cafe, 3811 Butler St., Lawrenceville, Pittsburgh, PA 15201; (412) 621-3171; www.cocacafe.net; Breakfast and Lunch, $$. Coca Cafe, in Pittsburgh's Lawrenceville neighborhood, is a tiny place on Butler Street with large windows and red walls with an impressive list of coffees and teas, Italian sodas, and fresh fruit smoothies.

During its Sunday brunch, you can order a made-to-order omelet and carb it up with your choice of cinnamon, seven-grain, herbed focaccia, pumpernickel, or country white toast. If you like your toast french, like we do, you're going to want to go for the almond french toast, served with fresh berries and lemon cream sauce. You'll be licking the plate afterward. For lunch, there are salads and paninis aplenty. Something that we love about Coca Cafe is the local artwork you can find when you look around. It's all for sale so you can get a cappuccino, a biscotti, and a painting to go! Coca Cafe also caters the cafe at the Mattress Factory so you know you'll be eating well if you decide to snack after peeping the art exhibits.

Dave and Andy's Homemade Ice Cream, 207 Atwood St., Oakland, Pittsburgh, PA 15213; (412) 681-9906; Ice Cream; $. The smell of handmade ice cream waffle cones is exhilarating. The sweet scent will fill your nose from outside, having you transfixed on ordering one upon entering the small ice cream shop. Since 1983, Dave and Andy's has been satisfying the sweet teeth of University of Pittsburgh students and anyone who comes in close contact with that sweet smell of waffle cones. There is a list of the flavors of the day on the chalkboard behind the freezers full of ice cream tubs. If you have a hard time choosing a flavor, try our two faves: birthday cake and chocolate chip cookie dough. The ice cream is rich and smooth, and you will want to get at least two scoops of your favorite flavors. Once you are done licking away your scoops, a surprise awaits you at the bottom of the waffle cone—a piece of chocolate candy, which is placed in the cone to prevent ice cream drippage. Sorbet, yogurt, and fat-free/sugar-free ice cream are also available.

Essie's Original Hot Dog Shop, 3901 Forbes Ave., Oakland, Pittsburgh, PA 15213; (412) 621-7388; Hot Dogs; $. Open until the wee hours of the morning, Essie's Original Hot Dog Shop, commonly known to Pittsburghers as "The O," is the perfect place to grab greasy food after a long evening of drinking. Be prepared to meet and mingle with all of the party-hardy University of Pittsburgh students. To prevent any kind of stampede for fries, there is a security guard stationed in the middle of the shop. Casing hot dogs and overloaded, twice-fried french fries are this landmark's specialty. Up front, you order your hot dogs and drinks, and then in the back is where all the french fry magic happens. The fries are piled high like skyscrapers, and condiments here don't come in those little packets. You get tubs of condiments large enough to jam all of those fries in. There are more than just fries and hot dogs at this place—you can get pizza, booze, and burgers, too!

Girasole, 733 Copeland St., Shadyside, Pittsburgh, PA 15232; (412) 682-2130; www.733copeland.com; Italian; $$. Girasole is a cozy, basement-level restaurant with stone walls that give the appearance of dining in a Tuscan wine cellar. This association is appropriate as the fare here references Italy as well. With seasonal menus for winter, spring, summer, and fall, you can anticipate slightly different variations of Italian classics depending on the time of year. Unchanging throughout the calendar is the excellent marinara sauce and the surprising house salad—no sad iceberg lettuce here! The salad, coined as the "Girasole," is prepared with mixed greens, garbanzo beans, gorgonzola cheese, and a flavorful sunflower vinaigrette. Girasole has a solid wine list spanning all regions of Italy and a bar that can serve you up a delicious bellini. If the weather is cooperating, a welcoming, substreet-level patio is the perfect spot for outdoor eating. Less than 1 block off Shadyside's busy Walnut Street, you'll still be in range to shout "ciao!" to friendly passersby.

Le Mardi Gras, 731 Copeland St., Shadyside, Pittsburgh, PA 15232; (412) 683-0912; www.lemardigras.com; Neighborhood Bar; $. Are you in the mood to be transported to a time when drinks were stiff and indoor smoking was prevalent? Then Le Mardi Gras is your new stomping ground. This small neighborhood bar has been around since 1954 and features a regular cast of locals just waiting for you to pull up a stool. Its cramped, dark quarters help it pull off that cool-without-trying vibe. Squeeze your way up to the bar and ask for a Greyhound. It's vodka and half of a freshly squeezed grapefruit. Be warned: it's heavy on the vodka, and light on the juice. The booze is the star in every drink the bartenders pour at Le Mardi Gras so find yourself a designated driver if you plan on staying for the long haul. If one of the four red retro

booths open up, be sure to slide in and make yourself comfortable. The jukebox is filled with blues, jazz, and countless classics and don't forget to play a round of Ms. Pac-Man. Oh, and watch those stairs when you're leaving. They'll make for a painful reminder of just how much fun you had.

Prantl's Bakery, 5525 Walnut St., Shadyside, Pittsburgh, PA 15232; (412) 621-2092; www.prantlsbakery.com; Bakery; $. If Pittsburgh had an official dessert, it would be Prantl's burnt almond torte. Just like a luxury purse, there are knockoffs out there. But don't give in to them. In Pittsburgh you must get a burnt almond torte from Prantl's. Plain and simple. You may ask, "What is a burnt almond torte?" Well, it is two layers of yellow sponge cake filled with custard, iced with buttercream, and covered in toasted almonds. The torte is so popular that it can be ordered online and shipped all over the country. Prantl's has been a Pittsburgh institution for over 100 years and bakes a wide variety of goods, ranging from breads, rolls, and doughnuts to cupcakes, cookies, and brownies. You can also special order cakes and have a Prantl's cake made for your wedding. Honestly, everything sold at Prantl's is excellent and enjoyable with your morning cup of coffee. Trust us. Additional location: Downtown, 438 Market St., Pittsburgh, PA 15222; (412) 471-6861.

Tessaro's, 4601 Liberty Ave., Bloomfield, Pittsburgh, PA 15224; (412) 682-6809; American; $–$$. Tessaro's has been crafting impossibly good burgers before gourmet burgers became the hottest menu item around. The meat is butchered on-site, and that freshness translates to a good meal. The menu has a lot more than burgers, but really, you should get a burger. You can order it plain, with cheese (American, bleu, Swiss, provolone, or cheddar), with bacon and cheese, with bacon, mushrooms, and cheese, or with coleslaw. On the side, decide from potato salad, coleslaw, chips, broccoli, or home fries. Always the home fries. Wood walls, paper placemats, and tablecloths create the perfect no-nonsense 'Burgh ambiance. There is a long bar and sports on the televisions. No better place to kick back and eat a burger the size of a small vehicle. Being a Pittsburgh tradition, sometimes a wait is inevitable. With all your time spent in anticipation, think of all the locals that have stood in your spot—waiting for a classic bite of the 'Burgh.

Tram's Kitchen, 4050 Penn Ave., Bloomfield, Pittsburgh, PA 15224; (412) 682-2688; Vietnamese; $$. You probably wouldn't notice Tram's Kitchen if you walked by. There's nothing fancy about it. Quite frankly, some might avoid it altogether. Tram's Kitchen serves inexpensive Vietnamese dishes to a typically packed dining room of patrons Tuesday through Sunday. Start things off with an order of fresh spring rolls. This appetizer regularly wins "best of" categories from the local media and you'll know why after the first bite. Each roll is tightly wrapped in translucent rice paper and pops with an explosive fresh flavor. As far as main dishes go, pho is king at Tram's. It arrives piping hot with thick noodles, choice of meat, and an array of mix-ins like bean sprouts and basil swimming in a perfectly seasoned broth. The vermicelli is also an excellent choice with thinly sliced meat, delicate rice noodles, broccoli, and peanuts sitting in a shallow pool of broth. Add a bit of complexity or spice to any dish you choose with one of the bottles of sauce found on the table. Don't forget your booze and cash. Tram's Kitchen is BYOB and cash only!

Uncle Sam's Sandwich Bar, 210 Oakland Ave., Oakland, Pittsburgh, PA 15213; (412) 621-1885; www.unclesamssubs.com; Sandwiches; $. Uncle Sam's Sandwich Bar has some pretty tasty cheese steaks for both meat and veggie lovers. Get the classic Uncle Sam's Special Steak, a cheese steak loaded with peppers, onions, and mushrooms. Fun fact: For a little up-charge, you can substitute chicken instead of meat on any cheese steak. Vegetarian? Uncle Sam's has you covered with five sandwiches on the menu, including the grilled portobello sub. We suggest you dine in at Uncle Sam's because you can take advantage of the free fries that come along with sandwiches. If you place an order to go, you must pay for fries. But they are definitely worth every penny. At Uncle Sam's, you always end your meal with a complimentary mint and make sure to get any part of your uneaten sandwich wrapped in butcher paper. Additional locations: See website.

Specialty Stores, Markets & Producers

East End Food Co-op, 7516 Meade St., Point Breeze, Pittsburgh, PA 15208; (412) 242-3598; www.eastendfood.coop. If you're in search of a healthy but hearty meal in Pittsburgh, the East End Food Co-op could be just what you're looking for. Open daily, the East End Food Co-op Cafe and market caters to the diverse East End crowd. House-made soups, smoothies, and juices, and sandwiches are available for dining in or taking with you on the go. Local and organic ingredients help you feel good about what you're eating. Visit during the weekend for their brunch and then fill your recyclable cotton bag with fresh fruit, vegetables, and all-natural snacks for you and the family and friends you're looking out for. The staff is friendly and knowledgeable so don't be afraid to ask questions, even if they look way cooler than you.

Groceria Italiana, 237 Cedarville St., Bloomfield, Pittsburgh, PA 15224; (412) 681-1227; http://groceriaitaliana.com. Long before chain grocery stores moved into town, communities shopped at their neighborhood market. Groceria Italiana in Bloomfield takes you back to a simpler time when life was homemade. The first thing you might notice is the counter where nimble fingers with years of practice are busy making fresh pasta and ravioli. Pasta includes fettuccine, linguine, vermicelli, spaghetti, angel hair, and about a dozen types of ravioli like artichoke and gorgonzola, mushroom,

ARSENAL CHEESE

Cheese makes everything better, especially when it comes from **Arsenal Cheese.** Jonathan Gaugler and his dad, Scott, started making curds in 2010 after noticing a void in the 'Burgh for local homemade cheese. The pair operates out of a small facility on Fisk Street in Lawrenceville and plan to expand the production with soft cheeses, camembert, and varieties of blues. It's located near Allegheny Arsenal, a storage and manufacturing site during the Civil War; Arsenal Lanes, a funky bowling alley; and Arsenal School—hence the name.

Arsenal Cheese currently makes two kinds of curds: cannonball curds and herb and bourbon. The cannonball curds are a fresh cheddar curd, and made from local hormone-free raw milk sourced from Le-Ara Farms in Worthington, Pennsylvania. These curds are a tad salty, have a chewy texture, and are meant to be eaten when fresh. If you eat them within 3 days, they squeak! The herb and bourbon curds are made by draining fresh curd then allowing them to settle into little rounds. Those are then salted and washed in bourbon that's full of thyme and tarragon then rubbed onto the cheese.

The tasty curds can be found at restaurants like **Brillobox** (p. 121), **Kelly's Bar & Lounge** (p. 141), **Meat & Potatoes** (p. 35), and **Station Street Hot Dogs** (p. 170). You can also purchase them at East End Food Co-op and the Whole Foods in East Liberty. For more information visit their website, http://arsenalcheese.com.

prosciutto, roasted red pepper, and spinach. Take a box home with you along with some homemade meat or marinara sauce and you have a quick, authentic Italian dinner. Next to the pasta is the deli counter where you can find cold cuts, dry cured meats, olives, and cold salads. If you need a hot quick lunch, check out the hot food section. Features change but expect to find dishes like meatball sandwiches, eggplant Parmesan, stuffed peppers, lasagna, and pepperoni rolls. Groceria Italiana also has shelves stocked with tomato sauces, olive oil, balsamic, and spices.

Shadyside Market, 5414 Walnut St., Shadyside, Pittsburgh, PA 15232; (412) 682-5420; www.theshadysidemarket.com. Shadyside Market has been a staple on Walnut Street for 50 years. This specialty grocer keeps stock in fresh produce, fresh meat, and interesting boxes, cans, and jars. No cheap alternatives here; this is higher echelon food product. We once went in for just regular old pasta sauce; when we realized this was not an option, we found ourselves with some of the best sauce ever. Thank you, Shadyside Market, for your off-the-beaten path finds! The market also has an on-site deli where you can indulge in a sandwich, salad, or daily entrees. Lunch and dinner can be picked up or delivered. Cookies and the like are often at the front register, which makes it hard to resist the charm. Pay for your groceries and snag some baked goods.

Waffallonia, 1707 Murray Ave., Squirrel Hill, Pittsburgh, PA 15217; (412) 521-4902; www.waffallonia.com. A mystical land dedicated to waffles? Welcome to Waffallonia! This tiny, tiny, blink-and-you-miss-it waffle shop specializes in Belgian liege waffles. The secret to the liege-y-ness is the specific, Belgian sugar that provides a different texture and outer crunch than other waffles. It's science. It's delicious. You can take your plain waffle and run, or you can kick back in the hip, minimalist space and get your waffle piled high with a variety of extras. Strawberries, whipped cream, Nutella, ice cream—take your pick. Perhaps you should be running toward Waffallonia right now. You can also order from a predetermined menu, which looks like a train schedule, on the wall with combos like the Antwerp, which includes chocolate sauce and whipped cream, or the Bruges, which includes strawberries and whipped cream.

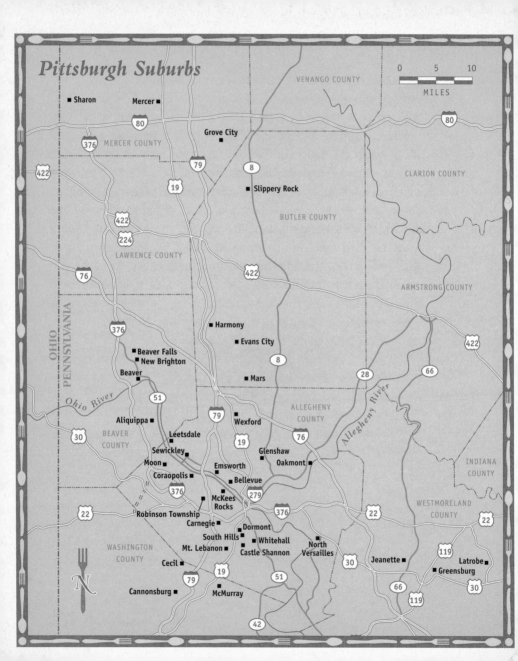

Suburban Gems & Places Worth the Drive

The suburbs are as varied as the collection of neighborhoods that make up the 'Burgh. Proud, tiny towns to posh, stately villages. We've outlined the best bets for tasty visits to these nearby hamlets. Your taste buds will delight in each area, and you'll continue to be a recipient of the Pittsburgh charm.

Sure, leaving Pittsburgh may be a struggle. Our roads are wacky, disjointed, and in no way parallel. Our drivers think they can turn left before you go straight through an intersection. And everyone—*everyone*—stops before going through tunnels. The reward for emerging on the other side is great for you and your stomach, as plenty of quality dining options abound beyond the city limits.

Yinz guys better get moving—the 'Burbs are anticipating your arrival.

Azul Bar y Cantina, 122 Broad St., Leetsdale, PA 15056; (724) 266-6362; www.azulbarycantina.com; Mexican; $$. Tucked away on a tiny street in Leetsdale, right past the pristine town of Sewickley, is one of the city's best Mexican restaurants. The dim blue lighting is romantic yet energizing. From the moment you walk through the doors you know you're going to get great service. Try not to drool as you stroll past other patrons happily munching on freshly made tortilla chips and what we're confident will be some of the best salsa that will ever grace said tortilla chips. Order a margarita while you think about which of the menu items will be the lucky winner dinner selection. Whether you're looking for

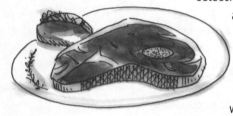

a mild fish taco or the more traditional pork, chicken, or steak option, you really can't go wrong. If you are feeling a bit hungrier, you'll want to go with one of the massive burritos, but don't stuff yourself before you get to try the fried ice cream. Seriously, you're going to want that. Get out to the suburbs pronto for an authentic Mexican meal that will leave you ready for a siesta.

B Gourmet, 428 Beaver St., Sewickley, PA 15143; (412) 741-6100; www.bgourmet-pgh.com; Neighborhood Cafe; $$. Sister eatery to

Avenue B (p. 118) in Friendship is B Gourmet, a neighborhood cafe and gourmet marketplace on busy Beaver Street in Sewickley. Different from the more upscale Avenue B, B Gourmet offers tasty lunches and meals-to-go. There are a handful of tables located at the front of the space where you can dine in during lunch hours and enjoy sandwiches, wraps, salads, and daily soups that are ordered off the wall menus behind the deli cases. In addition, B Gourmet has freshly prepared foods to go, including meat loaf, chicken, crab cakes, stuffed peppers, and quinoa salad, just to name a few. During the dinner rush, B Gourmet turns into a takeout-only restaurant. "Dinners to go" can be ordered in advance or you can swing by and pick up a meal-to-go. The dining space can be rented out during dinner hours if you have a large number of friends you want to take out and impress.

Brighton Hot Dog Shoppe, 1128 3rd Ave., New Brighton, PA 15066; (724) 843-4012; www.brightonhotdogshoppes.com; Hot Dogs; $. Hot dogs, burgers, fries, chili, cheese, milk shakes, and a fountain pop served in a take-home plastic cup with hot dog characters on it. You can get all of these tasty treats and more at the Brighton Hot Dog Shoppe. Started in 1959 in New Brighton, the Brighton Hot Dog Shoppe is a staple of Beaver County, which has since crossed county lines, opening up locations in Allegheny, Butler, and Lawrence Counties. When you visit you must order a chili sauce and onion hot dog, a side of cheddar and chili fries, and a milk shake. There are no fancy hot dog names here, no wacky toppings, and nothing gourmet. Just simple, good food that will stick to your ribs. Though the place is known for their wieners, their burgers are outstanding. Just plain, simple burgers with traditional toppings. You really don't go wrong with either a burger or a hot dog here. Several locations also serve breakfast of omelets, pancakes, french toast, and home fries, which are simple and delicious. Additional locations: See website.

Burgatory, Waterworks Mall, 932 Freeport Rd., Pittsburgh, PA 15238; (412) 781-1456; www.burgatorybar.com; Burgers; $$. Burgatory is all kinds of clever. Playing off the dichotomy of heaven and hell, Burgatory describes its offerings as "Helluva Burger" and "Heavenly Shakes." You know, just stuck between the two in Burgatory! There is no better place to be in limbo, folks. The burgers here really are sinfully delicious. You can build your own burger, starting with the specialty rub or seasoning (we really like the Angel Dust, a salt-and-pepper blend) and every condiment you can dream of. Each burger comes with house chips—a mix of regular and sweet potato. The shakes, good heavens the shakes, are absolutely fantastic. Using handcrafted ice cream, the team at Burgatory are miracle workers with both the nonalcoholic and alcoholic variety of frosty delights. We would go as far as saying the campfire s'mores milk shake, in particular, is the best milk shake we've ever had (and we have had a lot). A giant roasted marshmallow and expertly mixed graham cracker crumbs contribute to this magnificence. Word is out that this place is awesome, so the wait can sometimes be intimidating. You can check the wait time on the website before you go. Don't be deterred! Burgatory has additional locations: CONSOL

Energy Center (upper level), 1001 5th Ave., Pittsburgh, PA 15219; Robinson, 300 McHolme Dr., Pittsburgh, PA 15275.

Burgh'ers Organic, 100 Perry Hwy., Harmony, PA 16037; (724) 473-0710; www.burghersinc.com; Burgers; $$. In the mood for a road trip? Then hop in your car and drive about 50 minutes to Burgh'ers Organic in Harmony. Don't let the fact that it's in a strip mall fool you; Burgh'ers Organic offers an all-round quality dining experience. Its menu is primarily burgers made from a blend of local, all-natural, chemical-free beef. Like most burger joints, Burgh'ers Organic offers a build-your-own burger option, but where Burgh'ers Organic hits it out of the park is with its themed Pittsburgh neighborhood burgers. It offers a slew of tasty creations that melt together to form mini masterpieces. Try the Forest Hills burger with bleu cheese, sautéed wild mushrooms, spring mix, and finished with local honey, or the Polish Hill burger with caramelized onion, fried pierogie, cheddar cheese, and finished with mayo for a taste explosion. Each burger also comes with either thin fresh-cut fries or fresh mixed greens salad. If you decide on the fries, ask for the rosemary fries, which are tossed in extra-virgin olive oil and fresh rosemary. Burgh'ers also serves Coca-Cola (in a bottle!), thick old-fashioned milk shakes, and a nice variety of beer to accompany your meal.

Cafe Kolache, 402 3rd St., Beaver, PA 15009; (724) 775-8102; www.cafekolache.com; Coffee Shop; $. You are probably wondering:

What is a *kolache*? A kolache is a specialty pastry made from sweet dough with roots in Czechoslovakia. Though traditionally filled with cottage cheese, lekvar, and apricots, these kolaches have received  a major transformation at Cafe Kolache. Sweet kolaches come in the traditional flavors but are also filled with apples, blueberries, lemon, raspberry, coconut cream, and chocolate peanut butter, just to name a few. Savory kolaches for breakfast and lunch are also on the menu. Stop by for breakfast and grab an egg, cheese, and bacon kolache, a different take on your typical breakfast sandwich. For lunch, try the pepperoni and cheese and spinach and feta cheese kolaches. Be sure to get here early, because all of the kolaches are available while supplies last. In addition to these Czech treats, the Cafe also bakes cookies, biscotti, and cinnamon rolls, and brews coffee and teas to accompany the Czech and non-Czech pastries.

Cafe Notte, 8070 Ohio River Blvd., Pittsburgh, PA 15202; (412) 761-2233; www.cafenottepgh.com; Wine Bar; $$$. Complete with an extensive wine and liquor list, menu full of tapas and larger plates, and live music almost every night, Cafe Notte, in Emsworth, is truly a hidden gem. When dining here, be sure to ask the hostess to be seated where the live music performs. There is an additional quiet bar and dining room, but at Cafe Notte, it's all about dining amongst the lively entertainment. Order a few glasses of wine and share a few small or even large plates of the well-prepared dishes. Most of the menu is centered around seafood, including crab cakes and shellfish-stuffed ravioli, but a few chicken, steak, and other meat options are available. A full list of specials will accompany the regular menu, also indicating the preparation style of the tuna of the week and scallops of the week, so be sure to look at that before ordering. While savoring the cuisine and wine, don't be alarmed if you see the chefs pop out of the kitchen to enjoy the music or other patrons dancing around the tables. Everyone here is having a good time, and we think you will too!

Clifford's Restaurant, 514 Upper Harmony Rd., Evans City, PA 16033; (724) 789-9115; www.cliffordsrestaurant.com; American; $$$. Located literally in the middle of nowhere in Butler County, Clifford's is a definite destination restaurant worth every bit of the drive and gas money. The restaurant is located on farmland in an old stone house, which makes you feel as though you are going to your Great-Aunt Jennie's for dinner. It is only open for dinner Wednesday through Sunday and is BYOB with no additional cork charge. There is a standard menu of whole boneless trout, chicken romano, and grilled pork chops, to name a few, but Clifford's is known for their large daily menu, which is developed according to what is in season the day you go. Talk about freshness. With your meal, you receive homemade rolls so good you better take an extra-large purse to shove a few in for the drive back to civilization. Though you may be in the middle of nowhere farmland Pennsylvania, the meal you get will be as five star as any major restaurant in a metropolitan city.

Hank's Frozen Custard, 2210 3rd Ave., New Brighton, PA 15066; (724) 847-4265; http://go2hanks.com; Specialty; $. Frozen custard and Mexican food. Both sold at one place, through two different windows. Yes, it's strange, but once you think about it, both custard and tacos sound delicious to you, don't they? Hank's has been a Beaver County staple for over 60 years, though the Mexican food didn't show up until the 1960s. At the left window, you order your custard and other frozen goodies, like shakes, floats, and malts. But if you go to Hank's you must get a scoop of the custard (flavors vary each day). At the right window, tacos, enchiladas, burritos, and nachos can be ordered. Be sure not to order your custard at the wrong window. And it is okay in our book if you feel the urge to dunk a nacho cheese-covered chip into your vanilla custard.

Jean-Marc Chatellier's French Bakery, 213 North Ave., Pittsburgh, PA 15209; (412) 821-8533; www.jeanmarcchatellier .com; Bakery; $. Get out your passport, because Jean-Marc Chatellier's French Bakery will send you on a trip to France through the sheer power of tastiness. The baker, Jean-Marc, opened the space in 1992. Since that time, the Bakery has become renowned in the 'Burgh for its pastries and for its incomparable French macarons. If you haven't had a French macaron in your lifetime, get to Jean-Marc's immediately. If you have had a French macaron in your lifetime, get to Jean-Marc's immediately. These light, almond-based treasures are phenomenal. We are always partial to chocolate, but other creative flavors like salted caramel and peanut butter and

jelly are refreshing twists. Brightly colored, these stunning maca-
rons would be perfect presents for the sweet tooth in your life.
Other tempting treats include croissants (again, we like ours filled
with chocolate), cakes, cookies, and pies. The short trip to Millvale
for a visit will be worth it no matter what fills your bakery boxes.
Traveling never tasted so good.

Jerry's Curb Service, 1521 Riverside Dr., Beaver, PA 15009;
(724) 774-4727; www.jerryscurbservice.com; Car Hop; $. If you
want to experience a real-working car hop that isn't a part of any
chain restaurant, head up the Ohio River to Beaver. Jerry's Curb
Service has been hoppin' since 1947, dishing out burgers, fries, and
sandwiches from the kitchen to your car. Burgers and cheeseburgers
are stacked by the single, double, and triple patties, and there is
even a burger for your dog, the Mutt Burger, that comes plain so
your mutt can have some Jerry's lovin' too. If you are watching your
caloric intake, then don't get the Burnt Herbie, a deep-fried ham
and cheese sandwich. But you probably should just try it at least
once. The fries here are delicious, so definitely get them no matter
what. You can also get grilled chicken and fries or chopped steak
and fries, which come with cheese and dressing of your choice. We
will caution that the ketchup is bound to spill in your car as you
dunk your fries into the saucy goodness, so be sure to go prepared
with extra napkins.

Lincoln Bakery, 543 Lincoln Ave., Bellevue, PA 15202; (412)
766-0954; Bakery; $. Lincoln Bakery of Bellevue has been treating

Taking It Outdoors

There are a few months of the year when the skies open up over Pittsburgh and the sun shines down. During those precious moments you're going to want to get out and about to explore the city's outdoor dining options. Patios, rooftop bars, and sidewalk cafes are aplenty.

Whether we're eating breakfast at the few sidewalk tables outside of **P&G Pamela's Diner** (p. 62) in the Strip District, clinking martini glasses on the rooftop of **Six Penn Kitchen** (p. 40), Downtown, or downing a massive margarita in the back patio of **Round Corner Cantina** (p. 161) in Lawrenceville, you can be sure we're soaking in each magical moment. The deck at **The Church Brew Works** (p. 177) in Lawrenceville allows patrons a new view of the intricate stained-glass windows that line the back wall of the church and when you're nestled in a bistro table sipping wine at **Point Brugge Cafe** (p. 156) in Point Breeze, you can't help but have a cozy notion that it would be the perfect scene in a classic black-and-white film.

Some Pittsburgh restaurants open their doors on warm spring days and hot summer nights, and although you're actually inside, you

residents to deliciousness since 1945. This tasty spot is known for its holiday and theme cakes. The over-the-top cake decorations lure people in, and the airy frosting hooks 'em for life. The cake masters here could surely create whatever your heart desires. Maybe this Thanksgiving, try a cake turkey instead of a real one. You know, just giving the family something to be truly thankful for. Lincoln Bakery is well stocked in other amazing sweets as well. Try one of the many get the best of both worlds. **New Amsterdam** (p. 147) in Lawrenceville, **Burgatory** (p. 192) in Aspinwall, and **The Porch at Schenley** (p. 156) in Oakland open their doors and windows and it's enough to make you want to pray for Pittsburgh to have such glorious weather year-round. Margaritas always make us think of hot summer nights, so naturally, **Mad Mex** (p. 147) in Shadyside is a great place to hit up for a drink to cool you down.

Pittsburgh is all about al fresco dining, and the suburbs are no exception. **Willow** (p. 203) in the north 'Burbs has several outside dining options. Surrounded by natural woods and open air, you will quickly forget you are eating in the suburbs alongside a major highway. The dining experience at **Il Pizzaiolo** (p. 208) in Mount Lebanon is made even more exotic when you step through the back door of the restaurant into a garden with twinkle lights galore.

For more outdoor dining spots around the city, see "Outside Seating" in Appendix B.

flavors of cheesecake (you can score individual servings here, so try them all), or pick up a loaf of bread from the bread racks near the counter. If you are a fan of the simple things in life, you, like us, will be enthralled by the crazy devices that hang from the ceiling and dispense string to wrap up your baked good boxes. You will be taken by the simple goodness of your Lincoln treats, too!

Oram's Donut Shop, 1406 7th Ave., Beaver Falls, PA 15010; (724) 846-1504; www.orams.com; Bakery; $. Old-fashioned glazed dough-nuts are the name of the Oram's game up in Beaver Falls. It's been the name of the bakery game since 1938, when William and Lillian Oram moved to the Falls and started baking up their delicious fried treats. The most famous and most delightful doughnut on the menu is the signature cinnamon roll doughnut. This breakfast must-have is easily twice the size of any cinnamon roll we've ever encountered. They are a favorite of locals and out-of-towners alike, so much that they often sell out early morning. It's best to get a head start on your day if you'd like to try one of Oram's cinnamon rolls. We may be partial to the cinnamon rolls, but we will not turn away a black raspberry-filled doughnut sprinkled with powdered sugar, nor will we blink an eye before devouring a coconut-coated specialty doughnut. Get there early, folks, and if you run into the four of us, we'll happily wave as we stand hungrily over our box of dozen.

Quaker Steak & Lube, 101 Chestnut St., Sharon, PA 16146; (724) 981-9464; www.thelube.com; Wings; $$. We know that this chain wing restaurant is in 20 states and one Canadian province (Ontario), but before you call us out on including a chain in our book, you must know that the original Quaker Steak & Lube is in Sharon, about an hour and 20 minutes north of Pittsburgh. At Quaker Steak & Lube, the onion rings come high, stacked on a car antenna, and the wings come in over 20 flavors of hotness. Unsure of a flavor? Let us suggest the Louisiana Lickers, medium on the hot scale. It's the perfect combination of heat, garlic, spice, and barbecue. If heat is your thing, then sign the waiver and order the atomic or triple atomic wings. Wings so hot, your face might just burn off. It's really all about the wings here because they come traditional, boneless, on salads, with ribs, with fries, and the combinations go on and on. If your mouth isn't on fire when leaving, then you can enjoy our favorite part of the meal, the Twizzler that accompanies your check. Additional locations: See website.

Rachel's Roadhouse, 1552 Perry Hwy., Mercer, PA 16156; (724) 748-3193; www.springfields.com/rr_files/rachels.html; American; $$$. Rachel's Roadhouse, in the heart of Amish Country, gives patrons a taste of down home cooking with a few frills and a few surprises. The standout menu item are the New York–style pretzels that come with your choice of dippers. We recommend ordering all three—mustard, nacho cheese, and hot fudge! What?! Trust us. Rachel's is best known for their filet slices sandwich. Order that and you'll be served filet medallions on a garlic croissant topped with mozzarella. There are many accompaniments to the sandwiches, but we recommend the homemade chips, deep fried and served with a homemade dip. For dinner, you can't go wrong with one of the many varieties of reubens. We're partial to the Carolina reuben because it's smothered with barbecue pork, coleslaw, French dressing, and Swiss cheese and served on ciabatta bread. Speaking of barbecue, they rub their ribs with a special blend of seasoning, so if you're in the mood for a rack, we say go full and pair it with a pumpkin. Oh, excuse us, we mean sweet potato (but they're HUGE!).

The Sewickley Cafe, 409 Beaver St., Sewickley, PA 15143; (412) 749-0300; www.sewickley-cafe.com; Neighborhood Cafe; $$$. The Sewickley Cafe is a place where you can take just about anyone to break bread. Take your family for lunch, have a client meeting over a cocktail, and even court a date with dinner in the back garden patio. The Cafe has the feel of an old bar, but the food reflects a much fancier cuisine. Lunch service offers a variety of sandwiches from the gourmet lobster club to the classic grilled cheese. Complement your order with the truffle french fries because saying "I'll have the truffle french fries as my side" sounds really fancy. During dinner service, the menu completely transforms to include mostly entrees: seafood, pastas, chicken, beef, veal, lamb, and pork. No matter who you go with or when you dine at The Sewickley Cafe, save room for cake. A variety of cakes are on display in the pie case at the entrance. These cakes are stacked so tall, we don't know how they stand up straight.

Vivo Kitchen, 432 Beaver St., Sewickley, PA 15143; (412) 259-8945; www.vivokitchen.com; American; $$$. Vivo Kitchen, a minimalist space on the main drag in Sewickley, offers modern American fare in a sleek setting, both indoor and outdoor. (It should be noted that the restrooms here are all kinds of lovely. Do yourself a favor and freshen up at least once while you dine—you'll want to check them out!) Like a good number of its contemporaries, Vivo Kitchen has a changing menu due to its affinity for locally sourced ingredients prepared in its flavorful dishes. The freshness pops in starter plates like a local heirloom tomato and mozzarella salad. Vegetarians will have an easy time making a dinner selection as there are always several items sans animal (think a loaded butternut squash or a grilled fig). Meat lovers will rejoice over the variety on the menu, from duck to lamb to beef cheeks. And can we get a "mm hmm" from the bread lovers? Vivo Kitchen serves crusty bread with spiced-up olive oil. Nothing like a little kick-start to the meal!

Willow, 634 Camp Horne Rd., Pittsburgh, PA 15237; (412) 847-1007; www.willowpgh.com; American, $$. A special occasion calls for a night out on the town, right? Ditch the city and head to the suburbs to Willow. It boasts 9 different dining rooms including a patio, private dining room for parties, and a communal dining room for large celebrations. When we celebrate at Willow, we go all out and order the filet mignon and a glass of Shiraz, and we always stick around for an espresso and a slice of their decadent cheesecake. Though their menu often changes seasonally, some menu staples don't change with the weather. Some of our favorites include the signature crab cakes and the cranberry chicken, slow-roasted chicken breasts coated in corn flakes and served with a Vermont maple-cranberry glaze. We think we'll be celebrating at Willow the moment we see this book for sale. Whether your visit will be for a celebratory meal, like ours, or a casual lunch, we know you won't be disappointed.

Amel's Restaurant, 435 McNeilly Rd., Pittsburgh, PA 15226; (412) 563-3466; www.amelsrestaurantpgh.com; Mediterranean; $$. Amel's Middle Eastern restaurant in the South Hills is one of those rare gems that can take on whatever form of restaurant you're looking for. If you want a romantic dinner for two, Amel's is your place. Family fun night? Amel's. Drinks and appetizers with the girls (or guys)? Amel's. Its bar has a special almost every night of the week. If you get there on a Monday, you're definitely going to want to take advantage of the 33-cent wings (the wings are to die for). Amel's menu ranges from soups and sandwiches to pasta, seafood, and kabobs out the wazoo. It has traditional Mediterranean fare like hummus and grape leaves, and we hope you're no stranger to feta cheese because it's found on the majority of the menu items. If you are hungry for something a little more American, order a juicy filet cooked to perfection. Warm pita bread is complimentary so be cautious not to fill up before your entree arrives; trust us, we've made that mistake before!

Atria's Restaurant & Tavern, 110 Beverly Rd., Pittsburgh, PA 15216; (412) 343-2411; www.atrias.com; American; $$$. There are many Atria's around town, but if you want the true Atria's experience, go to Mount Lebanon where the original restaurant stands. You'll be dining in a house and you're probably going to wonder why you're paying to eat somewhere that looks like it could be your living room. The original chopped salad is one of our favorite menu items, made with chopped fresh veggies and is tossed with crumbled bleu cheese and garlic vinaigrette dressing. We can't shovel it in our mouths fast enough. Next course please! The pot roast nachos. Two things we love, together at last. It's topped with jalapeños, cheese, and sour cream. Atria's works with local farmers to provide Pittsburghers with a dining experience they can feel good about. We feel good ordering the tomato vodka Florentine, penne pasta and fresh, local chopped spinach swimming in their homemade tomato vodka sauce. Additional locations: See website.

Bistro 19, 711 Washington Rd., Pittsburgh, PA 15228; (412) 306-1919; www.bistro19.com; American; $$$. Bistro 19 is open for lunch and dinner, and brunch on Sunday. Bistro 19 is sophisticated and is the perfect place for a first date, a business dinner, or to impress the in-laws. The dinner menu is wide ranged and has items that include sea bass and duck. Whether you order the crab-encrusted tilapia or the boursin-encrusted filet you'll be enamored with Bistro 19, tenfold. The dishes are served with unique sides like sweet potato mash, pommes frites, and red pepper risotto. The restaurant's sauces are all house-made, as are the pickles that adorn the bacon cheddar bistro burger. Indulge in your inner child and opt for the beef short rib macaroni and cheese. Don't worry, you'll still be thought of as a full-fledged grown-up because it's made with beef short ribs. If you find yourself there on Sunday morning, our favorite menu items are the tiramisu pancakes, complete with cocoa, mascarpone, and coffee glaze, and the eggs benedict with prosciutto.

California Taco Shop, 2760 Saw Mill Run Blvd., Pittsburgh, PA 15227; (412) 885-5600; Mexican; $. We are so down with any restaurant that has a carnitas platter on their menu. That means we're down with California Taco Shop in Whitehall. You're blasted with yellow the second you walk in the door, and you're instantaneously hungrier than you were when you were standing outside (the color yellow is known to increase your appetite). Place your order at the counter and then take a seat. We recommend the carnitas. You can get the platter so it's served with rice and beans and authentic Mexican corn tortilla or you can get the burrito, rolled up in a tortilla with lettuce and salsa. Definitely go for the  corn chips on the side because you not only get salsa but also house-made guacamole and white queso. You can actually taste the freshness in every bite no matter what you order. It uses basic ingredients and pairs them together to create authentic Mexican dishes.

Dor-Stop Restaurant, 1430 Potomac Ave., Pittsburgh, PA 15216; (412) 561-9320; www.dorstoprestaurant.com; Breakfast and Lunch; $. The Dor-Stop has been serving up no-nonsense diner eats on the corner of Potomac and Glenmore Avenues in Dormont for over 25 years. The hotcakes here are legendary, as are the restaurant's

German potato pancakes—both worth a taste. Its reputation as one of the Pittsburgh area's must-eats was bolstered by a visit from Guy Fieri on Food Network's *Diners, Drive-ins, and Dives*. If you visit on a weekend, you are almost guaranteed a long wait on the sidewalk. Be patient and remember your reward: those giant, sweet Dor-Stop hotcakes. The menu includes lunch options as well, like a hot meat loaf sandwich, classic burgers, and homemade soups. There is a solid chance that you will see the owners, Bob and Vicki Lawhorne, making their way around the small, retro space. Look up the Food Network's *Diners, Drive-ins, and Dives* episode before you go so you can be aware when you have your brush with celebrity.

Golden Pig Authentic Korean Cuisine, 3201 Millers Run Rd., Cecil, PA 15321; (412) 220-7170; Korean; $. The Internet and GPS were created to find places like Golden Pig Authentic Korean Cuisine. Without either, word may have never reached the masses that a place like it exists. Golden Pig is in the middle of nowhere, about 30 minutes outside of Pittsburgh in a town called Cecil. The menu at Golden Pig is small. Really small. That's because it's a one-woman show in the kitchen. Actually it's a one-woman show entirely. The owner, Yong Kwon, does all the cooking and adds a little bit of her heart to each dish. She decided to open the 10-seat restaurant in 2008 during the Year of the Pig in honor of her grandson being born. So we'd like to take this opportunity to officially thank her grandson! All of Yong's dishes are made with the freshest ingredients, which make the simple yet complex flavor shine. Authentic dishes like *man-du*, beef and vegetable stuffed dumplings; *bibimbap*, white rice, seasoned vegetables, chili pepper paste, and sliced meat; *bulgogi*, beef marinated in a mixture of soy sauce, sesame oil, black pepper, garlic, onions, ginger, wine, and sugar; and spicy squid are as close to South Korea as you can get in Pittsburgh.

Il Pizzaiolo, 703 Washington Rd., Pittsburgh, PA 15228; (412) 344-4123; www.ilpizzaiolo.com; Italian; $$$. In the land of Mount Lebanon lies a magical place where one can feast on wood-fired pizza and sip wine while enjoying the sights and sounds of a garden patio reflective of any movie scene that takes place in Italy. That place is Il Pizzaiolo. Located in the heart of quaint Mt. Lebo, Il Pizzaiolo features something few restaurants in Pittsburgh do—a wine bar. If that doesn't sell you right there, there is also a brick oven where hand-tossed pizzas are cooked to perfection before being served to anxious patrons. The toughest

choice you're going to make is what to put on top of your pizza. The toppings are made in house and include sausage, meatballs, and mozzarella. If you're not the pizza-going type, don't worry; you can still have a Neapolitan experience at Il Pizzaiolo. Order up any of their veal menu items or lasagna made with pasta faella, San Marzano tomatoes, and fresh ricotta and mozzarella. You might forget you're in western Pennsylvania so don't be surprised if you're saying *grazie* as you leave.

Juniper Grill, 4000 Washington Rd., Canonsburg, PA 15317; (724) 260-7999; www.junipergrill.com; American; $$$. Giddyup! Juniper Grill's menu is based off cowboy cuisine, but you won't find beans on a tin plate here. From their street tacos (grilled chicken on soft corn tortillas with fresh salsa) to their seared tuna covered in southwest slaw, everything is spunk, spice, and everything nice. Start your meal with the Cajun spicy shrimp flatbread with poblano peppers and pineapple, and share it with a friend because you're also going to want to sample whatever the soup of the day is (our favorite is the roasted tomato). Cowboy up for the main course of meat. Any meat you choose, chipotle skirt steak with mashed potatoes, pork tenderloin with cherry demi-glaze and mashed potatoes, or barbecue beef brisket. Did we mention most of their entrees are served with mashed potatoes? Save room for dessert because you can't head off to the range without sampling some ice cream from local sweet shop, **Sarris Candies** (p. 229). Juniper serves it over homemade corn bread with fresh berry sauce or you can get it drizzled in Sarris's own milk chocolate hardcap.

Kous Kous Cafe, 665 Washington Rd., Pittsburgh, PA 15228; (412) 563-5687; www.kouskouscafe.com; Moroccan; $$$. It seems so unfair that the South Hills of Pittsburgh should be home to some of the city's tastiest Mediterranean restaurants, but here we are, folks. Kous Kous Cafe is a tiny place, seriously, it's very small—intimate is perhaps a more apropos term but we digress—it's a family-run Moroccan restaurant that serves food with flair and allows you to BYOB (with a small corkage fee). We love the beet salad, which is mixed with cumin, coriander, and gorgonzola cheese; it's a great way to begin your meal. A variety of meats and fish are available, including lamb, duck, beef, chicken, salmon, and sausage. These are combined with fresh vegetables and Moroccan spices like saffron, cilantro, and ginger. Try the beef in plums tangine with almonds for a dish that is a little sweet with a little crunch.

Little Tokyo, 636 Washington Rd., Pittsburgh, PA 15228; (412) 344-4366; www.littletokyopittsburgh.com; Japanese; $$$. No matter what kind of Japanese food you're craving, we think Little Tokyo is guaranteed to satisfy. Most of our cravings lead us to the sushi bar. The sushi chefs serve up some fresh fish combinations, including some standards like the spicy tuna roll and the shrimp tempura roll. Here's the fun part—if you're new to sushi, you're going to have to do a bit of chatting with your server. The menu, while extensive, doesn't list the ingredients in their maki sushi, which means *surprise!* If you aren't feeling particularly brave, order something safe like the tuna and avocado roll. Always, always get the sansai salad with Frank Lin's famous ginger dressing (he even bottles it and sells it in store!) and an order of edamame. If you don't roll with sushi, then you can go the hibachi route or one of their many spe-cials, beef and noodles, shrimp and noodles, chicken and noodles all served with soup and a salad. It's one of the pricier Asian restaurants in the 'Burgh but definitely worth the extra bucks. Additional location: Little Tokyo Bistro, South Side, 2122 E. Carson St., Pittsburgh, PA 15203; (412) 488-9986.

Luma Restaurant, 186 Castle Shannon Blvd., Pittsburgh, PA 15228; (412) 343-0355; www.lumapgh.com; American; $$$. Any restaurant that has "Wine Down Wednesday" is okay in our book. Luma Restaurant has half off bottles of wine on Wednesday and has an unbelievable menu filled with contemporary American foods with a twist every day of the week (except Sunday). For starters, try their Luma Chips. Kind of like nachos only better, made with homemade potato chips and topped with all the good stuff like cheese, tomato, onion, and sour cream, or a bowl of the she crab bisque. Our favorite entree has got to be the Muscovy duck breast. It's served over cranberry butterscotch gnocchi and the duck breast is marinated in a pomegranate chipotle marinade and pan seared. Seafood dishes, filets, and Korean barbecue flank steak round out the unique menu filled with fancy yet fun flavors. Don't dare leave without getting dessert, especially the humming bird cake, which is a unique take on carrot cake, baked with carrots, walnuts, and coconut smeared with orange cream cheese icing. Top that off with an espresso and you are living large, friends. Additional location: Aspinwall, 8 Brilliant Ave., Pittsburgh, PA 15215; (412) 781-0355.

Mineo's Pizza House, 713A Washington Rd., Pittsburgh, PA 15228; (412) 344-9467; www.mineospizza.com; Pizza; $. Mineo's is a family-owned pizzeria with two great locations and is a Pittsburgh staple. The Mount Lebanon and Squirrel Hill spots both serve pizza the way pizza should be served—slice by gigantic, cheesy slice. The best way to enjoy Mineo's is by ordering with your face pressed up against the glass counter, watching as your pizza is heated up (or if you're us—two slices) so it's warm and ready to eat. Be sure to work out before heading out to eat at Mineo's, though; they load enough cheese onto their pies that you'll swear you're holding onto an infant or a stack of three *Encyclopedia Britannicas*. They've also got your classic Italian dinners like manicotti, rigatoni, and ziti, and if you want to make it a complete meal, you can top it off with some of Pittsburgh's own Reinhold Ice Cream. Additional location: Squirrel Hill, 2128 Murray Ave., Pittsburgh, PA 15217; (412) 521-9864.

The Original Gab and Eat Restaurant, 1073 Washington Ave., Carnegie, PA 15106; (412) 276-8808; www.gabneat.com; Breakfast and Lunch; $. Under the Gab and Eat sign, complete with rooster, is a paper on the window that proclaims: "No whining." Eating at this authentic, Pittsburgh gem certainly won't provoke it. The long space has several booths that line a wall full of autographs from Pittsburgh news anchors, local sports heroes (high school included), and other hard-to-determine flourishes. If a booth isn't your style, saddle on up to the counter and watch the line cooks in action. Diner food rules the menu complete with absurdly low prices. It is possible to eat a week's worth of calories here for under $4. The breakfast options are all solid; the pancakes are the size of

Allegheny County, and the bacon has the perfect ratio of grease to crispness. The classic burgers will make your heart sing or, at the very least, bleed black and gold along with all of the locals eating beside you.

Potomac Bakery, 1419 Potomac Ave., Pittsburgh, PA 15216; (412) 531-5066; www.potomacbakery.weebly.com; Bakery; $. Looking for a soft cinnamon roll the size of a county? Potomac Bakery has you covered. This spot for sweetness has been cranking out the goods in the center of Dormont since 1927. Along with these cinnamon delights, Potomac has plenty to offer from breakfast pastries, breads, pies, and a long list of specialty cakes. You can't go wrong here, but the doughnuts are a standout as are the delicate petit fours, along with the aforementioned cinnamon rolls. The cake doughnuts are fresh and don't leave you with that "ugh, I just ate a doughnut" feeling. The petit fours are bite-size, moist cakes that come in chocolate or vanilla, dotted with a tiny flower. Like all of the treats at Potomac, they almost look too good to eat. Almost. Additional location: Mount. Lebanon, 689 Washington Rd., Pittsburgh, PA 15228; (412) 531-5067.

Sesame Inn, 715 Washington Rd., Pittsburgh, PA 15228; (412) 341-2555; http://sesameinn.com; Chinese; $$. Pittsburgh is home to few Chinese restaurants that we feel we can hang our hats on.

We'd hang our hat on Sesame Inn any day. It's so good there are multiple locations around the city, but our favorite is the original location in the Pittsburgh suburb of Mount Lebanon. Monday we go for chicken in curry sauce, a bit spicy but nothing you all can't handle. Tuesday is reserved for chicken with eggplant—gotta get that dose of vegetable in! Wednesday, why it's General Tso's of course, best in the city, we say. By Wednesday we need a bit of a pick-me-up and that usually comes in the form of crab rangoons. Don't judge. Thursday is mu shi beef because we tend to go a bit chicken heavy the first part of the week, and when we finally make it to Friday we celebrate with the crispy duck. OK, so we don't eat there every day but the portions are plentiful so you can get at least two meals out of one order! All of these delish dishes and more can be found at Sesame Inn every day. Additional locations: See website.

Sugar Cafe, 1517 Potomac Ave., Pittsburgh, PA 15216; (412) 341-1090; www.sugarcafepittsburgh.com; Neighborhood Cafe; $. Dormont is home to one of the cutest neighborhood cafes in the 'Burgh. Sugar Cafe has bright, blue-green walls, a cozy window nook with plush chairs and a bookshelf full of good reads, and frames of sweet, cartoon woodland creatures lining the perimeter. It is a place where one could easily spend a morning or an afternoon enjoying the free Wi-Fi. It sure helps that the food is equally as satisfying as the surroundings. Breakfast and lunch are served daily. The grilled cheese, with the choice of cheddar, monterey jack, or Swiss (or all three!) on sourdough, is a filling and comforting choice for a midday pick-me-up. Daily, house-made pastries, including cupcakes and tarts, fill the glass counter—trying to resist the deliciousness is futile. During summer months, Sugar Cafe offers Monday story times for children, so adult folk can enjoy their pastries with a side of peace.

East

Bulgarian-Macedonian National Educational and Cultural Center Soup Sega, 449–451 W. 8th Ave., West Homestead, PA 15120; (412) 461-6188; www.bmnecc.org; Specialty; $. Since 1999, the Bulgarian-Macedonian National Educational and Cultural Center in West Homestead has been cooking up and selling soup to support the organization. The Soup Sega is held Saturday from 9 a.m. to noon from September to May each year. Soups are available in quarts and half quarts, and are reminiscent of the soup your grandmother may have made during the winter months. Both vegetarian and non-vegetarian soup are available in flavors such as cabbage and tomato, potato leek, Balkan bean, and chicken and farina dumplings, the Sega's bestseller. The soups are low in sodium, and many are gluten free, in case you are watchin'. In addition to soup, you can take out other specialties, such as stuffed peppers and strudel.

Cafe Vita, 424 Allegheny River Blvd., Oakmont, PA 15139; (412) 828-5506; www.cafevitaoakmont.com; Italian; $$–$$$. Cafe Vita is an intimate spot in quaint Oakmont. The tiny storefront restaurant seats a couple dozen patrons, and food is prepared in the back of the dining room behind a divider. The menu changes often with comforting and original takes on Italian on rotation. Options will feature homemade selections, which should be at the top of your list. This could include homemade manicotti to homemade ravioli filled with asparagus. Regardless of your meal choice, you will receive a basket with thick cuts of crusty bread for dipping in seasoned olive oil. You will also get a side salad that is anything but ordinary, with walnuts, cranberries, mixed greens, and gorgonzola, on request. Breakfast and lunch are served, in addition to dinner, with options like paninis and frittatas. Reservations are necessary for weekend dining. We suggest a Wednesday or Thursday night for a quieter atmosphere.

Chef Robinson's Restaurant, 1225 Lowry Ave., Jeannette, PA, 15644; (877) 663-0048; www.bestbbqribsandchickenpa.com; Barbecue; $. Chef Robinson's Restaurant is a family-owned operation with sensational barbecue. An active smoker, which one can assume is full of meats for eating, sits near the road, beckoning customers to come on in and eat. The place is set up like a diner, so you can grab a stool at the long counter or settle in to a booth along the wall. The menu will help you get comfortable, as it features comfort food staples like meat loaf sandwiches and baked macaroni and cheese. Barbecue is the real deal here and not to be missed. Look up "perfection" in the dictionary and chances are you'll see a photo of Chef Robinson's pulled pork. The tender pork rests on a lightly toasted roll and a side of dipping barbecue sauce, either in hot or mild, is its plate neighbor. The lightly tangy barbecue sauce will drip down your arms, into your sleeves, as the sandwich melts in your mouth. You'll want to save it for later anyway.

The Earnest Gourmet, 646 S. Urania Ave., Greensburg, PA 15601; (724) 834-2020; www.earnestgourmet.com; Neighborhood Cafe; $. Certain things in life leave a lasting impression: graduating from high school; welcoming your first child into the world; and biting into your first sandwich from The Earnest Gourmet. This small operation, only open for lunch, is housed in what looks to be an old warehouse. The refined taste of every meticulously prepared lunch option transports you right out of that warehouse and onto a taste cloud of happiness. Chef Linda Earnest makes everything fresh from the soup to our favorite, herb mayonnaise chicken salad (on a croissant, of course). You can order a specialty sandwich like the Bistro Beef, with roast beef, red onion, and roasted red peppers on a baguette, or make your own creation. Other options behind the deli case include a rich and creamy vegetable lasagna and tomato basil tart, among others. The tomato basil tart is one of the best things we have ever eaten, ever. And we have eaten a lot of things. Chef Linda also does catering. Those events automatically become our favorites.

Ship Pittsburgh to You!

Say you're out of town and get a hankering for a taste of the 'Burgh. Sadly, to get most of our hometown favorites you may have to do some traveling. But here are a few classics you can have shipped to tide you over until you can get back to the City of Champions.

Pierogies from Polish Pierogi: Pierogies are a staple in the Pittsburgh diet, and there is nothing quite like homemade. **Polish Pierogi** makes traditional homemade pierogies from scratch using the freshest ingredients available. We're talking rich, thick dough stuffed with quality ingredients. Polish Pierogi makes around 10 varieties of pierogies like potato and cheddar, sauerkraut and mushroom, sweet cheese, and cabbage. You can purchase the various pierogies online by the dozen and in sampler packages. Go for the "One of Everything Pierogi Sampler" to get the full homemade effect. Polish Pierogi doesn't stop at pierogies. Traditional Polish favorites like *kolacky*, *haluski*, and mushroom soup are also available for online purchase. Visit www.polishpierogi.com for more details.

Eat'n Park, 245 E. Waterfront Dr., Homestead, PA 15120; (412) 464-7275; www.eatnpark.com; Diner; $. Pittsburgh's first carhop? Eat'n Park. In 1949 Eat'n Park opened up as a carhop and 13-seat restaurant in the South Hills. The day it opened, a traffic jam was caused. That's tells you how much Pittsburghers dig this place. The original carhop location is gone, but this local chain restaurant now

Original Barbecue Sauce from Isaly's: The chipped chopped ham sandwich, also known as a barbecue ham sandwich, is classic Pittsburgh. Recipes vary, but the best sandwiches are made with Isaly's chipped chopped ham, original barbecue sauce, and a crusty hard bun. The sandwich is hearty, tangy, and an instant hit at any Steelers tailgate. The good news is, if you live in a state around Pennsylvania, you'll have a good chance of finding Isaly's chipped chopped ham at Walmart. The really good news is that you can order several varieties of Isaly's barbecue sauce online. Visit www.isalys.com to get a full list of locations or to place an order.

Burnt Almond Torte from Prantl's: Whether you've had it for a special occasion or just because it's Wednesday, **Prantl's** (p. 181) burnt almond torte is famous in Pittsburgh. The torte begins with a layer of moist yellow cake followed by a generous helping of Prantl's special custard, then another layer of cake. It's then covered with a thick buttercream icing and covered with sugar-toasted almonds. It is as sinfully addictive as it sounds. And lucky for you Prantl's ships the torte anywhere in the United States. Visit www.prantlsbakery.com for more information on how you can enjoy the torte for yourself.

has over 75 restaurants in the tri-state area (Ohio, Pennsylvania, and West Virginia). Many locations are open 24 hours a day to satisfy your hunger at any hour of the day. Possibly the most noteworthy item on the menu is actually a cookie, a Smiley Cookie to be exact. The second most popular item, at least in our eyes, the Grilled Stickies, served a la mode or as a breakfast meal. Grilled

Stickies are Eat'n Park's signature sticky-bun type creation that coats your soul in sweet goodness. Besides these sweet treats, the menu includes a wide variety of salads, sandwiches, burgers, dinners, and buffets. A great spot if you are looking to take your family and kids. Additional locations: See website.

Jioio's Restaurant, 939 Carbon Rd., Greensburg, PA, 15601; (724) 836-6676; www.jioios.com; Italian; $. Pizza is always just pizza, right? Wrong. Jioio's Restaurant has created something truly unique with its Original Thin Crust Pizza. This crispy, squared pie is unapologetically sweet and gosh darn amazing. It is any good Greensburger's responsibility as a human to introduce outsiders to its goodness and sit gleefully by as the visitors take their first bites. Sweet sauce. Sweet crust. Savory cheese. The pizza comes in 4, 8, 12, and 30 cuts (if you must share). Jioio's serves other Italian favorites, like pasta and homemade ravioli, with that same sweet sauce. You can dine in at Jioio's in the no-frills space or call in for take out. Jioio's also takes pickup orders online. We know folks who will drive the 35 miles from the 'Burgh for so much as a slice. If you make the trip, order more than necessary. This is one of the best reheated or cold pizzas you will ever encounter.

Oakmont Bakery, 531 Allegheny Ave., Oakmont, PA 15139; (412) 826-1606; www.oakmontbakery.com; Bakery; $. The Oakmont Bakery is, not surprisingly, located in the town of Oakmont. About a 20-minute drive from Pittsburgh, by way of Allegheny River Boulevard, Oakmont Bakery should lay claim to the title "most likely to inspire joy-induced tears through cookie eating." Sweet, sweet sugar-filled tears. We think Oakmont Bakery is the producer of the best sugar cookies in the region (if the region includes all of North America and parts of Latin America, as well). Other gold-standard treats include the butter stars (soft butter cookies with chocolate frosting) and the variety of rich cakes. Breads, pepperoni rolls, and doughnuts also make a strong showing. Oakmont Bakery has been serving folks since 1988. It is an impressively large space with an overwhelming selection of baked goods under a long, L-shaped glass case. There is a second building across the parking lot where one can assume all the baking magic happens, making the Oakmont Bakery more like a compound of deliciousness. Tables are provided inside the bakery and outside, in nice weather, for eager snackers.

Smoke Barbeque Taqueria, 225 E. 8th Ave., Homestead, PA 15120; (412) 205-3039; Barbecue; $. Smoke Barbeque Taqueria feels familiar as soon as you walk through the door. Weathered hardwood floor and mismatched tables and chairs; it feels like you stopped by a friend's apartment for dinner. Only we bet your friend can't make a taco like this place can. Smoke combines perfectly smoked meats with hand-made tortillas and a hint of sauce and toppings. The pork taco comes with chunks of pork that easily shred and is lightly sauced with apricot habanero and caramelized onions. The brisket in the brisket taco is thinly sliced and falls apart in your mouth. A fiery spice is added with sautéed onions, hot peppers, and barbecue mustard sauce. Smoke's latest taco combinations are also worth a look. The chicken apple taco comes with bacon, cheddar, and a smoky jalapeño mayo. Breakfast tacos are also available all day long. While tacos are the main attraction at Smoke, we could die happy just eating items from the Snacks and Sides section. Macaroni and cheese is cooked to a creamy, cheesy perfection with roasted garlic, shallots, mascarpone cheese, and sharp white cheddar, and filling up Frito Scoops with pico de gallo queso will make you wonder why you ever ate it any other way.

The Supper Club, 101 Ehalt St., Greensburg, PA, 15601; (724) 691-0536; www.supperclubgreensburg.com; American; $$. The Supper Club is housed in the historic Greensburg train station and is adjacent to where the Amtrak train stops now. It is a beautiful space with soaring ceilings and old-timey transportation charm. The only thing more interesting than the location here is the farm-to-table menus, as the list of local purveyors the restaurant entrusts is truly impressive in length. The Supper Club serves from two menus: Gastropub and Farm-to-Table. From the more casual gastropub fare, do yourself a favor and order the house-made tater tots. These tots are not your normal tots—these beauts harbor mashed potato insides! The result is a surprising twist on a dish found on cafeteria trays across the nation. The pizza here is also quite delicious with topping combos that will elicit a "yes, please!"

We like the brie/pear/arugula/balsamic reduction mash-up. The Farm-to-Table menu is more refined than the Gastropub, with offerings like the Jamison Farm lamb steak, served with couscous and pumpkin seed pesto. For an even more memorable evening, dinners with the chef can be arranged at a table inside the working kitchen. Call The Supper Club for more details.

Zozo's Pub, 1517 Broad St., Greensburg, PA, 15601; (724) 420-5290; Neighborhood Bar; $. If at any point in your existence the thought "man, I wish I could try the best grilled cheese ever created" has crossed your mind, get to Zozo's Pub in South Greensburg. Immediately. This crazy cool little outpost is big on hipness and bold in menu choices. Bright paintings frame the space. A long bar eats up one side of the joint while tables with eclectic chair choices fill the rest. You could just come here for drinks, but you would be doing your stomach a disservice. Now let's talk about that grilled cheese. This bad boy is made with three cheeses: manchego, smoked gouda, and sharp cheddar. The bread is the correct thickness, and a tomato slice is perfectly situated in the melty inside. It's enough to make a sandwich lover cry. Other perfectly delicious menu options include inventive appetizers like quinoa fritters, grilled halumi, and fig and walnut bruschetta.

Bocktown Beer and Grill, 690 Chauvet Dr., Pittsburgh, PA 15275; (412) 788-2333; Neighborhood Bar; $$. Do you want a Fat Belly or a Beer Belly? Either way, you are going to get a mound of fresh-cut fries with toppings of your choice. In our eye, Bocktown is known for two things: fries and beer. The fry portions are large and are ordered in two sizes: Fat Belly for you and a friend, and the Beer Belly, enough for a few more friends. With your fry order, you can choose from a listing of toppings like cheeses, vegetables, sauces, and meats. Truly making your fries a complete (and well-balanced) meal. If you love fries so much, be sure to visit Bocktown  during the Beer Belly Challenge month. To complete the challenge (and win a free t-shirt) you must eat a Beer Belly fry, with three toppings of your choice, in 30 minutes. We did it, and we won. Boo-ya. Bocktown also has a menu full of sandwiches, salads, 'Burghers, and an impressive list of beers, if you can hold one down after the Challenge. Additional location: 500 Beaver Valley Mall Blvd., Monaca, PA 15061; (724) 728-7200.

Harold's Inn Restaurant, 2134 Brodhead Rd., Aliquippa, PA 15001; (724) 375-8992; www.haroldsinnrestaurant.com; Steakhouse; $$. Harold's Inn in Hopewell (about 20 miles outside of Pittsburgh city proper) is over 50 years old and a restaurant with more than just time under its belt. It's one of the first Pittsburgh area establishments to start serving mesquite-grilled foods. Harold's unique seasoning is sprinkled on everything. You won't hear us complaining. Dash a little of that on some wings, dash a bit more on their taters, and you've got yourself one of the best meals you're going to get north of the city. Its extensive menu features pasta, seafood, steaks, and sandwiches, and we pretty much recommend everything on the menu. But if you are a first-timer, it'd be a crime not to go for the steak or chicken salad topped with their seasoned taters. If you panic last minute and order something unseasoned, don't worry—it'll still be delicious and you can ask for their Mountain Seasoning to take home with you, as they now sell it by the shaker.

Pierogies Plus, 342 Island Ave., McKees Rocks, PA 15136; (412) 331-2224; http://pierogiesplus.com; Specialty; $. **Need gas?** Then don't head to Pierogies Plus. Because at this renovated gas station, you are not going to find fuel for your car. Instead, there's fuel for your stomach. Pierogies Plus was started by a Polish immigrant in 1991 and has been a Pittsburgh institution since. If you ask a 'Burgher where to get pierogies, he will tell you one of two places: the nearest church basement or Pierogies Plus. They are jam-packed so much, we wonder how they don't explode when cooked. Traditional fillings of potato, potato and cheese, sauerkraut and potato, and cottage cheese and chives, all come tossed in butter and onions. Are you salivating yet? These are a bit hard to eat on your drive back to the city, so you can order your pierogies cold so you can heat them up when you get to a stove or microwave. Just don't hurt yourself running to the nearest heating device!

The Sharp Edge Creekhouse, 288 W. Steuben St., Thornburg Bridge, Pittsburgh, PA 15205; (412) 922-8118; http://sharpedge beer.com; Neighborhood Bar; $$. Pittsburgh has a lot of bridges, and finding stuff under them can be sketchy. Not in Crafton. You can find a fine eating establishment located next to (and practically underneath) a bridge. The Sharp Edge Creekhouse has an extensive beer list of domestic and imported beers, specializing in the Belgian variety. And sometimes the beer ends up in an item on the menu, such as in the loaded beer cheese soup. One of the well-known Sharp Edge menu items are the buffalo bites, hand-breaded pieces of white-meat chicken fried golden brown and tossed in one of the house-made sauces of your choice. If chicken ain't your thing, you can order the tofu bites. The Sharp Edge also has a variety of burgers, like ostrich, buffalo, and duck, if you dare. Whatever you get, be sure to order a beer and sit on the outside patio. Additional locations: See website.

Wings Suds & Spuds, 8806 University Blvd., Coraopolis, PA 15108; (412) 264-1866; Wings; $–$$. So you flew into Pittsburgh International Airport and are dying for something to eat? Wings, perhaps? Before you make your way into the city, swing by Wings Suds & Spuds in Moon Township for just that: wings, suds (beer), and spuds (fries or chips). All three of these items are delicious in our book. The wings come in a variety of wet sauces and dry seasonings and can be ordered either small or large. If you are really hungry and think you can put away a large order, hold off because you must order the half pound curly fries here. We typically top our fries with cheese and ranch dressing. And to wash both of these down, beer of course. Besides wings, suds, and spuds, this neighborhood (dive-ish) bar has salads, sandwiches, chicken fingers, burgers, and other bar-food favorites that will please both wing lovers and non-wing lovers alike.

Specialty Stores, Markets & Producers

Giant Eagle Market District, 100 Settlers Ridge Center Dr., Pittsburgh, PA 15205; (412) 788-5392; www.marketdistrict.com. Literally anything you need to make a meal, from the produce to the plates, you can buy at the Giant Eagle Market District store in Robinson Township. This store is a beefed-up version of the regular grocery store and an adult food enthusiast's Disneyland. It has a cafe, complete with hot and cold food bars, coffee and juice bar, sushi station, crêpe station, and other freshly prepared foods. You can get these foods to go or eat in the second floor restaurant area. In addition to the regular grocery items, this Market District has a housewares store, charcuterie, sweets shop with house-made chocolates and gelato, and olive oil bar. In the fresh produce marketplace, the Market District grows its own herbs and lettuce in a Hydroponic Garden located in the middle of the produce section. If you don't know how to cook, you can learn here in the Cooking School. You can also buy beer here to dine in or take out. Remember: No drinking and buggy driving. Additional locations: See website.

McGinnis Sisters Specialty Stores, 700 Adams Shoppes, Rte. 228 and Adams Ridge Blvd., Mars, PA 16046; (724) 779-1212; www .mcginnis-sisters.com. Back in the day, people went to their local grocery stores almost daily and stocked up on fresh bread, fresh meat, and fresh produce for the day's meals. A place reminiscent of the grocery stories of years past is McGinnis Sisters Specialty Stores, a local chain of three family-owned grocery stores. The Mars location is located in a tiny strip mall off a busy highway. If you can make it through the traffic and red lights, it is worth the hassle. The meats are all sold fresh to order, as is the seafood. The produce is bright and colorful, and the bakery has muffins, breads, and other baked goods.

The aisles are tiny and small, so try not to bump your cart into a stranger. If you are on the go, you can pick up a meal from the prepackaged meal section or dine in at the in-store cafe. The cafe menu consists of pizzas, sandwiches, paninis, and fish sandwiches and dinners. Additional locations: See website.

Sarris Candies, 511 Adams Ave., Canonsburg, PA 15317; (724) 745-4042; www.sarriscandies.com. Pittsburgh icon Frank Sarris opened a small candy shop in 1963 in the heart of Canonsburg. Twenty years later, he opened a larger shop complete with an ice cream parlor that drew in crowds from all over the city. You seem to step through a time portal when you walk in the door. If you didn't know any better, you'd swear you walked into a soda fountain wearing Hush Puppies and humming "Mr. Sandman." Alas, it's present day, but the ambiance of Sarris Candies hasn't changed a bit. You can take in the bright colors of the ice cream toppings and almost taste the chocolate in the air as you ponder which delicate candies will grace your lips. Once you've created your own box of chocolates (lift the lid on ours and you'll find their famous chocolate-covered pretzels, coconut clusters, and dark chocolate pecanettes), you can enjoy a scoop of homemade ice cream topped with their milk chocolate hardcap. We dare you not to smile while you're there—and be warned, you'll be jitterbugging right out the door.

Soergel Orchards Family Farm, 2573 Brandt School Rd., Wexford, PA 15090; (724) 935-2090; www.soergels.com. Just 20 minutes north of Downtown lies Soergel Orchards Family Farm. Soergel's was started in the 1850s as an apple orchard by German-immigrant John Conrad Soergel and has expanded since to include much more than apples, though these are still the farm's namesake and a must-purchase along with the apple cider. When you visit Soergel's, the first place you will want to stop by is the Market Center, which is home to a bakery turning out delicious pies and pastries; a small deli providing take-home meats and cheeses as well as made-to-order sandwiches; a fresh produce section filled with colorful fruits and vegetables; gourmet grocery items; and a wine shop, which sells wines from Arrowhead Wines of North East, Pennsylvania (near Erie). If food allergies or healthy eating is of your concern, visit Naturally Soergel's (located directly behind the Market Center), which specializes carrying allergen-free and gluten-free products. In addition to the Market Center and Naturally Soergel's, Soergel's has a Plant Center, a Gift Barn carrying a variety of unique gift items from body scrubs to stationery, and an Amish Furniture shop. If you are looking for a quick getaway from the urban city, head north to Soergel's to enjoy the fresh air.

Stadium Food

Pittsburghers love a good sporting event. It is the City of Champions, after all. Since Pittsburgh teams are consistently amazing (with one major exception), tickets to games are at a premium and expectations exceedingly high: 'Burghers expect to see a winning team and expect to eat a winning meal. CONSOL Energy Center, Heinz Field, and PNC Park always deliver the latter.

The stadium food magicians of Aramark create culinary greatness off the field, diamond, and ice. We will take you behind the scenes, up close and personal with the nachos, hot dogs, and the mile-high ice cream cones. But the real magic here is found in what sports enthusiasts are not expecting: food that is fit for venues with tablecloths and metal utensils. Eating a nice meal, in a folding chair, while watching the home team score? We'd call that a victory.

CONSOL Energy Center, 1001 5th Ave., Pittsburgh, PA 15219; (412) 642-1800; www.consolenergycenter.com. The atmosphere inside CONSOL Energy Center is electric: the sounds of sticks hitting the ice, the organ melodies whistling through the air, and the shouts of "Let's go, Pens!" CONSOL Energy Center was built to be a state-of-the-art hockey arena for the Pittsburgh Penguins. The cuisine here echos this design achievement by being the cutting edge standard of arena dining. In the sublevel of CONSOL, you'll find Executive Chef Carl VanWagner holding court over a 6,000-square-foot custom kitchen and over 60 additional chefs during each game. All of these hands are needed for the expansive operations, from smoking hundreds of pounds of meat in-house to making gallons of condiments. The results are sent to outposts throughout the arena, like Smokehouse, Classics, and The Landing, where each spot offers a unique take on spectator dining.

For instance, **Smokehouse,** on the 200 level, provides fans will some of the best barbecue in the city. Order up the specialty nachos piled high with pork, cheese, and jalapeños, and you'll be chanting "Let's go, pulled pork nachos!" in no time. **Classics,** with stations throughout the arena, features fan favorites like Smith natural casing hot dogs and the most popular sandwich of all, the kielbasa grinder. This delicious beast starts with a BreadWorks bun, is then packed with enormous amounts of thinly shaved kielbasa (grilled to perfection), and is finally topped with sauerkraut and Thousand Island dressing. If you took a bite of Pittsburgh, it would taste like the kielbasa grinder. **The Landing,** located on the 100 level, on the landing from the escalators, offers something different each game, like fresh artisanal sandwiches or gourmet sliders. Other stations around CONSOL dedicated to carving offer similar fare.

CONSOL has a relationship with outside eateries as well: **Burgatory** (p. 192) and **Primanti Bros.** (p. 63) both have concession stands ready to fill fans up during the games. Ticket holders in the premium seat level have the option of dining at the **Lexus Club.** This epic buffet never has the same food twice (really!). The menu is inventive, from the salad table to the meticulously crafted dessert station, complete with truffles, ice cream sundaes, and decadent cake. At CONSOL, a level of care and attention to detail extends from the luxury dining section to the concessions, guaranteeing good, fresh meals throughout the arena. Serving tens of thousands of people is of course not easy work, and extra food is often a reality. Fortunately, Aramark has a relationship with the Pittsburgh Food Bank and donates over 28,000 pounds of food from CONSOL per year. Now, *that* is something to cheer about. See Chef Carl's recipe for **Smoked Pork** on p. 259.

Heinz Field, 900 Art Rooney Dr., Pittsburgh, PA 15212; (412) 697-7700; www.steelers.com. Home of the Pittsburgh Steelers, University of Pittsburgh Panthers football, rock concerts, and other events (including the 2011 NHL Winter Classic), Heinz Field opened in August 2001 with naming rights going to the H.J. Heinz Corporation. Probably one of the most eye-catching features of the stadium are the two Heinz Ketchup bottles on the scoreboard that pour ketchup onto the screen whenever the Steelers drive into the Red Zone at the 20-yard line. All this talk about ketchup is leaving you hungry for french fries, isn't it? Well, you can get those and sample a variety of food reflective of Pittsburgh cuisine. There are a few local chains located through the stadium, including **Primanti Bros.** (p. 63), serving up the Pitts-Burgher Cheese Steak and capicola and cheese sandwiches (Lower Level East 109 & 110; Lower Level West 132–133);

Papa Duke's, serving up gyros (Great Hall and Main Concourse section 141); **Quaker Steak & Lube** (p. 200), serving wings (Great Hall, Section 109 and 136); and **Nakama Japanese Steakhouse and Sushi Bar** (p. 100), preparing fresh sushi (West and East Club and Suites). In addition to our trusty local chains, Heinz Field has their own menu going on. You can continue your parking lot tailgate experience inside the stadium at **The Steel Pit,** located in the South Plaza End Zone, where burgers and hot dogs are grilled over an open wood pit. Your mouth will be watering when you smell the smoky goodness in the air. Heinz Field also rolls out unique menu options each football season, so be sure to keep your eyes peeled for unique sandwiches, and the chef's take on traditional Pittsburgh staples, like pierogies and kielbasa.

PNC Park, 115 Federal St., Pittsburgh, PA 15212; (412) 321-2827; http://pittsburgh.pirates.mlb.com. Opened in 2001, PNC Park is the fifth home of the Pittsburgh Pirates baseball team. The Park offers majestic views of Downtown Pittsburgh and the Allegheny River, and these views only get better when it's fireworks night at the Park.

Besides being home of the "Bucs," it's a Pittsburgh food destination. Tickets are cheap (some priced well under $20), which means you can visit many of the 82 games and try a different culinary item every time you go. Now, what should you eat when you are at PNC Park? First and foremost, we recommend the Pulled Pork Pierogi Stacker. This sandwich was introduced in the 2011–2012 season and became so popular it made it as permanent menu item. A pretzel roll is stacked high with pulled pork and topped off with two potato pierogies. This sandwich is available at many of the concessions and also at **Manny's BBQ** in center field, a definite must-visit at the park. At Manny's you can find beef brisket, pulled pork, burgers, and former Pirates catcher Manny Sanguillén. Though he isn't catching these days, you can find him at his barbecue stand signing autographs and posing for photos with fans. Besides the Pulled Pork Pierogi Stacker, PNC Park introduces new menu items each season, such as the Bucco Nachos introduced in 2012, featuring lime tortilla chips topped with smoked jalapeño peach salsa, nacho cheese, ground beef, and cilantro crème fraiche. Also in the 2012–2013 season, PNC Park introduced healthy choice concessions dedicated to providing baseball fans with gluten-free and vegetarian options. In addition to concession stands, PNC Park also hosts a few traditional dining restaurants. Diamond Pizza (Section 138) serves pizza by the slices, salads, wraps, and hoagies year-round. The Budweiser Bowtie Bar (Section 101) features a deck with views of the field and river and has guest chefs from local restaurants serving food and a bar. If traditional ballpark food is what you are after, then purchase one of the "All You Can Eat" seats. A ticket to this special outfield seat section will get you all-you-can-eat hot dogs, burgers, tossed salad, popcorn, pretzels, ice cream, and soft drinks. Like the other local sports stadiums, PNC Park hosts a few local chains, including **Primanti Bros.** (p. 63), **Nakama Japanese Steakhouse and Sushi Bar** (p. 100), **Quaker Steak & Lube** (p. 200), and Papa Duke's Gyros. To help plan your culinary take-over of PNC Park, visit the Park's website for an interactive map, complete with menus and locations of concession stands all over the Park.

Local Drink Scene

Pittsburghers love to eat, but Pittsburghers also love to drink. Maybe we are always thirsty because we are surrounded by water? Or we get inspired to wet our whistles by the lovely Pittsburgh rain?

Regardless, 'Burghers enjoy beverages with some kick. Luckily, craft breweries, wineries, and distilleries have been moving into town, and we are happy to have them as neighbors. We won't ask to borrow a cup of sugar, but we will ask for a growler fill-up.

Arsenal Cider House & Wine Cellar, Inc., 300 39th St., Pittsburgh, PA 15201; (412) 260-6968; www.arsenalciderhouse .com. Arsenal Cider House in Lawrenceville is dedicated to producing hard cider, mead, and wine coolers. If Arsenal feels like a home, well, it is; Owners Michelle and Bill Larkin live upstairs in this re-purposed house. What was once the Larkins' living room, dining room, and kitchen is now the Civil War–themed taproom. Bill brews in the basement. Using the local Soergel Orchards apple cider as a base, each brew has a distinct twist. Offerings rotate, with notes of blueberry to cinnamon to sour cherry, among others, popping up throughout the year. The names assigned to the drinks are as unique as their taste. The ciders categorized as "Bone Dry" are named after Civil War military terms (think picket and pioneer). All the other thirst quenchers are named after local Civil War servicemen. Always on tap, the Fighting Elleck Hard Apple Cider is a dry, crisp, and refreshing cider, which shares the nickname of Civil War General Alexander Hays. Purchase a 1-liter growler to fill with your pick of "Daily Rations" and included is a Civil War title of your very own.

Boyd & Blair Potato Vodka, 1101 William Flynn Hwy., Glenshaw, PA 15116; (412) 486-8666; www.boydandblair.com. Vodka made from locally grown potatoes? Sounds crazy but it's happening in Pittsburgh, and the world has taken notice. Boyd & Blair Potato Vodka was ranked #22 best liquor in the world (out of 140 spirits) according to F. Paul Pacult's *Spirit Journal* in June 2011. And it was the highest-ranking vodka on the list! Boyd & Blair Potato Vodka was started by Prentiss Orr and Barry Young of Pennsylvania Pure Distilleries in August 2008 and named after inspirational figures in each of their lives. The name Boyd comes from Young's father-in-law, James Boyd Rafferty, and Blair is the surname of Orr's great-grandfather, Dr. William Blair. The potato vodka is currently sold in Pennsylvania state liquor stores, as well as in other states in the

United States and in Ontario, Canada. If you don't want to purchase an entire bottle while you are here (though you may be persuaded after a few Boyd & Blair cocktails), many local restaurants craft cocktails centered around this smooth product, including **Olive or Twist** (Downtown, see p. 37), **Cioppino** (Strip District, see p. 52), and **Salt of the Earth** (Garfield, see p. 162). In addition to the Boyd & Blair Potato Vodka, Pennsylvania Pure Distilleries produces Boyd & Blair Professional Proof, a 151 proof version of the potato vodka.

The Church Brew Works, 3525 Liberty Ave., Pittsburgh, PA 15201; (412) 688-8200; www.churchbrew.com. We already talked about the food. Now, let's talk about the beer. You might feel a bit strange drinking in a church, but it's totally okay and actually encouraged at The Church Brew Works. For 20 years, The Church Brew Works has been brewing one-of-a-kind beers for the Pittsburgh beer-drinking community. The brews are crafted right on the altar in beautiful, shiny copper pots. The best-selling beer is the Pious Monk, a dark lager, but The Church Brew Works also offers several ales and stouts, as well as seasonal beers. You can take a few bottled brews with you, our favorite being the Cherry Quadzilla, a Belgian ale with cherry flavoring. Beer aficionados and newbies alike are welcome at The Church Brew Works. Feel free to ask questions about the brewing process, and the history of the building itself, a restored Catholic church.

Copper Kettle Brewing/Hough's, 563 Greenfield Ave., Pittsburgh, PA 15207; (412) 586-5944; http://houghspgh.com.

With over 200 bottled craft brews and over 50 craft taps, Hough's Bar in Greenfield is a great place to get craft beer in the city. While you're downing your frosty beverage, talk with the owners and staff about Copper Kettle Brewing next door. Copper Kettle is the first of its kind in Pittsburgh—you can brew and bottle your own beer. It has over 40 recipes that range from ales to stouts. Once you choose your recipe, you get started on the process. Take a few of your closest beer-loving friends and prepare to get your brewin' on. You'll be making the equivalent of five cases of beer so there will be plenty to go around. Once the beer has fermented for 2 weeks, head back to collect your prize! Extend the fun a little further and think of a great name for the custom label for your newly brewed bottles.

Duquesne Beer, 2555 Washington Rd., Suite 630, Pittsburgh, PA 15241; http://duquesnebeer.com. Once the leading brand of beer in Pennsylvania, Duquesne Beer was resurrected in 2010 by local entrepreneur and attorney Mark Dudash. Brewed in the South Side from 1887 to 1972, its new home is in Latrobe, Pennsylvania, alongside another Pittsburgh beverage legend, Iron City. The recipe is as close to the original as possible with a few ingredient upgrades. The Pilsner has a familiar golden color, bright white foaming head when poured, and tastes less hoppy than other similar-style beers. It can be found in various locations around Pennsylvania and comes in bottles, cans, and is soon to be on draft. Not only has the beer been resurrected but also its mascot, "The Prince of Pilsner." So be sure to salute the Prince as he raises his glass to you!

East End Brewing Company, 6923 Susquehanna St., Pittsburgh, PA 15208; (412) 537-2337; www.eastendbrewing.com. East End Brewing Company calls itself Pittsburgh's "micro-est microbrewery." While it may be a small outfit, word is out that these brews are super fine and 'Burghers can't get enough. East End has year-round beers and, like any quality microbrewery, a rotation of seasonal beers and some occasional one-off beers for the hops aficionado in us all. Our favorite year-rounder is the Black Strap Stout, a rich, dark beer made with black strap molasses and brown sugar. One of the seasonal ales, the Pedal Pale Ale, is kicked off with the brewery's annual Keg Ride  bike ride. The ride starts at the brewery and is led by the owner and volunteers who actually pull kegs of Pedal Pale Ale behind them on trailers. Hundreds of fans are led by the owner to a mystery bar location that receives the first kegs of PPA. Fun bonus: In late fall, the brewery leads a Reverse Keg Ride to pick up the kicked kegs from the lucky bar that got the first batch of PPA! Check out the website for event details and to get the Brewery's growler hours. You can also fill up your growler at the **Pittsburgh Public Market**, at the East End Brewing stand, at 2100 Smallman St., Pittsburgh, PA 15222.

Engine House 25, 3339 Penn Ave., Pittsburgh, PA 15201; (412) 621-1268; www.enginehouse25.com. In this former Lawrenceville firehouse, you will find a mixture of spaces—part rental space, part photography studio, part winery, and part Roberto Clemente Museum. The man running these unique businesses is celebrated advertising photographer, Duane Rieder. After years of making wine as gifts for his photography clients, Duane decided to start producing and selling Cabernet, Zinfandel, and Malbec to a more public consumer. The Engine House No. 25 Wine is produced in the engine house's cellar with Californian grapes, and the wine bottle labels all don photographs shot by Duane over the years, including portraits of Pittsburgh Penguins and Steelers and, of course, Roberto Clemente. The basement provides a dark and cool climate for aging wine, especially due to the 21-inch-thick walls (coincidentally, 21 was Roberto Clemente's Pirates jersey number). You can schedule a tour of the winery by contacting Engine House 25 via email or phone. And while you're at it, plan a trip to the Clemente Museum, too. Because a trip to Pittsburgh isn't really complete without learning a little something you didn't know about Clemente.

Full Pint Brewing, 1963 Lincoln Hwy., North Versailles, PA 15137; www.fullpintbrewing.com. What happens when beer-loving gents put their heads together over a few pints and start dreaming? They start a brewery! Full Pint Brewing combined the tasty talents of several local brewmasters and provides Pittsburgh with some of the best beers around. Most famous of those brews is the White Lightning. It's a light beer with citrus flavor, and it can be found in bars all over the city. While White Lightning is one of the favorites among 'Burghers, we recommend the Perc E Bust, their full-bodied porter brewed with coffee. Who doesn't love a two-fer? Full Pint is well-known for their sample tastings, which take place at local bars and restaurants around town. They also offer growler fill-ups.

North Country Brewing, 141 S. Main St., Slippery Rock, PA 16057; (724) 794-2337; www.northcountrybrewing.com. North Country Brewing is worth the 50-mile drive upstate. The brewery is a rustic building on the main street in Slippery Rock, Pennsylvania. Log cabin-esque, North Country is riddled with wood inside and out, from the sturdy deck out front to the long bar downstairs and the ceiling beams up above. It's definitely a place you can feel cozy in, especially when you're cuddled up in a corner booth with a frosty pint glass of their Liquid Love Double Stout. We think the brewery is one of the best places within a 60-mile radius that serves seriously slammin' bar- 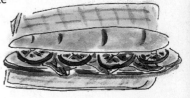 becue. Slap that smoked pork barbecue on a kaiser roll, slather it with North Country's dark and decadent barbecue sauce and famous slaw, and you have yourself one heck of a dinner date. It brews everything on location and beers can change daily, so if you find something you like, be sure to fill up a growler on the way out. We recommend the Vanilla Porter, always a fan favorite for its desserty aftertaste; the brewmaster's Fruit Bowl, which is the North Country Ale with whatever fruit the brewmaster is fancying that day; and the Double Vision I.P.A. that is so strong there is actually a 2-pint maximum.

Penn Brewery, 800 Vinial St., Pittsburgh, PA 15212; (412) 237-9400; www.pennbrew.com. Penn Brewery has an interesting claim to fame. The modern-day Penn Brewery opened back in 1989, under the name of Allegheny Brewery & Pub, and was the first "tied house" (restaurant tied to a brewery) in the entire state of Pennsylvania since Prohibition. The brewery cranks out numerous craft beers that can be found in many local bars. The flagship, Penn Pilsner, is by far the most popular, but Penn Dark and Penn Summer Berry Weisse are some of our favorites. Depending on the season, the Brewery crafts select beers, so be sure to ask your server or bartender what the current flavor is. One of our favorite seasonal brews is the St. Nikolaus Bock, available during the Christmas holiday season. The St. Nikolaus has subtle notes of chocolate and is the perfect adult beverage to enjoy on a cold winter night. The Brewery also offers unique menu items to complement the brews. We dig its buffalo chicken pierogis because there's nothing quite like a Pittsburgh twist on traditional fare to make our hearts skip a beat. We also recommend the Polish Hill Plate, which is a heaping helping of smoked kielbasa, potato cheese pierogis, grilled onions, and sauerkraut.

Pittsburgh Brewing Company, 3340 Liberty Ave., Pittsburgh, PA 15201; (412) 682-7400; www.pittsburghbrewing.com. If you ask any Pittsburgher what the most famous local beer is, chances are, he or she will tell you it's "Arn City," aka Iron City. If you are watching your calories, then it's I.C. Light. Why? Because Pittsburgh Brewing Company has been brewing Iron City Beer for over 150 years. In addition to Iron City Beer and I.C. Light, the

Pittsburgh Brewing Company brews up I.C. Light Mango, Iron City Amber Classic Lager, American, American Light, and Old German. Over 150 years ago, Iron City was brewed in Lawrenceville but has since moved brewing operations to Latrobe, PA. (Don't fret. The company's headquarters are still located in Lawrenceville.) Though the

beers are brewed on the city's outskirts, Iron City bleeds black and gold. Besides boosting Pittsburgh pride in every can, Iron City has achieved some firsts in the beer industry. In 1962 Iron City was the first beer to be sold in a snap top can. In addition, Iron City was the first draft beer to be packaged in cans, and in 2004 it was the first beer to be sold in aluminum bottles. So, when you are in Pittsburgh, you have to order at least one "Arn City" or I.C. Light on draft, because, well, that's just how it's done around here.

Pittsburgh Seltzer Works, 1971 Monongahela Ave., Pittsburgh, PA 15218; (412) 431-1898. Vintage charm and bubble-filled water await you at Pittsburgh Seltzer Works, just east of the Squirrel Hill tunnels. Pittsburgh Seltzer Works crafts crisp, carbonated water, bottles it up in gorgeous, antique glass bottles, and delivers right to your front door. Seltzer is sold in cases of 10 at just $1.50 per bottle, after a one-time, refundable deposit of $35. The absolutely lovely bottles steal the show, each one a happy hue and boasting a different town of origin. All the glass bottles pre-date the 1940s as the factory that manufactured the bottles was destroyed during

World War II. You'll be sipping your seltzer from a bit of history! So how do you fulfill your carbonation craving? The best way to order is by visiting the company's Facebook page and posting on the wall any form of "hey, I need some seltzer." Pittsburgh Seltzer Works delivers to the East End neighborhoods only, but you can always arrange a seltzer pickup and see the amazing bottle inventory first-hand. The Seltzer crew is usually around on Monday and Friday, but call ahead just in case. After a sample, your love for this specialty water will never fizzle.

Wigle Whiskey, 2401 Smallman St., Pittsburgh, PA 15222; www .wiglewhiskey.com. Wigle Whiskey might be new in town, but its ties to history are not. The distillery, located in the Strip District, is the first of its kind since Prohibition. It's named after Phillip Wigle a rebellious whiskey-lover and igniter of the Whiskey Rebellion.

 Paying close attention to tradition while implementing modern innovation, Wigle Whiskey produces two varieties of Pennsylvania-style whiskey: White Rye and Wheat. Both whiskeys are made with local resources and by following a similar process Phillip Wigle once used. Group and private tours of the distillery are available, during which you'll get a complete history lesson of the distillery's namesake. But let's not forget about the best part of a distillery tour—tasting the product! Whiskey is available to sample and purchase in the tasting room. Be sure to look up while you're slowly savoring the flavor: a lighting fixture made from its glass whiskey bottles brighten the room.

Recipes

Jumbo Lump Crab Rangoon

Elements Contemporary Cuisine is a place where you can get modern fare inspired by traditional cuisine classics. Chef Robert Courser puts his own spin on dishes, layering flavors, altering textures, and pairing with proper accoutrements. He has taken a traditional Chinese restaurant appetizer, the crab rangoon, and given it a new flavor palette. After years of ordering mediocre "crab cheese" at restaurants, Chef Robert made the best one he ever had. He then put it on the Elements menu. He says that it's a staple menu item for two reasons: Pittsburgh's love of jumbo lump crab and its affinity for Chinese-American restaurants.

1 pound cream cheese
3 ounces crab claw meat
1 large scallion, thinly sliced
1 teaspoon sriracha

2 tablespoons low-sodium soy sauce
Wonton skins
24 whole jumbo lump crab chunks, about 4 ounces

In large mixing bowl, combine softened cream cheese with claw meat, sliced scallion, sriracha, and soy sauce, and mix thoroughly to combine. Allow mixture to refrigerate at least 1 hour. Place 1 ounce mixture in center of wonton skin and place 1 whole jumbo lump crabmeat chunk in center of filling: use water on edges of wonton to make tacky. Fold in half diagonally and fry till golden.

Courtesy of Executive Chef Robert Courser of Elements Contemporary Cuisine (p. 28)

Short Rib Pierogies

Pittsburgh's culinary scene is a mixing pot of cultures and flavors, a city where old-world dishes meet modern flavors. One such dish that we are absolutely in love with is the short rib pierogies at Braddock's American Brasserie. Executive Chef Dean Gress and Chef de Cuisine Brian Volmrich work seamlessly together to create unique dishes that are new takes on traditional Pittsburgh classics. This recipe makes enough to feed about an army, which is necessary because these little guys will disappear quickly!

Short Ribs

5 pounds bone-in short ribs, approximately 4 inches cut

Salt and pepper as needed

3 quarts beef stock

2 cups tomato paste

Parchment paper

Foil

Liberally season the short ribs with salt and pepper. Heat a medium-size roasting pan and place ribs in the pan. Quickly sear the short ribs on all sides; remove from the heat. Add the stock and tomato paste; the stock should cover the ribs. Place parchment paper on top; this will keep the ribs submerged. Cover with foil or lid and place in the oven at 350°F for 1 to 1½ hours or until the ribs are tender. Remove from the oven and cool to less than 41°F. After they are thoroughly cooled, remove the fat from the top of the cooking liquid and remove the ribs. Reserve the liquid for the sauce. Pull all of the meat from the bones and place in a mixer. Mix the meat on a low speed until it is pureed.

Pierogie Dough

¾ pound cream cheese

12 eggs

9 cups all-purpose flour

Water if needed

Combine all ingredients, adding water if the moisture is needed. Roll dough to a ⅛-inch thickness. You can use a rolling pin or pasta machine if you have one. Using a 3-inch ring mold, cut the pierogie rounds.

To assemble the pierogie, place approximately ½ to 1 ounce rib meat in the center and fold over. Pinch edges closed with the tines of a dinner fork and par-boil for 2 minutes, then cool.

Creamed Leeks

1 bunch leeks

Canola oil as needed

1 pint heavy cream

Salt and pepper as needed

Remove the green from the leeks and cut in half lengthwise. Thoroughly clean the leeks under cold running water. Cut into thin strips across the width of the leek. Place into a sauté pan over medium heat with a small amount of canola oil. Sweat the leeks for 3 to 5 minutes. Add the heavy cream and simmer for 5 to 8 minutes. Season to taste.

Pan Jus

1 cup burgundy or red wine

3 cups braising liquid from the ribs

Salt and pepper to taste

Place the wine and braising liquid in a small saucepan and reduce by half over medium heat. Thicken slightly if needed using a cornstarch and water mixture.

Heat a sauté pan over medium heat with 3 tablespoons of butter. Add the pierogies and brown slightly on both sides. Add the pan jus and continue cooking for 2 to 3 minutes. Place a small amount of leeks on the plate and arrange the pierogies around them. Finish with a drizzle of the pan jus and chopped fresh herbs.

Courtesy of Executive Chef Dean Gress of Braddock's American Brasserie (p. 25)

Sweet Onion Sauce

Clearly, you can see from our book that there are a lot of hot dog joints we love. But the one we love the most is Franktuary. The concept of the restaurant was born out of a love affair of the New York–style frankfurter, made from quality cuts of beef enclosed in a snappy natural casing, served with sauerkraut, spicy brown mustard, and sweet red onion sauce. Franktuary co-founders Tim Tobitsch and Megan Lindsey based their initial menu around this New York street food staple and have crafted their own unique Sweet Onion Sauce. Though they say this recipe works best with Vidalia onions, you can substitute any variety of onion you have on hand, as long as you cook them low and slow until soft. The ending result of this recipe will be a sauce that is delicious not only on franks but also on burgers, salads, sandwiches, and tofu.

2 large onions (Vidalia will make the sweetest sauce, but yellow or white onions may be substituted)

2 garlic cloves

2 tablespoons oil

½ teaspoon salt

½ teaspoon cornstarch or arrowroot powder

½ cup water

1 tablespoon balsamic vinegar

1 tablespoon brown sugar

1 tablespoon tomato paste

1 teaspoon dijon mustard

½ teaspoon dried basil

¼ teaspoon cinnamon

Peel the onions and cut in half along the line running from the root to the plant end. Place onions cut side down and slice into thin strips. Dice the garlic cloves.

Heat the oil on medium heat in a large skillet or soup pot and add onions. Sprinkle the salt over top, which will pull the water out of the onions. Cook, stirring occasionally, until the edges start to brown, but do not burn. Then add the garlic and turn the heat down to low.

Whisk together the cornstarch and water. Add remaining ingredients and whisk until smooth.

Stir onions frequently, scraping up any browned bits from the bottom of the pan. When they are uniformly softened, add the liquid.

Combine mixture thoroughly and cover pan with a lid. Simmer on low, stirring occasionally, for 45 minutes or until soft. If sauce gets too dry, add a few tablespoons of water.

Makes enough to liberally top 10 or 12 franks. Keeps in the fridge for a week, possibly more.

Serve on an all-beef natural casing frank with sauerkraut and a spicy white-wine-and-horseradish brown mustard.

Courtesy of Megan Lindsey, Owner of Franktuary (p. 29)

Candied Yams

Carmi Family Restaurant is home to fantastic Southern cooking and hospitality to match. Carleen Kenney, owner along with partner and chef Michael King, never actually lived in the South, but she got schooled on soul food from her aunts and grandparents starting at a very young age. Soul food preparation was always treated as a special occasion, with all the women of the family gathering to cook . . . and gossip! "This is where I developed my poker face. The trick was not to react to anything you heard," says Carleen.

After years of absorbing juicy stories and delicious culinary tips, while quietly shelling peas and peeling potatoes, Carleen is full of good secrets. She shares one with all of you in the form of a sweet side dish. Assemble your relatives; start cooking and start talking.

5 pounds fresh yams, peeled
and sliced 1 inch thick

3 cups sugar

1 cup brown sugar

⅛ teaspoon nutmeg

½ teaspoon cinnamon

1 tablespoon lemon juice or
¼ teaspoon lemon zest

1 teaspoon vanilla extract

1 cup butter

½ cup water

Preheat oven to 350°F.

Mix all ingredients together in a large bowl.

Bake loosely covered for approximately 2 hours.

Courtesy of Carleen Kenney, Owner of Carmi Family Restaurant (p. 75)

Falafel

Root 174 Chef Keith Fuller has a playful approach to food preparation, with creative food ideas peppered into every dish that leaves the kitchen. Chef Keith was inspired to cook up this recipe because of a childhood trip to a Middle Eastern restaurant that left a lasting impression and love for falafel. This love had a catch, though, as falafel texture was always dry and gritty. So Chef Keith resolved to make his own dish creamier and less gritty, while still staying true to its falafel roots.

Enjoy the product of Chef Keith's experimenting—a creamy falafel packed full of fresh herb flavoring—and don't forget to have a little fun!

2 15-ounce cans chickpeas, drained and rinsed
½ teaspoon cayenne pepper
3 cloves garlic chopped
3 cloves roasted garlic
½ teaspoon paprika
½ teaspoon ground coriander
½ teaspoon granulated garlic

2 teaspoons lemon juice
3 tablespoons olive oil
Salt and pepper to taste
¼ cup each chopped parsley and chopped cilantro
2 eggs, beaten, for dredge
1 cup panko bread crumbs, for dredge

Add all ingredients except for herbs, eggs, and bread crumbs to the work bowl of a large food processor. Process on high until uniform and creamy. Remove to a large mixing bowl. Fold in herbs. Using a 1-ounce disher, portion and dredge in egg wash followed by panko bread crumbs. Fry in 350°F oil until crispy. Yields approximately 30 1¼-ounce portions. Serve with tzatziki (recipe follows).

Tzatziki

½ cucumber, seeded and diced
½ red onion, finely diced
Zest and juice 1 lime
1 tablespoon chopped mint
1 tablespoon chopped cilantro

2 tablespoons red wine vinegar
1 cup plain yogurt
¼ cup sour cream
Salt and pepper to taste

Mix all ingredients thoroughly and let stand in refrigerator for at least 20 minutes or up to 1 hour.

Courtesy of Keith Fuller, Chef and Owner of Root 174 (p. 160)

Chicken Potpie

At Meat & Potatoes, the menu is filled with much more than these two food staples. Chef Richard DeShantz's menu at this Downtown gastropub is filled with items he would eat himself after a busy day in the kitchen. Bone marrow, wings, burgers, tacos, and of course, steaks fill the menu, as well as his take on a traditional chicken potpie. In his recipe, chicken skin is deep-fried golden brown and added to the pie's flaky crust. Though the recipe has a few extra steps in the preparation, you will never want to have another frozen potpie again after making this one.

Chicken Stock

1 whole chicken	2 bay leaves
2 cups chopped onion	1 bunch thyme
1 cup chopped carrots	1 bunch parsley, with stems
1 cup chopped celery	1 tablespoon peppercorns
1 cup chopped leeks	

Pull skin off chicken and reserve. Add all ingredients to a stockpot and simmer on low for 2 hours. Pull chicken out, dice into medium-size pieces, and set aside. Drain stock and return stock liquid to a pot and reduce by half.

Crust

Skin from chicken, cut into medium pieces	1¼ teaspoon salt
2½ cups all-purpose flour	2½ sticks butter, cold
	5–6 tablespoons ice water

Cut chicken skin into medium-size pieces and deep-fry. In a bowl mix flour and salt together. Add butter and mix until butter is no larger than the size of a pea. Add in water and chicken skin. Knead dough into a ball and set aside.

Pot Pie Base

1 cup pearl onions

1 cup medium diced carrots

1 cup red-skinned potatoes, cut into quarters

Roux (recipe follows)

Place all ingredients into reduced chicken stock and simmer on low for 45 minutes. After 45 minutes, add in roux.

Roux

1 tablespoon butter

6 tablespoons flour

Cook on stovetop until light golden color for about 4 to 6 minutes. Add cooked roux to potpie base 1 tablespoon at a time until the base becomes thick.

Assembling the Chicken Potpie

To thickened chicken stock, add in reserved chopped chicken, 1 teaspoon thyme, 2 tablespoons parsley, 1 teaspoon chives, 1 teaspoon tarragon, and season with salt and pepper. Place mixture into a pie pan. Roll out dough and place on top. Crimp pie edge and slice a center vent into the crust top. Brush with egg wash (1 egg mixed with 3 teaspoons water) and bake at 375°F 30 to 40 minutes until top is golden brown. Cool for 10 minutes before slicing.

Courtesy of Tolga Sevdik at Meat & Potatoes (p. 35)

Smoked Pork

Aramark Executive Chef Carl VanWagner cooks up thousands of meals for hungry hockey fans at every game. His goal is to offer quality, exciting cuisine in a place typically reserved for nachos and beers. A self-taught master of the kitchen, Chef Carl has a fondness for food festivals and excellent barbecue.

CONSOL serves about 500 pounds of pork per game. Can't make it into the arena? Fire up the smoker, because this scaled-down recipe will take you to the game, and the glorious food stands, without leaving the comforts of your own kitchen.

Pork Brine

1 cup Worcestershire sauce
2 pounds brown sugar
2 cups kosher salt

1 gallon water
1 4- to 6-pound pork shoulder
   or Boston butt

Dry Rub

1 cup paprika
2 cups brown sugar
½ cup dry mustard

1 cup kosher salt
½ cup granulated garlic
½ cup onion powder

Mix Pork Brine ingredients and marinate the pork shoulder or Boston butt in brine for 2 days. Take pork out of brine and let dry for 2 hours.

Mix dry rub ingredients together and rub the pork with dry rub.

Preheat smoker to 220°F. Use 2 pounds apple wood chips in smoker.

Let cook for 8 to 10 hours until fork tender.

Courtesy of Executive Chef Carl VanWagner of Aramark at CONSOL Energy Center (p. 231)

Spaghetti Carbonara

According to E2's Chef Kate Romane, Spaghetti Carbonara is a hearty, tasty, and easy meal to make. Her recipe here serves 2, though it could easily be doubled or quadrupled because it's sure to be a tasty meal that you will want to make for everyone in your life. Chef Kate suggests making this meal for a cold night or a snuggle date, but we suggest you make it whenever you want. She says that this dish is also known as "the coal miner's pasta." It is very Italian but also representative of the coal mining history of Pennsylvania. Whoever you make this dish for, the fresh ground pepper and the bacon are the key ingredients.

½ **pound spaghetti**
3 **thick-cut strips slab bacon, par cooked and cubed**
¾ **cup heavy cream**
⅓ **cup green peas**
Salt

Pepper
1 **local egg of choice (E2 uses local eggs from Churchview Farm)**
Parsley (to taste)
Grated Parmesan cheese (to taste)

Cook the spaghetti. When the spaghetti is almost done, sauté the bacon in just a touch of olive oil. When the bacon begins to crisp, add in heavy cream and peas. Heat until cream begins to reduce. Add salt and lots of fresh cracked pepper. When spaghetti is perfectly al dente, drain and add to sauté pan then take off the burner. Crack egg directly into pasta and toss. The heat of the pasta will lightly cook the egg and thicken sauce. Add more salt and pepper to taste. Top with parsley and Parmesan cheese and serve.

Courtesy of Kate Romane, Chef and Owner of E2 (p. 130)

Carrot Cake with Cream Cheese Icing & Caramel Sauce

Pineapple in a carrot cake? Crazy, but delicious. Pastry Chef James Wroblewski at Habitat has taken his mother's original carrot cake recipe and classed it up with pineapple and caramel sauce. This recipe was one of the first dishes his mother taught him to make, and throughout the years since, he has found a way to make the original his own. This more sophisticated carrot cake reflects the cooking style of both him and Habitat: using quality ingredients, bringing out their natural flavors, and creating a killer presentation. Chef James says not to be intimidated by this recipe. The preparation is easy and the few extra steps definitely make a world of difference.

Roasted Pineapple

1 fresh pineapple
10 ounces brown sugar
¼ teaspoon cinnamon

¼ teaspoon vanilla bean seeds
  (beans split and scraped)
2 ounces honey
¼ cup Myers's Rum

Peel, quarter, and core pineapple. Spread brown sugar evenly on the bottom of a roasting pan and place pineapple on brown sugar. Sprinkle with cinnamon and vanilla bean seeds. Pour honey and rum over pineapple and roast at 350°F for 30 minutes. Flip each piece and roast for an additional 30 minutes or until tender. Cool and dice, then store in an airtight container in refrigerator.

Carrot Cake

10 ounces peeled and shredded carrots	¼ ounce cinnamon
6 ounces granulated sugar	¼ ounce salt
4 ounces brown sugar	10 ounces all-purpose flour
6 tablespoons vegetable oil	½ ounce baking soda
5 ounces whole eggs	9 ounces diced roasted pineapple
2 teaspoons whole milk	1 ounce raisins

Grease an 8-inch x 8-inch pan and line bottom with parchment paper. Mix carrots, sugars, and oil. Whisk eggs and milk together, add to carrots, and mix well, scraping occasionally. Add dry ingredients and blend until well mixed. Add diced pineapple and raisins and mix until just incorporated. Pour mixture into pan. Bake at 350°F for about 40 to 50 minutes. Allow to cool.

Cream Cheese Icing

4 ounces unsalted butter	18 ounces cream cheese
8 ounces powdered sugar	1 teaspoon vanilla extract

Beat butter and powdered sugar in mixer until light and fluffy. Scrape bowl to prevent lumps. Add cream cheese and continue to mix until smooth, scraping frequently. Add vanilla extract and blend well. Store in an airtight container.

Caramel Sauce

4 ounces unsalted butter	1 ounce heavy cream
8 ounces granulated sugar	

Cook butter and sugar over medium-high heat until dark amber color; do not stir. Remove from heat and add cream slowly, whisking to incorporate. Strain and cool. Store in an airtight container in refrigerator.

To assemble the cake, trim top of the cake so that it is even. Flip the cake over so the cut side is down. Spread cream cheese icing over top, ¼ inch thick. Refrigerate for at least 20 minutes. Cut into bars 4 inches x 1¼ inch. Drizzle with caramel sauce.

Makes 10 individual servings.

Courtesy of Pastry Chef James D. Wroblewski II of Habitat Restaurant (p. 32)

PB & J Milk Shake

Beyond dessert, milk shakes are the perfect way to end a meal or even to have as a meal on their own! In Pittsburgh, we have The Milk Shake Factory by Edward Marc Chocolatier, which can shake up over 50 flavors. In the summer of 2010, The Milk Shake Factory held a contest for customers to pick their favorite out of five flavors. The PB & J Milk Shake won as the most popular and was placed on the menu. It is still one of the most popular milk shakes on the menu, and we can see why. Both a milk shake and a PB & J sandwich are reminiscent of our childhoods, and having them blended together is the perfect combination.

Strawberry Syrup

1 pint fresh strawberries
¼ cup sugar

2 tablespoons orange juice
1 cup chilled water

Milk Shake

8 ounces strawberry ice cream
1 ounce creamy peanut butter
1 ounce strawberry syrup
6 ounces whole milk

Whipped cream
½ ounce crushed honey-roasted
    peanuts
1 whole strawberry

Strawberry Syrup

Combine all ingredients in a saucepan and simmer over medium heat for about 6 minutes, stirring constantly. Puree the sauce in a blender and strain if preferred. Chill for milk shake.

Note: If using frozen berries, use ½ cup water.

To assemble the Milk Shake

Using milk shake mixer or blender, blend ice cream, peanut butter, strawberry syrup, and 4 ounces milk. While blending, add remaining milk slowly and blend until smooth. Serve in a tall glass and top with whipped cream, crushed peanuts, and a fresh strawberry for garnish. Serve immediately.

Courtesy of Christian Edwards, Co-owner of The Milk Shake Factory
by Edward Marc Chocolatier (p. 112)

Bangkok Tea

Soba's fundamental cocktail characteristics make up this signature drink. Made with house-made green tea vodka, fresh squeezed sours blend, and house-made ginger-honey syrup, Soba's recipe makes a refreshingly unique cocktail.

1½ ounces green tea-infused vodka (recipe follows)

1 ounce ginger-honey simple syrup (recipe follows)

½ ounce sours mix

1 ounce club soda

In a shaker half-filled with ice, combine the infused vodka, ginger-honey syrup, and fresh sours. Shake well. Strain into a collins glass almost filled with ice cubes. Add club soda. Stir and garnish with a lemon slice.

Green Tea Vodka

750 ml bottle vodka

6 teaspoons sencha green tea leaves

Place tea leaves into the bottle of vodka and let sit for 2 days. Strain and re-bottle.

Ginger-Honey Simple Syrup

1 cup roughly chopped fresh ginger (skin on)

2 cups honey

½ cup white sugar

3 cups water

In a medium saucepan add all ingredients and bring to a boil. Reduce to simmer; let simmer for 30 minutes. Turn off heat and let cool for 1 hour. Remove ginger and strain.

Courtesy of Ryan Burke, General Manager of Soba Lounge (p. 166)

The Captain Spaulding

The Smiling Moose has character, and so does its cocktail menu. Each cocktail is named after legendary movies, movie characters, and props. One of those drinks that best represents The Smiling Moose is The Captain Spaulding because, like the menu says, it's "Tutti F-ing Frutti!"

1 ½ ounces vodka   ½ ounce Triple Sec
1 ounce peach schnapps   ½ ounce Grenadine
1 ounce Malibu rum

Fill shaker with above ingredients and add 1 part orange juice and 1 part cream. Shake and serve with ice in a pint glass.

Courtesy of Mike P. Scarlatelli, Owner of The Smiling Moose (p. 107)

Appendix A: Eateries by Cuisine

Tazza D'Oro Cafe & Espresso
Bar, 171
21st Street Coffee and Tea, 60

Creole
NOLA on the Square, 36

Deli
Carson Street Deli, 91
Deli on Butler Street, 128
Kevin's Deli, 142
Market Street Deli & Grill, 34
Smallman Street Deli, 63

Diner
DeLuca's, 60
Eat'n Park, 218
P&G Pamela's Diner, 62
Taste of Dahntahn, 42
Tick Toc Restaurant, 42

Eclectic
Cafe at the Frick, The, 122
Cure, 126
Legume, 145
Root 174, 160
Salt of the Earth, 162

Toast! Kitchen & Wine Bar, 173
Yo Rita, 109

Ethiopian
Abay Ethiopian Cuisine, 115

French
Crêpes Parisiennes, 126
Paris 66, 149

Gastropub
Alchemy N'Ale, 116
Church Brew Works, The,
177, 198
Meat & Potatoes, 35
1947 Tavern, 148

German
Max's Allegheny Tavern, 82

Hot Dogs
Brighton Hot Dog Shoppe, 191
Essie's Original Hot Dog
Shop, 179
Franktuary, 29, 30
Joe's Dog House, 139
Station Street Hot Dogs, 170

Ice Cream

Dave and Andy's Homemade Ice Cream, 178

Klavon's Ice Cream Parlor, 61

Mercurio's, 146

Oh Yeah! Ice Cream & Coffee Co., 149

Razzy Fresh, 158

Indian

People's Indian Restaurant, 151

Sree's Foods, 41

International

Backstage Bar at Theater Square, 24

Cafe Phipps, 123

Cafe Zinho, 124

Gypsy Cafe, 94

Habitat Restaurant, 32

Isabela on Grandview, 95

Jozsa Corner Hungarian Restaurant, 140

Kaya Island Cuisine, 56

Piper's Pub, 102

Irish

Monterey Pub, 77

Italian

Cafe on the Strip, 51

Cafe Vita, 216

Caffe Davio, 90

Del's Bar and Ristorante DelPizzo, 128

DISH Osteria and Bar, 92

Enrico Biscotti Co. and Enrico's Cafe, The, 53

E2, 130

Girasole, 179

Il Pizzaiolo, 208

Jioio's Restaurant, 220

Joseph Tambellini Restaurant, 139

La Tavola Italiana, 96

Legends of the North Shore, 76

Osteria 2350, 57

Papa J's Centro, 38

Piccolo Forno, 151

17th Street Cafe, 106

Stagioni, 108

Japanese

Little Tokyo, 210

Nakama Japanese Steakhouse and Sushi Bar, 100

Umi, 174

Korean

Golden Pig Authentic Korean
  Cuisine, 207

Latin American

Alma Pan-Latin Kitchen, 117

Seviche, 39

Mediterranean

Amel's Restaurant, 204

Casbah, 124

Mike and Tony's Gyros, 99

Salonika Gyros, 39

Mexican

Azul Bar y Cantina, 190

California Taco Shop, 206

Las Velas Mexican Restaurant, 33

Mad Mex, 147

Madonna's Authentic Mexican
  Food, 34

Round Corner Cantina, 161

Verde Mexican Kitchen &
  Cantina, 176

Middle Eastern

Khalil's II Restaurant, 142

Moroccan

Kous Kous Cafe, 209

La Casa Wine and Tapas Bar, 143

Neighborhood Bar

Big Jim's Restaurant & Bar, 119

Bloomfield Bridge Tavern, 120

Bocktown Beer and Grill, 224

Brillobox, 121

D's SixPax and Dogz, 127

Elbow Room, The, 134

Fuel & Fuddle, 134

Harris Grill, 137

Hemingway's Cafe, 138

Kelly's Bar & Lounge, 141

Le Mardi Gras, 180

Library, The, 97

Local Bar + Kitchen, 97

Lot 17, 145

Mario's South Side Saloon, 98

New Amsterdam, 147

Olive or Twist, 37

OTB Bicycle Cafe, 100

Park House, The, 83

Redbeard's Bar & Grill, 105

Shady Grove, 163

Sharp Edge Creekhouse, The, 226

Appendix B: Dishes, Specialties & Specialty Food

Sausalido, 162
Smiling Banana Leaf, 166
Smoke Barbeque Taqueria, 221
Tram's Kitchen, 182

Car Hop
Jerry's Curb Service, 197

Cheese
Pennsylvania Macaroni Company, 70

Chicken & Waffles
Carmi Family Restaurant, 75

French Fries
Bocktown Beer and Grill, 224
Essie's Original Hot Dog
    Shop, 179
Lot 17 (Sweet Potato Fries), 145
Uncle Sam's Sandwich Bar, 183

Fried Chicken
Kaya Island Cuisine, 56

Gluten-Free
Gluuteny, 135

Grilled Cheese
Hemingway's Cafe, 138
Pittsburgh Pretzel Sandwich
    Shop, 154
Zozo's Pub, 223

Hot Dogs
Brighton Hot Dog Shoppe, 191
D's SixPax and Dogz, 127
Franktuary, 29
Joe's Dog House, 139
Station Street Hot Dogs, 170

Hungarian
Jozsa Corner Hungarian
    Restaurant, 140

Live Music
Backstage Bar at Theatre
    Square, 24
Bloomfield Bridge Tavern, 120
Brillobox, 121
Cafe Notte, 194
Gypsy Cafe, 94
Leaf & Bean Company, The, 66
NOLA on the Square, 36
Papa J's Centro, 30

Six Penn Kitchen, 40
Tamari Restaurant and Lounge, 171
Vivo Kitchen, 202
Willow, 203

Pancakes
Dor-Stop Restaurant, 206
P&G Pamela's Diner, 62

Pepperoni Rolls
Mancini's Bread Company, 67

Pierogies
Braddock's American Brasserie, 25
Pierogies Plus, 225

Pizza
Aiello's Pizza, 115
Bella Notte Pizza Pasta &
    More, 50
Beto's Pizza, 86
Dinette, 129
Fiori's Pizza, 93
Il Pizzaiolo, 208
Jioio's Restaurant, 220
Mineo's Pizza House, 211
Piccolo Fornio, 151

Pi Coal Fired Pizza, 101
Pizza Sola, 104
Spak Bros., 167

Popcorn
Pittsburgh Popcorn Company, 71

Ravioli
Groceria Italiana, 184

Shepherd's Pie
Monterey Pub, 77

Soft Pretzels
GO Pretzel, 48
Max's Allegheny Tavern, 82
Pittsburgh Pretzel Sandwich Shop,
    The, 154
Rachel's Roadhouse, 201

Stadium Food
CONSOL Energy Center, 231
Heinz Field, 233
PNC Park, 234

Sushi
Little Tokyo, 210

Nakama Japanese Steakhouse and
  Sushi Bar, 100
Penn Avenue Fish Company, 57
Plum Pan-Asian Kitchen, 155
Umi, 174

Tacos
California Taco Shop, 206
Reyna Foods, 72
Round Corner Cantina, 161
Smoke Barbeque Taqueria, 221
Yo Rita, 109

Tapas
Bar Marco, 50

Ibiza Spanish Tapas & Wine
  Bar, 95
La Casa Wine and Tapas Bar, 143
Silk Elephant, 164
Tamari Restaurant and
  Lounge, 171

Waffles
Waffallonia, 186

Wings
Quaker Steak & Lube, 200
Redbeard's Bar & Grill, 105
Wings Suds & Spuds, 226

Index

Getaway ideas for the local traveler

Need a day away to relax, refresh, renew?
Just get in your car and go!

travel

To order call 800-243-0495 or visit www.GlobePequot.com